...For
Dummies

COMPUTER
BOOK SERIES
FROM IDG

GUI Design For Dummies®

Cheat Sheet

D1210778

Goals & Key Info

- ✔ What does the GUI have to be like for the project to succeed?
- ✔ Set three design goals in priority order
- ✔ Find out about *users, tasks, technology,* and *environment*

Early Design

- ✔ Almost GUI, Standard GUI, or One-time GUI?
- ✔ Multiwindow, MDI, Multipane?
- ✔ Draw the conceptual model
- ✔ Prototype top and key windows

Making it Work

To create a design, start with the task.

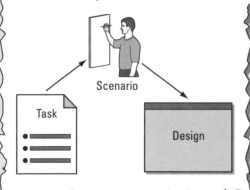

Scenario

Task

Design

Reality Checks

Test with users for the best and cheapest design education going.

- ✔ Decide what you want to know
- ✔ Define a task that will answer your question
- ✔ Choose how to represent your program: a sketch, a paper prototype, a few windows, a live system
- ✔ Beg, borrow, or hire users
- ✔ Give a user the task and the system
- ✔ Button your lip, but keep your eyes and ears open
- ✔ Pay attention when the user does something you didn't expect; that's how you find out the really good stuff
- ✔ For best cost/benefit, test with four or five users

Sure, you can call it a user error. But there's more insight to be gained by asking, "What did my program do to make the user believe this was a right action?"

...For Dummies: #1 Computer Book Series for Beginners

GUI Design For Dummies®

Cheat Sheet

Visual Design

- ✔ Communicate purpose and use
- ✔ KISS. Keep it Simple (if you don't want to look) Stupid
- ✔ Send the same message with all your visual cues
- ✔ Squint test: Does the most important stuff stand out best?

Making it Easy

- ✔ Give fast, fitting feedback
- ✔ Use affordance: Let the design *show* what it can *do*
- ✔ Good mapping: Natural one-to-one match between task and GUI
- ✔ Use idioms: Once learned, never forgotten
- ✔ Reuse what the user knows. Choose a good analogy!

Window Layout Tips

Menus are maps for new users. Make them complete.

Establish few, clear vertical "left margins" in the window to guide the eye quickly to starting points.

Good icons are distinct, not similar. They are easy to associate with their purpose.

Arrange widgets so work goes from top to bottom, left to right.

Color (contrast) draws eye; use where you want to focus attention.

A white text field invites the user to type or edit freely.

Omit leading texts where the user does not need them.

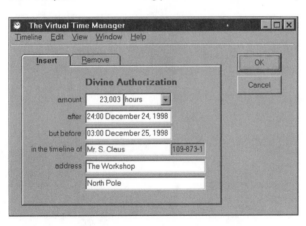

Main action buttons always here or always bottom center.

Limit yourself to one row of tabs.

Allow breathing space on windows, in frames and in buttons.

Right-align amounts, but not codes.

Gray field background tells the user, "you can't change this now."

...For Dummies: #1 Computer Book Series for Beginners

GUI DESIGN
FOR
DUMMIES®

GUI DESIGN FOR DUMMIES®

by Laura Arlov

IDG Books Worldwide, Inc.
An International Data Group Company

Foster City, CA ♦ Chicago, IL ♦ Indianapolis, IN ♦ Southlake, TX

GUI Design For Dummies®

Published by
IDG Books Worldwide, Inc.
An International Data Group Company
919 E. Hillsdale Blvd.
Suite 400
Foster City, CA 94404
www.idgbooks.com (IDG Books Worldwide Web site)
www.dummies.com (Dummies Press Web site)

Library of Congress Catalog Card No.: 97-80124

ISBN: 0-7645-0213-1

Printed in the United States of America

10 9 8 7 6 5 4 3 2 1

1B/SY/QY/ZX/IN

Distributed in the United States by IDG Books Worldwide, Inc.

Distributed by Macmillan Canada for Canada; by Transworld Publishers Limited in the United Kingdom; by IDG Norge Books for Norway; by IDG Sweden Books for Sweden; by Woodslane Pty. Ltd. for Australia; by Woodslane Enterprises Ltd. for New Zealand; by Longman Singapore Publishers Ltd. for Singapore, Malaysia, Thailand, and Indonesia; by Simron Pty. Ltd. for South Africa; by Toppan Company Ltd. for Japan; by Distribuidora Cuspide for Argentina; by Livraria Cultura for Brazil; by Ediciencia S.A. for Ecuador; by Addison-Wesley Publishing Company for Korea; by Ediciones ZETA S.C.R. Ltda. for Peru; by WS Computer Publishing Corporation, Inc., for the Philippines; by Unalis Corporation for Taiwan; by Contemporanea de Ediciones for Venezuela; by Computer Book & Magazine Store for Puerto Rico; by Express Computer Distributors for the Caribbean and West Indies. Authorized Sales Agent: Anthony Rudkin Associates for the Middle East and North Africa.

For general information on IDG Books Worldwide's books in the U.S., please call our Consumer Customer Service department at 800-762-2974. For reseller information, including discounts and premium sales, please call our Reseller Customer Service department at 800-434-3422.

For information on where to purchase IDG Books Worldwide's books outside the U.S., please contact our International Sales department at 415-655-3200 or fax 415-655-3295.

For information on foreign language translations, please contact our Foreign & Subsidiary Rights department at 415-655-3021 or fax 415-655-3281.

For sales inquiries and special prices for bulk quantities, please contact our Sales department at 415-655-3200 or write to the address above.

For information on using IDG Books Worldwide's books in the classroom or for ordering examination copies, please contact our Educational Sales department at 800-434-2086 or fax 817-251-8174.

For press review copies, author interviews, or other publicity information, please contact our Public Relations department at 415-655-3000 or fax 415-655-3299.

For authorization to photocopy items for corporate, personal, or educational use, please contact Copyright Clearance Center, 222 Rosewood Drive, Danvers, MA 01923, or fax 508-750-4470.

is a trademark under exclusive license to IDG Books Worldwide, Inc., from International Data Group, Inc.

About the Author

Laura Arlov lives and works in Norway, where she consults for developers designing graphical user interfaces (GUIs), writes for *PC World Norge,* and teaches GUI design.

Laura has a Bachelor of Science degree from the University of California at Berkeley. After moving to Norway, she wrote user handbooks and worked as a user interface designer for Norsk Data, a minicomputer company that produced office automation software. Laura went on to work for Andersen Consulting as an international expert in GUI design, consulting for custom development projects and devising GUI design training for developers. She is an active member of the Norwegian Computer Society, where she serves on the steering committees of two special-interest groups: User-friendly Computer Systems and User Documentation.

Laura shares working quarters with her Norwegian husband, Per, a technical writer who also translates *...For Dummies* books; their son, Jon; an Airedale Terrier named Chewie; five computers; and a panoramic view of Oslo.

ABOUT IDG BOOKS WORLDWIDE

Welcome to the world of IDG Books Worldwide.

IDG Books Worldwide, Inc., is a subsidiary of International Data Group, the world's largest publisher of computer-related information and the leading global provider of information services on information technology. IDG was founded more than 25 years ago and now employs more than 8,500 people worldwide. IDG publishes more than 275 computer publications in over 75 countries (see listing below). More than 60 million people read one or more IDG publications each month.

Launched in 1990, IDG Books Worldwide is today the #1 publisher of best-selling computer books in the United States. We are proud to have received eight awards from the Computer Press Association in recognition of editorial excellence and three from *Computer Currents*' First Annual Readers' Choice Awards. Our best-selling *...For Dummies*® series has more than 30 million copies in print with translations in 30 languages. IDG Books Worldwide, through a joint venture with IDG's Hi-Tech Beijing, became the first U.S. publisher to publish a computer book in the People's Republic of China. In record time, IDG Books Worldwide has become the first choice for millions of readers around the world who want to learn how to better manage their businesses.

Our mission is simple: Every one of our books is designed to bring extra value and skill-building instructions to the reader. Our books are written by experts who understand and care about our readers. The knowledge base of our editorial staff comes from years of experience in publishing, education, and journalism — experience we use to produce books for the '90s. In short, we care about books, so we attract the best people. We devote special attention to details such as audience, interior design, use of icons, and illustrations. And because we use an efficient process of authoring, editing, and desktop publishing our books electronically, we can spend more time ensuring superior content and spend less time on the technicalities of making books.

You can count on our commitment to deliver high-quality books at competitive prices on topics you want to read about. At IDG Books Worldwide, we continue in the IDG tradition of delivering quality for more than 25 years. You'll find no better book on a subject than one from IDG Books Worldwide.

John Kilcullen
CEO
IDG Books Worldwide, Inc.

Steven Berkowitz
President and Publisher
IDG Books Worldwide, Inc.

Eighth Annual
Computer Press
Awards ≥1992

Ninth Annual
Computer Press
Awards ≥1993

Tenth Annual
Computer Press
Awards ≥1994

Eleventh Annual
Computer Press
Awards ≥1995

Dedication

There are people who count things, and people who make things. This book is for the people who make things.

Author's Acknowledgments

Thanks to Kjell Gytrup, Jill Pisoni, Joyce Pepple, Joe Jansen, Bill Barton, and E. Shawn Aylsworth and the rest of the production staff at IDG Books Worldwide, Inc., for helping this project on its way. Special thanks to Project Editor Robert Wallace for constructive and good-humored leadership, and to Drew R. Moore for his wonderful drawings of the "Squirt."

Thanks to Margaret Tarbet for technical comments that kept me laughing even as they placed my feet on the straight and narrow path.

Thanks to colleagues at Andersen Consulting and Norsk Data A/S, where much of the experience behind this book was gained. I am especially grateful to the Oslo practice of Andersen Consulting for permission to rework material I originally developed there.

Thanks to Jonathan Grudin, Michael L. Wright, Jakob Nielsen, and Gautam Ghosh for permission to quote or describe their work.

Thanks to SINTEF and Jan Martins for the photograph of their usability lab.

Thanks to Lars Flikkeid, my partner at GUI Design School, whose discussions and questions helped me to formulate my ideas. And to Mike DeBellis for inspiration for some of the example files on the CD-ROM.

Thanks to Jorulf Beitland of Lotus Development Norway and to Ole Tom Seierstad of Microsoft Norway for help in obtaining software.

Thanks to some of my favorite techies: Julie Karr, Bernadette Eirheim, Tone Pettersen, and Torunn Brandt, for reading and commenting on various versions of the book.

For the long-term association that has nourished the ideas behind this book, thanks to my fellow committee members at the Norwegian Computer Society: Svein Arnesen, Simon Clatworthy, Tor Endestad, Jacob Thyness, and Erik G. Nilsen — as well as Gautam and Lars, already mentioned.

Thanks to SHARE, the online community that kept me company while I seemed to be living my whole life in front of the PC: Frances, Jane, Judith MerriAngela, Linda Kat, Marilyn, Don, Tom, and Suzanne.

The last and biggest thank you to my husband, Per Arlov. Without your support, I'd never have started this book. And with your support (and distractions), writing it has been more fun than anything else — so far!

Publisher's Acknowledgments

We're proud of this book; please send us your comments about it by using the IDG Books Worldwide Registration Card at the back of the book or by e-mailing us at feedback/dummies@idgbooks.com. Some of the people who helped bring this book to market include the following:

Acquisitions, Development, and Editorial

Project Editor: Robert H. Wallace

Senior Acquisitions Editor: Jill Pisoni

Media Development Manager: Joyce Pepple

Associate Permissions Editor:
Heather H. Dismore

Copy Editors: William A. Barton, Joe Jansen

Technical Editor: Margaret Tarbet

Editorial Manager: Leah P. Cameron

Editorial Assistant: Donna Love

Production

Project Coordinator: E. Shawn Aylsworth

Layout and Graphics: Steve Arany,
Cameron Booker, Lou Boudreau,
Linda M. Boyer, Angela J. Bush-Sisson,
Angela F. Hunckler, Heather N. Pearson,
Brent Savage, Michael A. Sullivan

Special Art: Drew R. Moore, "Squirt" Creator

Proofreaders: Arielle Carole Mennelle,
Christine Berman

Indexer: David Heiret

Special Help

Mark Kory, Media Development Intern;
Dwight Ramsey, Reprint Editor;
Publication Services

General and Administrative

IDG Books Worldwide, Inc.: John Kilcullen, CEO; Steven Berkowitz, President and Publisher

IDG Books Technology Publishing: Brenda McLaughlin, Senior Vice President and
Group Publisher

Dummies Technology Press and Dummies Editorial: Diane Graves Steele, Vice President and
Associate Publisher; Judith A. Taylor, Product Marketing Manager; Kristin A. Cocks, Editorial
Director; Mary Bednarek, Acquisitions and Product Development Director

Dummies Trade Press: Kathleen A. Welton, Vice President and Publisher

IDG Books Production for Dummies Press: Beth Jenkins, Production Director; Cindy L. Phipps,
Manager of Project Coordination, Production Proofreading, and Indexing; Kathie S. Schutte,
Supervisor of Page Layout; Shelley Lea, Supervisor of Graphics and Design; Debbie J. Gates,
Production Systems Specialist; Robert Springer, Supervisor of Proofreading; Debbie Stailey,
Special Projects Coordinator; Tony Augsburger, Supervisor of Reprints and Bluelines;
Leslie Popplewell, Media Archive Coordinator

Dummies Packaging and Book Design: Patti Sandez, Packaging Specialist; Lance Kayser,
Packaging Assistant; Kavish + Kavish, Cover Design

♦

The publisher would like to give special thanks to Patrick J. McGovern,
without whom this book would not have been possible.

♦

Contents at a Glance

Cartoons at a Glance

By Rich Tennant

page 9

page 51

page 109

page 183

page 253

page 301

Fax: 508-546-7747 • E-mail: the5wave@tiac.net

Table of Contents

Chapter 6: How Users Get Around: Navigation Models 85

Chapter 7: The GUI Standard 99

Part III: Designing GUIs that Work 109

Chapter 8: Learning How Users Work 111

Introduction

● ●

*W*elcome to *GUI Design For Dummies.* You've got a project that uses a graphical user interface, and I've got 15 years of experience with users and design to put at your disposal. You've got looming deadlines, uncooperative development tools, and users with attitude. *GUI Design For Dummies* walks you through the entire GUI design process, skirting the pitfalls.

You probably already have some technical background. In this book, you find the material you need from other disciplines to help you create great graphical user interfaces:

- ✔ Industrial design contributes a market-oriented product design process
- ✔ Software design aims for a fast, feasible, elegant solution that takes advantage of the technology, and includes both task-oriented and user-centered design
- ✔ Psychology helps you to investigate and predict user reactions
- ✔ Graphical design helps you to make a clear, attractive interface

Some people think GUI design is an art form. They think that you must be born with a special talent in order to do GUIs well. Others wish that it were a purely mechanical skill: "Just hand over the standard, please!" I think GUI design is a craft: part inspiration and part skill. A well-crafted interface is sturdy and useful as well as beautiful. Like any craftspeople, GUI designers must pay careful attention to materials, functions, and users. *GUI Design For Dummies* can take you through your apprenticeship and point the way to eventual mastery. As in any craft, your own willingness to practice, seek criticism, and learn is your key to success.

Who Should Read GUI Design For Dummies?

GUI Design For Dummies is for everybody who creates or helps to create software that other people will use. That includes not only experienced programmers, but also the students, business analysts, user representatives, managers, human factors experts, and graphic designers who take part in software development projects.

Even if you're one of the nonprogramming software developers, you'll feel welcome in *GUI Design For Dummies.* The material here doesn't presume that you know how to write programs, but it does assume that you are interested in technology and in getting technology to work for users — even those users who, for some strange reason, don't *like* the stuff!

Regardless of your job title, if you're developing software, you should think of yourself as a designer — and as part of the audience for this book.

What Is This Gooey Stuff?

GUI stands for Graphical User Interface. Most people pronounce it *gooey,* appropriately enough: Implementing your first one can be a pretty sticky proposition.

I'd rather not go for a formal definition of *graphical* here. Just consider graphical interfaces to be those in which you are likely to tangle with issues of pictures or icons, color, pointing devices (everything from rodents to fingers), and maybe even pull-down menus — or then again, maybe no menus at all.

Interface means the place where two things meet. In this book, I talk about the meeting between your computer program and the people who use it, about how your program works when seen from the user's point of view, and about how users work when seen from an interface designer's point of view.

That leaves *user* — the person who uses your program. I introduce you to methods by which you can meet the user and painlessly gather information from her. For a designer, one very helpful thing to know about your users is what they expect from the program. You can take into account a lot of variation. For example, users who are active on the Internet may think your screens are boorrinng if you don't provide animated graphics and hyperlinks. Other users who are new to GUI environments will just have trouble hitting small screen areas with the pointing device.

The GUI environment itself is an important factor in determining both what your users will expect and what you will be able to do. The screen shots in this book come from the Microsoft Windows graphical user environment. However, the design method, the techniques, and most of the advice that you find in this book are also relevant whether you develop interfaces for UNIX, IBM OS/2, or Apple Macintosh programs.

This Book Follows a Method

Except for The Part of Tens, that traditional ...*For Dummies* goody, all the parts of this book correspond to the parts of a simple model of the design process shown in Figure I-1. You start by choosing a direction and defining a goal. You get ideas, and then refine them and make them more concrete until you have a finished design or a finished product. Each part of the book covers what you need to know during one step in the GUI design process.

Of course, you are welcome to read from cover to cover if you're the methodical type. But it isn't really necessary. If it suits you better, feel free to pick out the parts or chapters that interest you, or the chapters that seem relevant to what is happening in your project right now. Each topic has all the information you need built right in, and also points you to related topics elsewhere in the book.

Part I: Identifying Goals and Constraints

Read Part I if you find yourself at the beginning of a project, if your project team is having trouble reaching agreement on design questions, or if you just want to know where designing a graphical user interface all starts.

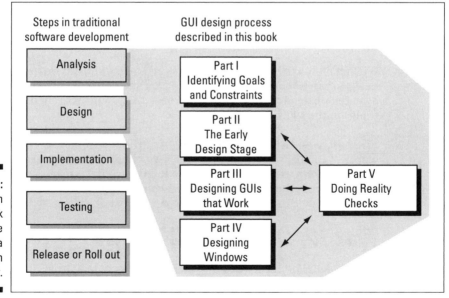

Figure I-1:
The parts in this book match the steps in a GUI design project.

Part II: Surviving the Early Design Stage

Putting pencil to paper and sketching those first tentative examples of how you want your GUI to appear can be a creative bungee jump into a sea of possibilities — from a height that can really make you wonder if your bungee cord is well-fastened. Read Part II if your project is currently working with questions like the following:

- What should the menu system look like?
- What are the main features, and how do they fit together?
- What kinds of windows do you need? How will the user move from window to window?
- Do you need a project standard? What should be in it?

If you're in the early design phase of your project, this may also be a good time to take a look at Part V, "Doing Reality Checks," because you'll find it cheaper to catch and correct problems if you do it early in the design. Wait longer, and watch prices skyrocket.

Part III: Designing GUIs that Work

GUI design involves a lot of trial and error. Because bosses don't like to hear terms like "trial and error," GUI designers call the process *iteration* instead. Iteration means that you return to the same design question several times, aiming to find a better and more detailed answer each time.

When it's time to get some real functional meat on the bare bones of your design, you're ready for Part III. This part shows you how to use task-oriented design techniques to make sure that your program does the right things in the right way.

However, your GUI doesn't just consist of the right functions. In order to work, a GUI has to work for the user. Two chapters in this part show you how to make a user interface easy to learn and effective to use, using concepts from the academic field of *Human Computer Interaction* (HCI).

Part IV: Designing Windows

In an ideal world, every project team would include a professional graphic designer. If you've got your own graphic designer, go ahead and skip Part IV. Otherwise, take heart. You don't need an artistic temperament or three years at a prestigious design school in order to do a workmanlike job. Just keep your eyes open and your little gray cells in gear, and check out the chapters on visual design, color, and graphics.

Part IV also seems like the right place for the chapter on GUI components or widgets. You know the things I mean: menus, check boxes, drop-down lists, and the like. I assume that you already know what these different components are and how they behave, so Part IV focuses on how these GUI components work from a user's point of view.

Part V: Doing Reality Checks

The techniques in Part V are useful at any stage in an interface design project. Part V tells how to conduct what is commonly called *user testing* or *usability testing*. I think of these activities as reality checks. A reality check is not about testing the users, and it doesn't result in a grade for the software developers, either. A reality check is a practical test with users that provides designers with the feedback that they need about what works the way they thought it would, and what doesn't. Even better, such tests provide clues about *why* things work or don't work. Over time, this kind of feedback improves your batting average at creating successful designs.

Like graphical design, usability testing is a discipline in its own right, with qualified specialists who have taken degrees in fields such as Human Factors or Human Computer Interaction (HCI). If you have access to specialists, learn everything you can from them. If not, Part V has the information you need for do-it-yourself reality checks.

Part VI: The Part of Tens

All ...*For Dummies* books have a Part of Tens — I haven't figured out if that's because The Part of Tens is the most fun to read or because it's the most fun to write. Anyway, *GUI Design For Dummies* is no exception: In Part VI, you can find lists of goodies that don't fit elsewhere.

For example, Murphy's Law — if something can go wrong, it will — has lots of axioms, corollaries, and theorems that explain why GUI design is a perpetual challenge. They've got their own chapter in The Part of Tens. Since project leaders never have time to read a whole book, I've awarded them their own chapter: everything project leaders really need to know about GUI design compressed into one tidy list.

I sincerely hope that you'll enjoy designing a GUI with the help of *GUI Design For Dummies*. In fact, I hope you'll get so hooked on the subject that you'd like to learn more. The Part of Tens winds up with a resource chapter that will guide you to Web sites, books, publications, conferences, and organizations that may be of use in your advanced GUI design work.

Icons Used in This Book

How do you find what you want in this book? Graphical user interfaces are dripping with icons, right? Icons show the user where to find the good stuff in a program. So, it seems appropriate that this book about GUIs should have icons, too. The icons in this book help you spot the very best stuff easily. Here's what to look for:

Tips are the best. A tip is some action, insight, or technique that has worked several times for me in the field, and will work for you, too.

Nontechnical Stuff indicates material about things like feelings, psychology, or even aesthetics. Some people find this to be the most fascinating part of GUI design. Some, however, like to keep everything nice and objective and factual. If that description fits you, then Nontechnical Stuff serves as a warning that things may get just a wee bit fluffy or general. Feel free to skip ahead to safer territory.

You may work in the systems division of a bank or an insurance company, a utility or a retail chain. You may be a consultant or an independent contractor. If you are doing custom software development for specific clients — internal or external — you'll run into problems that are specific to your situation. The "Custom" GUI icon marks advice especially for you.

You may be developing package software for any computer user to buy from the computer store at the mall, or from a catalog. Package development has its own set of challenges and problems. How do you please most of the people most of the time? The "Package" GUI icon flags advice especially for you.

I don't know about you, but I'm lost without my Apple Newton. The old gray cells are glitchy. The Remember icon points out information that you probably already know, but shouldn't forget at this particular point in the project.

The picture says it all. When you see the Warning icon, there's a potentially threatening loose cannon somewhere in the vicinity. The text that accompanies this icon tells you how to keep that cannon tied down.

You probably already noticed the shiny CD-ROM that's attached to the back of this book. The On the CD icon marks those paragraphs that refer to something you can find on the CD-ROM. How's that for added value?

The CD-ROM

At the back of the book, you'll find a CD-ROM to help you on your way. Several of the files that it contains, such as GUI standards for Windows-based projects and the glorious "Design Considerations Memo," are ready for you to edit and use in your own project. The CD-ROM also contains shareware and freeware that may be of interest to a GUI Designer. Check out the Appendix for more information about the compact disc.

Take the Plunge

I don't know too many people who actually read introductions, but if you're still here, thanks for sticking around. You deserve a reward, so after you've browsed through Rich Tennant's great cartoons at the beginning of each part (the gray pages), why don't you look up the part of GUI design that you find the most daunting, whether it's Visual Design (Chapter 13) or keeping all the different gizmos straight (Chapter 16) or even just getting started (Chapter 1). After all, well begun is half done, especially given the elastic way in which progress is measured in software development: The first 90 percent of the project takes the first 90 percent of the time, and the last 10 percent of the project takes the last 90 percent of the time.

Part I

Identifying Goals and Constraints

"...AND YOU'RE CLAIMING THAT THE SOURCE CODE USED FOR THE MICROSOFT CORP. GUI WAS ACTUALLY AUTHORED BY YOU AS THE GUMBY USER INTERFACE?!"

In this part . . .

Congratulations — you're a designer! Soon hundreds or thousands of real people will be searching through the menus *you* have organized, peering at the icons *you* have chosen, clicking on *your* buttons, and knitting their brows over *your* helpful and educational error messages. Your brainchild will be someone else's workplace.

Design is a serious responsibility, but that doesn't mean it isn't fun, too. In fact, starting your design work is a lot like playing with a toy construction set. First you've got to get all the pieces out on the table and see what you've got to work with. Then you can give free rein to your creativity. Part I shows you how to start your design work by picking a direction, getting familiar with your "pieces," and making a plan.

Chapter 1

Deciding Where You're Going

. . . .

. . . .

*H*ow to get started? Whether you perceive infinite possibilities or merely an infinite vacuum at the start of a GUI design project, you probably agree that the first steps are the difficult ones.Try thinking of yourself as a hunter. In a GUI design project, the first thing you want to figure out is what you're hunting *for,* so look around you. If a hunter is tromping around in Kansas, he's probably not hunting for elephants. Similarly, if you're designing a system for a medical practice, you aren't looking for user entertainment. On the other hand, if you're designing a computer game, finding user entertainment is your most important goal.

You must know what you want to accomplish in a user interface design project in order to do a good job. If you're just starting out, this chapter can help you set appropriate, achievable design goals. If you're already deeply into a GUI design project and are having a lot of noisy design debates, a quick time-out with this chapter may help you to agree on a set of priorities for resolving your differences.

Aim for Perfection, Settle for Excellence

What makes a good GUI? The volumes of design guidelines published for each graphical user environment, whether Windows, Mac, UNIX, or Java, will try to convince you that a graphical user interface should be all things to all people. Don't believe them. As you can see from the following list that I assembled, some of the desirable attributes are in conflict with others. Often you are forced to choose between them.

✔ **Consistent with the standard:** If the user already knows how to use some other Windows program, it'll be easier for her to learn to use yours (provided that both programs follow the standard, of course).

✔ **Easy to learn and understand:** The program requires minimal training, communicates clearly, and is based on ideas familiar to the user, such as familiar tasks or objects. The interface contains visual cues such as text, buttons, and icons so that it does not burden the user's memory unnecessarily.

✔ **Fast to use:** Typing, waiting, clicking, reading, navigating, and even thinking or remembering are kept to a minimum.

✔ **Effective:** Differs from *fast to use* in that the interface should help the user to produce a good-quality result. A favorite goal, but it requires some serious analysis to determine what the desired result is, and how the user defines good quality.

✔ **Forgiving of user errors:** The program does not get stuck or destroy data if the user has made an error. The program may ignore errors or may help the user to recognize and correct the errors easily.

✔ **Attractive to look at:** Well-thought-out and professional-looking graphics and layout.

✔ **Comfortable to work with:** User comfort issues include readability/legibility of text, appropriate language, user control of colors, allowing the user to choose between using the mouse or the keyboard. User comfort is related to ease of use, too. Users feel uncomfortable with systems that make them feel stupid or ineffective.

✔ **User-driven:** This quality especially distinguishes GUIs from the older, character- and screen-based systems, which were often called *menu-driven*. A user-driven system allows the user to decide in what order to perform tasks and to take the initiative about what to do next. A user-driven system is comfortable for many kinds of people to use: Each user can work in the order that she finds natural, rather than following a single path preset by the system designers.

✔ **Satisfying to use:** Systems are usually judged *satisfying to use* when the user feels in control of the system and is able to produce the desired result without difficulty or undue effort.

✔ **Flexible:** A flexible system offers the users more than one choice, path, or way to perform tasks. Flexibility allows the user — and the system — to respond to needs that may have been unforeseen during development.

✔ **Task-centered:** The system is organized around the user's tasks and the way the user works, rather than on how data are organized in the database.

The truth is that if you try to create a user interface that always fulfills every requirement in the list, you are doomed to failure — not because you lack a degree in HCI (Human Computer Interaction), but because the inherent conflicts in the specifications for the perfect GUI set you up to fail. For example:

- ✔ Suppose you want to make a user interface *flexible* and *user-driven,* so you create quite a few alternatives and allow the user to take the initiative in deciding how to use them. For new users, especially new users who are performing an unfamiliar task, it can be hard to take initiative and difficult to sort out the alternatives. Adding too much flexibility can make the interface harder to learn. Oops.

- ✔ Say that you want to make a user interface *quick to use* and *task-centered.* Well, you could tailor the interface precisely for a specific task, omitting unnecessary choices, information, and steps — which, by the way, makes the GUI less flexible.

- ✔ Perhaps you want to make the GUI *effective* and *time-saving* for experienced users; you therefore assume that the users have a certain level of expertise (they have memorized codes, for example, or don't need on-screen reminders in which they have to click OK). But now the interface is harder to learn.

- ✔ Suppose that you want to include those gorgeous graphics that make the interface more *attractive.* But what if those graphics cause the windows to appear more slowly on the average user's PC?

Face it: I'm talking real life here. Effective GUI design is about making the right tradeoffs. The key to designing a great GUI is to face the fact that you cannot design a perfect GUI. You can't design so that the interface is always equally fast, flexible, easy, attractive, and effective for everybody all the time. But by prioritizing your top design goals and sticking to them, you can create an interface that will be good in the ways that are most important for your particular project.

Carefully consider the overall project goals, the type of users you have, and the working situation of those users. Pick three items from the list of desirable attributes — just three — and put them in order of priority. Say you pick flexibility first, ease of use second, and attractiveness to users third. Try to design the whole interface with those three characteristics in mind. Any time you are forced to make a tradeoff, choose the solution that best matches your priorities.

Don't pick design goals all by yourself. Involve project stakeholders — client leaders, user representatives, your own project leaders, marketing, and such others — in selecting the design goals and putting them in order of priority. Hang a list of the prioritized goals up on the wall to remind you to be fearless, determined, and unflinching in your pursuit of the quarry: an excellent user interface.

Choosing appropriate GUI design goals does not guarantee that you will produce a good interface design, but it does get you started off in the right direction. Start this way, and at least you won't be hunting elephants in Kansas . . . or going on a camera safari only to find yourself derrière-deep in a bunch of hungry alligators.

Different Projects, Different Design Goals

When you develop custom software, look at the overall goals for the project before you set design goals for the user interface.

Suppose an insurance company, Central Calamity, has a new product: a policy to cover costs due to loss or damage of computing equipment and software. Central Calamity wants you to design the user interface for an application that contains functions to estimate the customer's degree and extent of risk, suggest the policy amount, calculate the premium, register necessary information about the customer and the equipment to be insured, and then create the policy. I can think of at least three completely different projects that might ask for an application with this functionality.

Project 1: Letting the customer do the work

In order to reduce its own personnel costs and to capture as much of the "new" market as possible, Central Calamity intends to let customers enter their own data and purchase policies via the World Wide Web (with suitable protection against fraud, of course). What goals would you select from the list at the beginning of this chapter? Here are my suggestions:

1. **Attractive to Net surfers:** The GUI should display leading edge technology, graphics, or both. The interface should offer some form of content that has value to the visitor independent of the proffered insurance policy — bait. Making the interface attractive to users is first priority — no "if you build it they will come" guarantee is in effect here. If the user interface is not attractive, surfers won't stay and all other efforts will be wasted.

2. **Easy to understand:** Users can walk away from a Web site at any time, so you don't dare irritate or offend them with an interface that they have to struggle with. Make sure that the interface clearly communicates what you can do with it. Central Calamity's site, for example, should say that you can estimate your premiums and set up your own policy.

3. **Either fast *or* interesting to use:** Data entry for users of the site should be kept to a minimum. If Central Calamity wants the users to enter quite a bit of data, perhaps a running comparison of total coverage

and premiums might keep the user riveted. (Maybe you could also include a little humorous animation of the catastrophes that can befall computers.)

Project 2: Signing up the best customers

Central Calamity wants to increase its revenues from large businesses. Central Calamity plans to offer a new insurance policy to its 5,000 largest business customers during a concentrated campaign of personal visits by top sales agents. The agents will use your application on a laptop computer, creating the policy together with the customer during a single visit. Would the salespeople be well served by the same interface you designed for the Internet users? Not really. How about these design goals:

1. **Easy to use:** Central Calamity will send the sales agents who already have strong relationships with the best customers — whether or not those agents are proficient with their computers. Furthermore, an agent needs to give the customer most of her attention; she won't be able to concentrate on using the program. Make "easy to use" your top priority.

2. **Interesting/attractive to the customer:** This application actually has two users: the sales agent and the customer. If you can design the application so that it is interesting for the customer, your interface will help to make the sale. What about including a dynamic graph that shows the ratio of risk to premiums? Or how about small video clips of executives describing the consequences of theft, sabotage, or flooding on their business systems?

3. **Effective:** Make sure the interface allows the agent to get through the task as quickly as possible. Customers are busy; you don't want them to get restless and conclude the interview before the agent can finish creating the policy.

Project 3: Grabbing market share

Central Calamity invented computer insurance to have a product that would appeal to younger customers and to attract customers from rival insurance companies that don't offer computer insurance. Naturally the other insurance companies will quickly create rival products, so Central Calamity plans to market computer insurance with an intense telephone campaign. Trained agents will create the policies while speaking with the customers on the phone. Time for a new set of design goals:

1. **Effective:** You're looking for volume here — users are going to be asking customers the same questions, in the same order, over and over again. Unnecessary steps, long response times, or unnecessary typing all cause stress for expert users, and the stress increases when a customer is waiting on the phone.

2. **Task-centered:** You can tailor this system to the standard sales conversation. For example, organize the input fields so that the agent can start at the top of the screen and ask the customer sequential sales questions as the agent fills in the fields from top to bottom.

3. **Error-preventive:** The high-pressure sales campaign can create a stressful working environment — users may make typing mistakes as they tire, or they may make incorrect judgments. Therefore, you can make your interface error-preventive by integrating the telephone and the computer system. For example, you can implement automatic dialing to avoid wrong numbers. You can also reduce errors by setting up the system to automatically retrieve any existing computer data about the customer, so that users can simply confirm data rather than reentering it.

Pleasing Most of the People

Goal-setting is equally important when you're developing *shrinkwrap* software (for the retail market) as it is when you're working on a project for a specific client, but the process is a little different. The overall goal of a commercial development project is to make a good profit from selling the software. If you intend to sell as many software packages as possible to as many people as possible, this section is for you.

Here's the solution, what's the problem?

When developing commercial software, make sure that your program can solve a real problem (or meet a real or strongly perceived need) for the potential users. Do enough people want the software that you're developing? Are you sure?

To demonstrate the importance of gauging user needs, let me tell you a cautionary tale about a particular telecommunications application. This software was intended to allow private telephone customers to use their personal computers for programming their telephones with information about who they were willing to take calls from, and when. By doing so, phone users could ensure that only Grandma or Uncle Joe could interrupt Thanksgiving dinner.

While it is doubtful whether you actually would want to look up all those phone numbers and type them into your PC in the first place, the bigger issue is that people evaluate incoming calls as interesting or uninteresting based on *who* is calling, not *where* they are calling from or *when*. For example, I want to receive that incoming call from my teenage daughter, even if she is calling at 2 a.m. from an unknown telephone booth.

This project was unable to recoup its development costs. Nobody wanted to buy the product.

Consider how people spend money: Techies like to try out the new stuff. Techies invest their money sensibly in personal digital assistants, tiny cellular phones with faxes, and ISDN phone lines. Non-techies will cheerfully waste their money on boring things like new clothes, new furniture, or new movies, but they tend to view new technology with more reserve. "Another new monster to tame? Is it worth my trouble?" you can hear them thinking.

So, rule one for commercial software development is to find something that non-techie users experience as a real problem, and then design a solution to that problem.

Make it easy, but make it yesterday

To dress for success in commercial software development, you need to focus on the following:

- ✔ Be first to identify and develop new functions or new technology that are important to help your users get their work done. And, of course, you always have those market-driven goals — make sure that the program is bug-free, compatible with all conceivable hardware, and on the market yesterday.

- ✔ Offer these functions in a user interface that is visibly easier, prettier, faster, or cheaper than the competition — preferably all four.

- ✔ Offer new versions in which existing users can use their present knowledge, but don't puzzle new users with commands that seem irrelevant. Add new functions constantly without making the program more complicated or too unwieldy.

Commercial software development always involves tradeoffs. On one hand, the goals for the software development are always the same; on the other hand, those goals always conflict. You'll never have time to make a perfect system. Your ability to choose *what the users will care about most* will be continually tested.

The goal that's neglected most often is making an interface user-friendly for nondevelopers. Why does this happen? You attend design meetings and live with the code for weeks or months. You've got the project in your bones, in your jokes, and in your dreams. You can't imagine what it would be like to not know how the program works.

User testing will solve this problem for you. By holding a user test, you don't need to imagine how users will figure out your program — you get to see for yourself. Part V, "Doing Reality Checks," tells you how.

Your program needs to be easy to understand for several reasons:

- ✔ Expert users are few and far between. While you may boldly seek out new functions that you've never used before, many users are content to understand the working basics. Many users simply stop at the beginner level and never progress to become experienced or advanced users.

- ✔ Nobody ever complained that a program was too easy to use, but many people complain about the opposite.

- ✔ Users are not keen on deferred gratification. They want to be productive right now. A lot of them go straight to work, ignoring handbooks, help programs, and interactive tutorials. Commands that are easy to overlook or difficult to use just don't get used.

- ✔ Is your product the only one of its kind? If not, a competitive advantage for your product can be that it is easy to understand. Make your users feel smart and productive rather than dumb and frustrated, and you'll sell more.

Expert users of WordPerfect 5.2 for DOS claim that it was superior in functionality to the most common Windows-based word processors in use today. What displaced WordPerfect 5.2 from the market? Why did people move like lemmings to Windows-based applications? It certainly wasn't to hang around in the operating system playing solitaire and using Program Manager. Maybe it was because users experienced Windows-based word processors as being significantly easier to use.

I'm a User — Can't I Design What I Like?

I enjoy computers. I like to work with them, and I like to play with them. If you're like me, you may need to think about the fact that the way *you* react to computers does not predict how the average user reacts to computers.

Because this book is for people who are interested in software development, I'm going out on a limb with a few guesses about you: I bet that, if you were to choose the qualities you prize most in the programs that you use, you'd choose flexibility and speed. I'd also guess that learning any new computer program is pretty easy for you, and that you choose the programs with the most powerful functionality.

Many software developers share these preferences, and if you are designing a GUI for software developers, go right ahead and design something that you'd like to use yourself. Everyday computer users have different working situations, different preferences, and different interests than do software developers. Table 1-1 summarizes just a few of the differences. When your users differ from you in important ways, consider the project's overall goals and the users' working situations rather than your personal taste when you pick design goals.

Table 1-1	Techies versus Users
Techies . . .	*Users . . .*
Like figuring out how things work.	Like things to work. Are educated to work with computers. May have trouble getting permission to attend a two-day course on a new application.
Choose to work with computers.	May be under pressure to use computers if they wish to keep their jobs.
Use the newest, fastest computing equipment that money can buy.	May be working on slower, hand-me-down computer equipment. (The 386s, 486/25s, and 14-inch monitors that techies refused to work with had to go somewhere, didn't they?)
Can focus complete attention on what they are doing with the computer.	May be subject to continual interruptions when working on the computer. For example, doctors, air traffic controllers, or salespeople may be required to use the system while interacting with other people.
Feel that they control the computer.	Often feel controlled by their computers.
Get a kick out of tinkering with something to make it work.	Get a kick out of getting their job done well and quickly.

Unless you are developing interfaces for other system developers, rid yourself of the pernicious illusion that you or other members of your project are typical users. In fact, research shows considerable evidence of temperamental differences between techies and the non-techies (above and beyond techies' tendencies to enjoy science fiction, hang up *Dilbert* cartoons, and dine on pizza). The next few sections discuss these differences.

What type are you?

A quick look at the Myers-Briggs categories for personality types reveals that an unusually high percentage of technical people share the same preference — Intuition — which is less common in the population as a whole. The Myers-Briggs Type Indicator measures a person's inherent preferences in four areas:

1. How you prefer to relate to other people: Introvert/Extrovert.

2. Whether you prefer to collect information through your five senses or through your own thought processes: Senser/Intuiter.

3. Whether you prefer to base decisions on objective rules or on your subjective value system: Thinker/Feeler.

4. Whether you like your time planned, organized, scheduled, and determined, or whether you prefer to keep things open, see nuances and shades, and be spontaneous: Judger/Perceiver.

Myers-Briggs tests have been in use since the 1950s. According to personality type research, about 72 percent of the U.S. population are Sensers, and only 28 percent are Intuiters.

- ✔ In *Tog on Interface* (published by Addison-Wesley), Bruce Tognazzini mentions that 75 percent of Apple Computer's engineers are Intuitive.

- ✔ A personality type test is available on the World Wide Web. By June 1997, 1.4 million Web-surfers had taken the test, and almost 62 percent of them had tested as Intuiters. (Currently you can find an online version of the test at http://sunsite.unc.edu/personality/keirsey.html.)

- ✔ A Web page for the Sibley School of Mechanical and Aerospace Engineering reported that 51 percent of 181 students who took a personality type test were Intuiters.

So why are Intuiters overrepresented (75 percent, 62 percent, and 51 percent instead of 28 percent) among people who are technically-oriented or computer-oriented, and what does that mean for interface design?

An Intuitive personality (or a Senser who has developed his or her Intuitive abilities) finds it easy to work with abstractions, theories, and models; to perceive complex relationships and interdependencies. The invisible structures of system development are real to intuitive developer-types in ways that may seem frustrating for the pragmatic Senser. Typical Intuiters think nothing of talking about "logical disks," "the file system" or virtual reality. Their reality *is* virtual. Only an Intuitive person could seriously call a programming language "object-oriented." A dyed-in-the-wool Senser doesn't see any objects there, and can't touch them either.

The Myers-Briggs classifications remind system developers that their preferences are probably different from those of their users. Intuitive developers will tend to create interfaces that are abstract, generalized, or generic, whereas Sensing users like to see interfaces that are concrete, down-to-earth, and related to the physical world.

Who likes what in GUIs

An Intuitive designer groups commands in the Options menu for changing views, changing editing behavior, and changing where files are saved. To the Intuiter, all these commands share the common attribute of being parameters. A down-to-earth Senser probably looks for the View commands under View, the Edit commands under Edit, and the File commands under File.

An Intuiter remembers there's a pop-up menu on the right mouse button. A Senser, lacking the visual clue, is more likely to forget.

Intuiters did okay with DOS; they could imagine the file structure and remember the commands. Sensers preferred Macs, or waited for Windows to make visible the imaginary structure inside the computer.

An Intuitive developer may put a single tab on a properties window because the design standard says "all properties windows have tabs." A Senser looks at one window at time; seeing a window with a single tab, he may be puzzled about the purpose of the tab.

An Intuitive developer is fully capable of building a database application that reports only to the screen and doesn't print. "You can copy, cut, and paste the database screen into a word processor if you need to," says the Intuiter. The Senser may feel that the database application is incomplete if it doesn't produce physical results: paper reports.

Why the Right Answer Is "It Depends . . ."

"Can't I just follow the standards?" I am often asked. Of course, you can follow the standards for your platform. That still leaves you with myriad design decisions to make on your own. Just consider the enormous differences in appearance between three presumably standard-compliant Microsoft products: the multimedia encyclopedia Encarta, the word processor Word, and Windows Paint.

_____

Furthermore, at least for Windows and Apple Macintosh, the platform standards are created by people who produce an operating system and some personal productivity tools — like word processors. The platform standards often fail to address the issues faced by designers of database applications or transaction systems. Sometimes the right answer for a transaction system is to ignore part of the standard that is not applicable.

Only about 20 percent of your design decisions are covered by the platform standards. If you create a project GUI standard, you can cover an additional 20 percent of the decisions. The remaining right answers aren't written down anywhere — you have to figure them out on the spot, while you're doing your design work.

The right answers depend on your users, their tasks, and the market in which you are competing. Just consider these examples:

- ✔ In a self-ticketing system in which airline passengers can use touch screens, pull-down menus are not a good answer: Many airline passengers don't regularly use a GUI and won't recognize pull down menus when they see them.

- ✔ Touch screens require larger command buttons than regular screens do. Inexperienced users generally need larger command buttons, and so do some user groups that have reduced motor control.

- ✔ Bright colors are distracting in an application that you use all day long; however, these same colors may be appropriate in the graphics of a Web page that you visit for only a few minutes — though perhaps not at a serious-minded site, such as one on world hunger. Many other factors can affect the way that you design a GUI; Chapter 2 gives you a good overview. For now, understand that the right answers are not written down in this or any other book. Your job as a GUI designer is to make the best design decisions for your particular project. *GUI Design For Dummies* shows you how.

Chapter 2
Asking the Right Questions

• •

In This Chapter

▶ Using the Design Considerations Memo

▶ Asking the first questions about users

▶ Coming to grips with project technology

▶ Assessing users' tasks

▶ Understanding the working environment

• •

A good GUI designer asks a lot of questions before starting to draw windows. Find out as much as you can about the factors that will influence the design — the things that you need to take into consideration in order to create a really good solution. As a non-GUI example, suppose I design children's play clothes that can't handle a trip through the washing machine. I've forgotten to consider what children *do* when they play. If I design a GUI that's beautiful on my 17-inch monitor, but the users have to resize the windows or scroll around in them to use the interface, then I've forgotten to ask what size monitors the users have.

You need to ask different questions for different projects. Here's a mental image that will help you figure out what to ask about. Imagine that you're working on a table like the one shown in Figure 2-1. The four legs of the table are technology, users, tasks, and environment. If you pay too much or too little attention to any one leg, it becomes out of proportion to the others. Your table will be an uncomfortable, unstable place to work, and your design will reflect the imbalance.

Most GUI designers have a stronger affinity for one or two of the design areas that need investigation. If you lean toward the technology side of design, pin up the table drawing in your workspace to remind you to do more research on users, tasks, and environmental considerations while you lay the groundwork for your design.

Figure 2-1:
Asking the
right
questions in
all four
areas puts
your GUI
design on a
firm footing.

Preparing a Design Considerations Memo

No matter where you are in the project, take a couple of hours to run through the questions in the upcoming sections of this chapter with your bosses or with your client.

For many of the questions you can safely say, "This doesn't make any difference for our project." Where you agree that the answer to a question should have some influence over the design, jot down the answer. Your collection of answers forms what I call the *Design Considerations Memo* for your project. In a longer project, get the memo out and review it with the top brass once in a while as an aid to communication: You'll scare up some new information out of the bushes each time you review the memo.

I like to add the three top-priority design goals to the end of the Design Considerations Memo. Review these goals with top brass at regular intervals, too.

You'll return to the facts in the Design Considerations Memo over and over again throughout your project's development. In the early design phase described in Part II, for example, you refer to information about users and use patterns in order to select an appropriate windows structure. The task information you gather now will come in handy when you draw the conceptual model (Chapter 5) and the navigation model (Chapter 6).

The memo also acts as documentation for your plans and estimates. When the run-time platform is changed or when a new user group is suddenly discovered, you'll find it easier to bargain for a little more time or help when you can prove that the new information represents a significant change in the project.

The CD-ROM at the back of the book contains both an empty, ready-to-edit Design Considerations Memo and a filled-in memo from a sample project. If paper is more convenient for you to look at, Table 2-1 shows the headings and the main questions for the memo. Feel free to add or skip questions as needed; the template is meant to get you started thinking about what's important for your project within each heading.

Table 2-1	Contents for Design Considerations Memo
The headings	*The main questions*
Users	How many users?
	How much turnover?
	What is the use pattern?
	What are the important user groups?
	What are the characteristics of each group?
	How are the users different from the developers? From non-users?
	How can we learn to know the users better?
Technology	What is the build platform?
	What is the run-time platform? The run-time environment?
	What are the strengths and weaknesses of the development tool?
	How will we ensure acceptable response times?
	What are the storage, recovery, refresh, and locking strategies?
Tasks	From a user's point of view, what are the tasks we must support?
	What tasks are frequently repeated?
	What tasks are mission-critical?
	With the current system, which tasks are most disliked?
	What sources of information can we use to learn more about tasks?

(continued)

Table 2-1 *(continued)*

The headings	The main questions
Environment	What is the physical environment in which the system will be used?
	What is the cultural environment for this system?
	What training or support will users receive?
	What attitudes do people have about this product/system?
	What marketplace considerations should influence our design?
	How much time and money can we use?
Design goals	What are the design goals for the user interface, in order of priority?

Rarely will you be able to fill in complete answers to the Design Considerations Memo at the beginning of the project. Let the group make its best guesses. Perhaps some members can be assigned the responsibility for further research. You can always update the memo as you collect new information; just be sure to ask yourself, "What do I need to do differently in the design as a result of this change?"

Asking about the Users

If the users are real people to you, designing an interface that meets their specific needs is much easier. You won't make the same mistake as the GUI designer who created a system for truck drivers to enter delivery data into palmtop computers. The system flopped because the keys on the palmtop were too small for the truck drivers' fingers. Notice that I did not say the drivers' fingers were too big for the keys. The drivers had fingers all along — the designer failed to identify a user characteristic that was important for the design.

If you're doing custom development, begin by asking the following questions about the users, or about each important group of users. (You find more about categorizing users into groups in the following section.)

✔ **How many users are there?** Just 100? Or 2,000? Or possibly 20,000?

✔ **What kind of turnover does the user group experience?** Do 10 percent of the users leave per year? Or 10 percent per month?

✔ **What is the normal pattern of use?** For example, how many hours per day will they use your application? Will the users' tasks be repetitive or will they be complex and unpredictable?

The answers to these questions should reinforce your sense of direction for the design, help you to judge how much effort to invest in the design project, and help you justify your plans to project leadership or to clients. You can draw the following conclusions from the answers:

✔ High numbers of users and/or a high turnover mean that it will pay to make the user interface self-explanatory or very easy to learn. For example, if you're designing a cash register for a fast food chain (which has many users and a high employee turnover rate), the GUI design should be intuitive to use and easy to figure out; the chain can't afford much training time for each new employee.

✔ If the program will be used occasionally or only for short periods (for example, a utility program or an interface for generating quarterly reports), the GUI design should be easy to understand and easy to remember.

✔ If the system use pattern is intense (people use the system for hours at a time), it is especially important to note whether users are performing tasks that are primarily simple and repetitive, or whether the tasks are complex, varied, and unpredictable:

  • **Repetitive tasks:** You need to focus on making the interface effective. For example, besides keeping keystrokes to a minimum and ensuring snappy response times, look carefully for any factors that can contribute to user comfort and user motivation — such as the opportunity to personalize the interface with color or graphics.

  • **Complex tasks:** Make sure to give the users a good overview of the system. Make navigation paths between functions clear and effective, and allow for flexibility in switching between tasks or between steps in a task. Windows wizards, for example, allow the user to back up in the process step-by-step as an alternative to scrapping the whole effort and starting again at the beginning.

Of the three questions you need to ask regarding users, the issue of *use pattern* is especially important for package software development. Users keep their word processor, spreadsheet, or graphics program open and maximized most of the day. With this type of program, users quickly become "old hands." Even though all users do not become advanced users, the time they spend as true beginners is relatively short. For a GUI with the "all day, every day" use pattern, don't neglect keyboard shortcuts, toolbars, or any other convention that makes life more comfortable for experienced users.

A quarter's worth of cost-benefit analysis

Use the information on numbers of users and use pattern to do some quick-and-dirty calculations. Estimate the possible benefit from improvements to the interface so that you can compare these numbers to the costs of extra design effort and user tests.

For example, suppose that a frequently performed user task takes an average of five minutes. With extra design and testing efforts, you create a GUI that lets users accomplish the task in four minutes instead. Plug in your estimates for number of users and use pattern:

> 3,000 users × 10 repetitions per day × 1 minute saved = 500 user-hours per day, or 90,000 user-hours saved per year.

How many development hours can you afford to invest to save 90,000 user hours?

Look at turnover and training time to see whether it is important to spend time making the design easier to understand and easier to learn. Suppose that 1,000 users take one work week to learn a new system, and that the user group has 10 percent turnover per year. In addition to initial training costs of 5,000 person-days, plus instructor time, your clients will be using 500 person-days per year for training. If you can design a program easy enough to be learned in three days instead of five, you've reduced training-associated costs by 40 percent.

If you need to provide thorough cost-benefit analyses for your leaders or clients, get this specialized yet readable book on the subject: *Cost-Justifying Usability*, edited by Randolph G. Bias and Deborah Mayhew (published by Academic Press).

If you design an interface for a program with an *occasional use pattern* (such as a virus checker, a file compression utility, a screen capture program, or other program used for a specific, short-term task), take care to show the user clearly what the program does and make it easy to see how to perform the task. Don't rely on the user's memory; use visible command names. If you use icons, add text. Remember that your program represents a minor task for the user; don't hog screen space.

Grouping users

If you suspect that different users may have significantly different wishes for, and opinions about, your program, you then need to define several user groups. Try to define distinct groups. Keep the number of groups as small as possible. Check for differences among groups like these:

- ✔ **Professional groups:** Doctors and nurses need access to the same patient information, but may want the data organized and presented in different ways. A nurse giving patient care follows a few individual patients and needs detailed information, perhaps arranged chronologically. A doctor making rounds sees many patients briefly, and may want information focused to support decision-making: changes in patient condition, summaries, and test results.

✔ **Geographical location:** Head-office users are often specialists in one area. In a bank, a head-office user might work on loans for a single large account, using one or two programs at the expert level. Users from the local branches work with many customers and many different kinds of accounts. They have broader knowledge of many programs, but don't have time to become expert at any one program.

✔ **Setting for use:** Home users may enjoy variety, frivolous features, and informal output; at the office, the same person might prefer that the word processor has a more subdued behavior and appearance.

✔ **Degree and source of expertise:** Users with different computer backgrounds tend to have different expectations; users like what they are familiar with. If you have to create a new program to be used by one group that currently uses Windows 3.1 and a second bunch currently using X-Windows applications, the sooner you get the conflicts out in the open, the better.

Negotiating a truce between conflicting user groups

One reason you want to identify conflicting groups up front is that you won't be able to please them all, all the time. The sooner everybody understands this, the better chance that your project will be judged a success. Still, there are a few constructive things you can do:

✔ Analyze the conflicts by deciding on a set of design goals for each user group.

✔ Will some parts of the user interface be used by a single group? If so, let that group's design goals prevail in that part of the design.

✔ Which groups are most critical to project acceptance and success? Let their needs take priority.

✔ Can problems be exported, for example to the training department? If new users' interests got sacrificed, encourage leaders to compensate by providing more training time.

✔ If the conflicting user groups are aware that they are in conflict, how about getting them together to negotiate some tradeoffs?

Whatever else you do, keep your head down when the rotten fruit starts flying.

Gathering information about users

"Phooey! Don't do what I *tell* you to, do what I *want* you to!" Across our facing desks, my husband berates his word processor. He's not alone in his frustration. Ideally, users want you to read their minds correctly at all times and to provide them with both exactly what they want and what they need. That's why the single most-repeated piece of advice in the GUI design trade is "know your users."

Have you ever done the same work that your users do? Some lucky developers have first-hand experience of their users' workplace and tasks; others need to collect the information secondhand. If you're working in the shrinkwrap software industry some of the best people to ask are either inside your own company or work for you as contractors:

- ✔ **Documentation experts:** The people who write the handbooks usually do an audience analysis. Have you read it?

- ✔ **Marketing people:** These folks may have conducted surveys or focus groups with users.

- ✔ **Course instructors:** Instructors can give you excellent feedback on what new users understand easily and what they struggle with.

- ✔ **Support personnel:** Support personnel are a great source of ideas for new functions — they man the phones and hear the user questions such as, "Isn't there a way to make this program. . . . ?"

- ✔ **Trade shows and user association conferences:** These events give software developers a chance for frontline contact with users.

If you're doing in-house or custom interface development, check out some of the following sources of information:

- ✔ **User representatives:** User representatives usually get picked for the job because they like computers more than typical users do, so take their opinions with a grain of salt. Ask the user representative to tell you about her colleagues and their work, rather than just asking the rep what she likes and doesn't like about the interface.

- ✔ **Reference groups:** A random bunch of users collected together in a reference group can give you a variety of opinions. You get a more realistic impression of the diversity in your user group.

- ✔ **Site visits:** Site visits are a great way to pick up information about tasks and working environment. Chapter 19 tells how to conduct a site visit.

- ✔ **Interviews with client management:** Managers can usually estimate the size of and the shared characteristics of a user group quite accurately. You don't need to do an expensive survey asking, "How long did you attend school?" and "How long have you used a computer?" if you can wrangle an hour or so with a clued-in manager.

Users with special needs

Be aware that some of your users are disabled. Users with motor handicaps and computer users who are blind, for example, use GUIs with the help of adaptive devices. An adaptive device may convert computer-based text into Braille, or a speech synthesis attachment may read out loud text appearing on the screen. A disabled user may prefer a speech-recognition system to input commands. In many cases, an interface that contains information stored *solely* as graphics causes problems. The two most important guidelines for ensuring accessibility are:

✔ All commands must have keyboard equivalents so users with impaired vision — and adaptive devices — can interact with the program.

✔ Particularly in Web pages, content must be separate from format so that adaptive devices can locate and translate the meaningful information for the user's benefit.

For further information, visit the Equal Access to Software and Information (an affiliate of the American Association for Higher Education) Web site at http://www.rit.edu/~easi/ or contact EASI at: EASI c/o AAHE, One DuPont Circle, Suite 360, Washington DC 20036; 202-293-6440, extension 48.

Hanging your users on the wall

Make your users a true presence in the interface development project. You can try hanging posters around your work area, showing the names, pictures, and workplaces of real users you have met (as shown in Figure 2-2). Add interview quotes and samples of the output they produce with your program.

If you're working on a design team, help each other to see the users as real people by including notes on their families and favorite amusements. You can even do this with fictional people. After a couple of weeks, you will hear conversations like this: "But do you think Jerry-the-shipping-clerk-in-the-warehouse is going to understand this?" "No, but he won't be using it. That's for Marilyn-the-foreman-on-the-night-shift."

Identifying Technology Issues

Even if you feel that technology is your strong point, you may want to read this section just to see which aspects of the technical architecture need special focus from a GUI design standpoint. If you happen to think of yourself as a non-techie, this section will help you shrink the technology issue from a nightmarish monster down to a manageable, if energetic, pet poodle.

Figure 2-2:
Keeping
users on
the walls
helps you
keep them
in mind.

Build and run-time platforms

The *build platform* is the hardware and software that the development team uses to create the program or application. The *run-time platform* is the minimum hardware and software environment that the user must have in order to run the program or application.

When you determine the minimum hardware configuration that users must have in order to run your application, don't forget to define minimum screen size in number of pixels (for example, 800×600) and minimum number of colors. The user's minimum size represents the largest window you can safely design; the user's minimum number of colors is the maximum number that you can use. Software for different audiences will have different requirements; for example:

✔ In commercial software development, restrictions to screen and window size will be a strategic decision. You naturally prefer to demand that the users have bigger, newer, faster machines so that your program can have plenty of resources to play with; marketing wants your program to have all the nice new features but run on every PC produced since 1990, in order to have the largest possible market. Nonetheless, you must come to agreement (or compromise) on these points, preferably before you do much design work.

✔ In custom development, you probably need to ask for information on what configurations the client's users already have. Be skeptical to wishful declarations from client technical personnel that "oh, it'll all be upgraded by the time the project is finished." Record the information and the source in your Design Considerations Memo.

Software developers tend to have more powerful computers and bigger and better screens than the users. In order to get a realistic idea about the way your interface will appear to users (including the color palette, window sizes, display time, and response times of the interface), you should view the interface on one or more typical user workstations. To see how your design works, look at it on the users' machines, not on the developers'.

The development tool

You need to ask: What are the development tools? What are their strengths and weaknesses? Which window types and components are ready-made? What has to be done the hard way?

You want to know these things because as the GUI designer, it's in your best interests to work *with* the development tool rather than against it. Take the time to get familiar with the tool before you attempt to make design decisions, especially decisions regarding the project standard (Chapter 7).

Technical architecture issues

This section is where you get into the truly juicy technical issues. Meet with the project's top technical expert and trace the path of a demanding user command through the technical architecture of your single-user or client/server system. Where are the bottlenecks? What actions might you take in the user interface that would affect response times adversely? What actions might improve response times?

Long response times give users purple fits. Begin as soon as possible to understand what contributes to slow response, and design your interface to minimize the problem.

You may have to resort to guerrilla design tactics to keep response times acceptable, for example:

✔ Build in default search criteria to narrow searches

✔ Reduce graphical complexity in windows to free up memory or graphical resources

✔ Limit the number of dynamic relationships between components in one window

Don't forget that time is subjective. A dynamic progress bar, an hourglass that turns over, or a loony animation can make users *underestimate* the time they spend waiting and reassure them that the system is working on their last command.

What — and why — to ask about packet size

If the application sends data over a network, how much data can the application send at one time? This amount is sometimes called the *packet size*. What is the estimated capacity and activity on the network? What is the chance that users will experience a noticeable wait between the receipt of related packets?

Ask about packet size and network capacity because the answers can impact the way you design search functions, windows containing large amounts of data (especially if you have a window with lots of tabs), tables, and lists, and can influence how you save the user's data and changes.

Storage and recovery strategies

At what point will user changes be saved? What triggers a save? Will it be possible to save incomplete information? How much work might a user lose in the worst case, if the client, server, or network fails at a bad time?

The answers to these questions can make a difference when you are trying to divide a task between several windows, or to consolidate it into a single window. These answers can influence your design and placement of the Save, New, and Undo functions.

Saved by the leg

I once preserved my own professional reputation by using the "legs of the table" concept discussed in this chapter as a mental checklist. As I was about to turn thumbs down on a user interface I'd been hired to review, I paused to ask the *technology* question: "What development tool did they use?" The tool was unfamiliar to me, so I took an extra day to learn about it.

It turned out that most of the undesirable "features" in the interface resulted from limitations in the development tool, which was in its first GUI-supporting version. I was able to link my criticisms to the weaknesses of the tool, rather than reporting incorrectly that the developers had done a poor job on their design.

Give me a sensible Save

When I take the trouble to type something into a computer, I do so because I want to keep what I am typing — almost every time. I don't type for recreation, or at random. My computer does not really need to wonder, "Is she typing this because she really means it, or is she just doing finger calisthenics?"

Given that the uncertainty factor about what I want is so low, why do I afterwards have to tell my computer, every single time, as if it were something really exotic and unheard of, "Hey, know what? I think I'll save this!"

I could understand it if I were storing in Read Only Memory, so I could never take it out again if it were wrong. I could understand it if we were back in 1983 when the complete storage capability of my word processor was four pages in one file.

With today's technology, I can't understand it.

Saving is normal, but most programs act as if it were an error situation. I think an intelligent program should save everything I type, and let me take a little extra trouble to get rid of things I put in by mistake.

True, we'd need a good Undo feature, and that would mean extra work for software developers. But sensible saving will come someday, and the first people to implement it are going to look a lot better in the marketplace than the laggards.

Would you rather be first, or last?

In a multiuser system based on a large database, make sure that you understand the *locking* and *refreshing* strategies in your project: When are records available to be viewed or changed by more than one user at once? What happens if Betty in Boston changes the data while Bill in Butte is looking at it on his screen? Does Bill get a signal that the data has changed? Does Bill's data change automatically? Your interface design must let the users know what they can change and what is locked; they must be able to see whether data is reliable or possibly out-of-date.

Asking about Tasks

By asking users about the specific tasks that they perform, you open up a gold mine of information on how your interface should work.

What is your program or application supposed to do? Hopefully, you already have the answer to this question in the form of a *functional specification,* which is a horribly boring and very detailed document that explains what operations users can perform with the program, what data it must accept, and what results it is supposed to produce. If not, somebody needs to get to work on it right away. But *functions* (save, search, draw a circle) are not the same thing as *tasks* (register a new member, draw a poster), and a GUI designer needs to know the difference.

For example, consider a customer database. Like most database applications it has the functions create, update, delete, read, and search. But you can't design windows until you know what specific *tasks* the user is performing when she uses these functions.

The task "register a new customer" may mean nothing more than create, fill in, and store one customer record. However, the task could include assigning the customer to an account manager or creating and sending out a customer ID card, in which case you would need to add additional commands and fields to the window that displays the customer record. Does the user merely register information, or does she open an account? Perhaps she must evaluate credit history before registering the new customer. Your design may need to include space to display credit data from another system.

At the beginning of a design project, you simply need to be able to describe what the user will be doing with the system, from her point of view.

See Chapter 9 to find out more about the task descriptions that you need in order to perform task-oriented design.

Because time is at a premium in most GUI development projects, you need to select a few user tasks where you concentrate your best efforts. There are three types of tasks that deserve special attention:

- **Frequently performed tasks:** Make sure that frequently performed tasks require no unnecessary steps, no extra typing, and no unnecessary mouse navigation. Nobody will raise an eyebrow at good design here, but they'll be at your throat if you mess up. Did I say life was fair?

- **Mission-critical tasks:** When you ask what the mission-critical tasks are, somebody will try to give you the non-answer, "everything." Try not to settle for less than a real answer. Be stubborn and inquisitive. Go on, it's fun. Try referring to the overall project goals: "If this system is really going to succeed in reducing personnel costs, what tasks will make the biggest contribution to reduced costs?"

- **Tasks that are tedious to perform with the current system:** Any new system means extra work for the users. They have to learn new ways to do things. Why should they greet this extra work with open arms and smiling faces? Usually, the *FUD* factor (fear, uncertainty, and doubt) is high. So you should try to discover what the users really detest doing under the current system. If your design can make the worst jobs go more easily, users will be more positive to the new system.

Try to set up your list of frequently performed, mission-critical, and most-detested tasks before you start your interface design work — these tasks should get the lion's share of your time and attention during the project.

Design the user interface for these tasks early in the project so that you have time to make *prototypes,* which are imitations of one or more windows — much simpler to create than a finished program. (See Chapter 6 for more about prototypes.) I like to make prototypes for the important tasks because I get more useful comments on a visual prototype than on a narrative description of how the interface will look. You can also use a prototype to do early user testing.

Evaluating the Environment

According to real estate agents, three factors determine the cost of a home: location, location, and location. You should also ask three "location" questions to help you evaluate the environment in which your design will be used:

- ✔ In what type of *physical environment* will the interface be used?
- ✔ What is the *culture* in which the interface will be used?
- ✔ What is the *marketplace* in which the interface will be used?

As you think about each of the location questions, you'll discover additional specific questions that relate to your particular project.

Physical environment

In assessing the users' physical environment, you may ask questions like the following:

- ✔ **Where is the user in relation to the workstation?** Is the user seated at a desk or standing at an information kiosk? I've seen a measurement system for assembly line use where the user stood 4–6 feet from the PC, tapping parts of a car with a light pen and reading figures off the screen. That system used BIG fonts.

- ✔ **What are the physical surroundings?** What are the lighting conditions like? Is there a lot of dust? If so, maybe you need to supply a keyboard cover, or consider a different input device.

  Does the users' work environment generate a lot of noise? If so, don't choose audible warning signals for your program.

- ✔ **What other equipment typically surrounds the user?** How much is the user on the phone? Will the program be used while the user is on the phone with a customer? If so, quick response times and fast navigation through the interface are particularly critical.

  Is the fax machine down the hall? If so, you may find it worthwhile to integrate a fax package into a sales order application, for example, so the user needn't run up and down the hall continually.

> Does the user have both hands free for the GUI? Air traffic controllers, for example, run their radio/telecommunication panel with one hand borrowed from the scanning and routing systems. When the telecom system went digital, it seemed like a good idea to put the interface on a PC with a GUI — so much more flexible! — until a controller pointed out that the proposed interface would require two hands, and he had only about half of one to spare.

Cultural environment

Living in a world blessed with increasingly effective communication and transportation technology, we have begun to see that *culture* is far more than music, art, and culinary style. Culture has been described as "software of the mind." It permeates our thought patterns and our responses. And culturally based conflicts can be among the most difficult to resolve, because they threaten our sense of identity.

Cultural differences are not limited to differences between national groups. You and I are really cultural onions. At the outer layer of the onion are our national and ethnic cultural differences, but we can have inner layers of regional culture.

Deeper into the onion, we may be part of a company culture, a professional culture, or both. Imagine what might happen if a software developer from Wild n' Woolly Multimedia's office in a converted dockside warehouse magically changed places with a business-suited individual from Incredibly Boring Machines' corporate finance department. The crises that you are imagining stem from cultural differences.

Naturally, I don't expect you to get to know all the cultural layers of your onions — excuse me, *users*. After you have an idea of what culture is, you just need to consider: Do my users share my national culture? How about my company culture? If not, you'll need to learn about the culture you're designing for.

Interfaces for international usage have to cope with problems such as these:

- Symbols acceptable in one culture may be offensive in another. The "thumbs up" symbol that is positive in the U.S. makes an unfriendly suggestion about where you should put your thumb in Sicily. A piggy bank looks cute to many people, but pigs are unclean for Moslems and orthodox Jews.

- Symbols well-known in one country may be unrecognizable in another. Official mailboxes have different colors and shapes in almost every country.

✔ Colors may have different emotional content. Red is a happy color in China; in India, on the other hand, red is associated with life or creativity. In the United States, red usually means stop or danger.

✔ You cannot assume that a "Western" reading direction is natural — all users will not tend to start at the top left of a window and work towards the bottom right.

The requirements and pitfalls for multinational GUI development are beyond the scope of this book. If you have such a project, you might like to get hold of the book *International User Interfaces,* edited by Elisa M. del Galdo and Jakob Nielsen, published by John Wiley & Sons.

Corporate culture or professional culture often determines what people think is an appropriately formal (or informal) tone of speech or dress at work; what degree of respect/subservience is appropriate between leaders and subordinates, and who is allowed access to which information. These issues can in turn influence how your GUI design is received:

✔ Terminology and tone of language in windows, help, error messages, and reports may be judged appropriate or inappropriate in different corporate cultures.

✔ Corporate or professional culture may include positive or negative attitudes toward computers in general or toward a new system. Today many Scandinavian health professionals are united in skeptical resistance to more technology "between" them and their patients.

✔ Old-school corporate attitudes towards clerical workers are still present in computer systems that attempt to control users or that monitor worker effectiveness with little regard for privacy. The degree of freedom and responsibility offered to the individual users is definitely a cultural issue.

✔ Culture influences attitudes towards security requirements, information accessibility, and information distribution. If your system is too relaxed, some companies won't accept it; other companies (often smaller) will reject the same system as too rigid.

✔ Some professional cultures — for example, that of the social sciences — are prepared to work with approximate and partial data; others such as auditors and accountants, want their data complete and correct or not at all.

✔ Products for the U.S. market have serious problems if they seem to discriminate, deny access, or refer to some group in a derogatory manner. Few products on the European market meet such tough scrutiny — yet.

Watch out for cultural differences when members of the development project communicate with users during site visits or in meetings with user representatives and focus groups. Cultural differences cause people to interpret actions and information differently.

To check your understanding of what a user tells you, repeat to the speaker what you think you heard, in your own words. When a user tells you what he wants, check by offering a concrete example that you believe will meet the requirement. Watch out for company cultures that are consensus-seeking or for the kind in which everybody follows the leader; if you're working with a group of users, it may be difficult to get useful criticism or feedback. Try meeting one-on-one. Present several alternatives for discussion instead of one design that must be either accepted or rejected.

Marketplace environment

When you develop a commercial software package, you must always be aware of the current state of your market environment. Who are the main competitors? What are they likely to do? How quickly are market demands changing in your field? What can your company afford to spend to produce the software? What will the customers be willing to pay? What features will make customers abandon a previous version of the software or a competitor's product for your new version?

The most wonderful interface in the world may be wasted if it arrives in the market a year too late. Your evaluation of the market environment should be a powerful influence when you choose the "right" design answers for your product. If you've only got three months to get the product to market and three people to work with, then you'll need to make design choices that are simple to implement.

For in-house or custom development, you still have to ask, "How much time and money can we use without getting into trouble?" When the Car Insurance Department at Central Calamity asks for a new application, they would like it in three months, not in three years. If they have to wait so long that they feel they are losing customers to Western Catastrophe, grouchy messages will travel up the line to some vice president and then down again to the Data Processing Development Dudes: "You're making us lose money! You're not doing your jobs well enough!" Nobody wants to hear that. So ask, right at the beginning, when this project needs to be finished. And then start trying to convince your internal clients to accept the application that can actually be built in the period they are willing to allow.

The marketplace question also helps you to focus on your client's marketplace. If you understand the market pressure (unacceptably high turnover, difficulty in recruiting desired candidates) that caused the Personnel Department to ask for a new Human Resource Management System, it will be easier to choose which functions to prototype and implement first. Understanding how your customers and users deal with *their* customers and users will give you better insight into the tasks your system must support.

Chapter 3
Organizing the Work

· ·

· ·

*G*UI design is a lively task, with lots of give and take between people. When you're writing program code, the number of people looking over your shoulder is limited to those who are willing to do the hard mental labor of reading code. If one of these observers takes the trouble to comment on your code, they're probably worth listening to. On the other hand, everyone in the general vicinity of a development project with a GUI can *see* the user interface as it takes shape. They can all form opinions about the GUI at a glance, and they are all touchingly eager to give you the benefit of their insight. You can see why a GUI designer gets no peace, and why it's a continual challenge just to carve out a little respect.

To produce a successful design in a timely manner, you as the GUI designer must get the feedback and decision-making processes organized. You need to know roughly when the GUI design work should take place within the context of the overall development project. Also, you probably need a plan for the GUI design process. I cover all these topics in this chapter, but first I start off with a down-on-my-knees plea that someone in your project act as the primary GUI designer to oversee the interface development.

Putting GUI Design on the Map

If you've got a one-person project, you can skip this section. If you stick around, I'm going to do everything I can to persuade you to put "GUI Design" somewhere on one of your project's most important maps — either on the project organization chart or on the project delivery schedule.

I admit that assigning one person as the GUI designer doesn't seem necessary or sensible at first glance. With modern development tools, each developer designs one piece of the user interface while creating each window. In this way, the design work is divided among many people. The design process is spread out in time as well. The user interface emerges gradually, like the picture on a jigsaw puzzle assembled by a family. Wouldn't it be very disruptive to separate GUI design from the actual development process?

Well, what if the family members were unknowingly working with several puzzles jumbled together — and no one had the box with the picture on it? That's essentially what happens when the GUI is not consciously, separately designed, and that's why it *is* necessary and sensible to see GUI design as a separate part of the development project.

If your development project treats the GUI as a kind of side effect of the system development effort, the result will be just that: a side effect — unplanned, undesirable, and not what you expected.

In order to create a good GUI, you have to actively *design* the interface, not just let it happen. Define the GUI design as a deliverable product, or a sub-project, or a job title. Any of these solutions can help your project focus on the user interface as a product that must be completed and tested, a product for which some specific person or team is responsible. Which solution or combination of solutions you choose depends on the size of your project; how it is already organized; and what you, your colleagues, and your leaders prefer.

✔ To make the GUI design a separate product in the project delivery schedule, decide what deliverables (usually documentation or code) your design must consist of: a prototype of the top windows, a project GUI standard, and a drawing of each window, for example. Set a deadline for completing this work, and subject it to the same quality assurance and technical reviews as any other part of the development work.

✔ In a large project, define the GUI design as a project-within-the-project. You may need to assign a whole team to the job, or you may assign several people to spend part of their time on the GUI design job. Like any project, the GUI design sub-project should have a defined goal or result and a plan for reaching the goal.

✔ In a small- to medium-sized development team, assign the overall responsibility for the GUI design to the person who is most qualified for the job. Give this person the title of GUI Designer and place the GUI Designer in the project organization chart with authority to guide the rest of the development team on this aspect of the design work.

For quite a few developers, deciding how their windows should look is one of the fun parts of the development job. They naturally resist giving up autonomy, and they lose motivation if they feel like they're getting pushed around. Although it is more time-consuming to share the GUI design work and still control the quality and consistency of the finished design, you may find that this is the most effective overall solution in an ongoing project. Follow this plan to give "distributed GUI design" a chance to succeed:

- ✔ **Train together.** You wouldn't let a development team start programming in, say, Java, without some training, so train team members before you entrust them with the GUI design. Hire a good GUI design consultant to hold a few days of training for the whole team. A seminar will help team members to develop a uniform level of competence and a shared design vocabulary. If a seminar is impossible, at least have everybody read *GUI Design For Dummies*!

- ✔ **Perform early design together.** Write the Design Considerations Memo (Chapter 2) as a group. Choose GUI type and windows structure together (Chapter 4). Draw the models together (Chapters 5 and 6). Finally, design a few sample windows together.

- ✔ **Write the standard together.** On the basis of the sample windows, draft a short project GUI standard (Chapter 7).

- ✔ **Put design and review on the project schedule.** Require team members to document their window designs. Schedule review and delivery dates for window designs.

- ✔ **Review each other's work.** Set up review meetings so that each developer reviews the work of at least two others (Chapter 19).

- ✔ **Do tests with users** (Chapter 17). A distributed GUI design effort often degenerates into acrimonious discussion or, worse yet, each developer goes his or her own way if they cannot agree. However, let two developers observe a test with users, and they then have a shared experience to replace conflicting personal opinions. Besides, testing with users is the best education available about your design!

Managing Too Many Cooks

As I mentioned at the beginning of this chapter, when it comes to GUI, everybody within earshot of a development project is convinced that they're an expert. If you are responsible for GUI design, your challenge is to collect useful input and remain open to new ideas from all of the self-appointed assistant GUI cooks, and still compose a coherent design. If you're the chief cook, be prepared to wield a firm spoon.

Ask for input or get swamped by it

Try to set up a list of the individuals or groups who are bound to have opinions about your user interface. Candidates for your list are other development groups, leaders, marketing, graphic design, sales, support, documentation, training, clients, customers, reference groups, and user groups. I call these people *stakeholders*. Stakeholders are people who feel they "own" a piece of the interface design, for good or ill. Like shareholders in a company, these people cause less trouble if you take preemptive action to keep them happy.

Consider what type of input each stakeholder individual or group will have to offer, what background they have, and what aspects of the interface will be especially important to them. Marketing, for example, will be most interested in what the product looks like, what equipment users need to run the program, when it will be available, and how it compares to competing products. Marketing may be able to provide graphical design input, statistics about users, sales statistics, and competitor information. Ask for the information that you want from them, and tell them how you plan to use it. By asking questions first, you sometimes can preclude getting detailed, and unwanted, advice.

Set up a plan for discussing, reviewing, or testing the design (as appropriate) with your various stakeholders. Consider *when* you will need the type of input that only they can give. You should also try to consider the different needs of each group to comment about the interface and to feel that they have influence on it. Take the trouble to put your plans in writing and to distribute the plans early on. After you assure them that you *will* be listening to them, your stakeholders will be less clamorous.

By taking control of the input process rather than allowing input to rain down on you, you establish the psychological upper hand: leadership of the design process.

How to decide who's right

Design discussions can get unpleasantly heated. Simply letting the victory go to the person who can talk the fastest, hold out the longest, or be the nastiest if they lose is *not* design.

Try using the design decision pyramid shown in Figure 3-1 to resolve conflict or evaluate any form of input to the design.

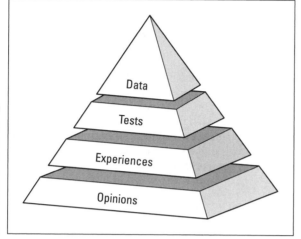

Figure 3-1:
The design
decision
pyramid.
Start at the
top and
work down.

The pyramid indicates that proven facts, or *data,* are the tip-top basis for a decision — when you can get your hands on accurate data. For example, if you're trying to decide how to indicate which fields in the GUI are obligatory, when you find relevant research on the subject you can safely say, "This proves the right way to show obligatory fields; no more discussion is necessary."

Unfortunately, good data is hard to find (though Chapter 23 can give you some clues). If you're reviewing research papers, read the description of the experiment carefully. Research experiments are strictly defined to eliminate as many variable factors as possible — preferably all except one. For example, in a recent experiment on obligatory fields, researchers chose random fields to be marked as obligatory so that users would have no clues other than the marking. Outside the laboratory, users have all kinds of knowledge that they use *together* with marking to understand which fields are obligatory. Sometimes experimental conditions are so unlike the real world that you cannot be certain that the results of the experiment will apply to your users.

If you haven't the time to go look for research data, or if what you have found is not relevant to your design project, move down one level in the decision pyramid. The next best basis for a decision is the results of your own usability test (find out more about testing in Part V).

You rarely benefit from performing a usability test as formally and carefully as a research experiment, so I must admit that the results can't be applied as general truths. But when you do a good job of usability testing, what you observe is *factual.* You see what happens with actual users. If you're making a design choice that might have a big impact on whether you reach your design goals, base your decision on a usability test. You should do usability tests or some form of evaluation at each stage in the design. Part V shows you how.

Often you have to go down to the third level of the pyramid and make design decisions on the basis of experience. When you can say, "We've done this before, and it worked," then you are speaking from experience. Users' knowledge of their work can also be classed as experience. For example, a user may report, "We get very few credit applications from people with addresses outside the United States, so let's use American format for the zip-code field." The user speaks from experience; he is not offering an opinion.

As with research, ask whether the experience is relevant to the decision you want to make. For example, my experience that the right mouse button works well *for me* is not necessarily relevant when we are considering whether it will work for a group of users who are quite different from me. If you can't get facts or test results, try to base your design decisions on relevant experience.

At the base of the decision pyramid, opinions are the biggest part — simply because more opinions are floating around than anything else. For example, comments like "Yellow fields look nicer than gray ones," "Lists should always be in alphabetical order," and "All GUI applications should be modeless," are subjective opinions. Learn to recognize opinions and consider their sources. You can base unimportant design decisions on opinions.

Share the design decision pyramid in Figure 3-1 with project members and stakeholders, and you may find that arguments can be more quickly and amicably resolved, just by asking "Is that data, test results, experience, or an opinion that you're asking us to believe?"

Predicting Your Workload

Did you know that many experts now believe that designing the user interface may consume up to half the development resources in a modern project? Modern programming tools reduce the effort that goes into construction of windows and dialog boxes, but not the effort needed to decide what goes into the windows and dialog boxes and how they should look.

"Reusable objects," I hear someone mumble hopefully. Well, yes, but these, too, save more implementation time than thinking time. It's the customization that costs.

How much time do you need to devote to GUI design in your project? I can't give exact answers, but Figure 3-2 shows how the time required for GUI design probably will be distributed throughout the duration of your development project.

Expect the design workflow to be concentrated in the two "camel humps" shown in Figure 3-2 when the project has the following:

- ✔ A large numbers of future users
- ✔ High-speed or high-quality user performance as a high-priority design goal for the GUI
- ✔ Intense use patterns

The first workflow hump represents your goal-setting, early design, task design, and checking activities near the beginning of the development project. The second hump comes near the end of the project because you need a very realistic version of the program — perhaps a beta version — to check user effectiveness. The second hump grows even larger when your design needs to meet objective, measurable usability criteria such as: "Experienced users should be able to complete the average customer service call in less than four minutes." Because nobody likes late-breaking changes, it's important for you to warn your project group to expect the second hump.

Expect the work to be distributed in the wedge-shaped pattern shown in Figure 3-2 when:

- ✔ You know little about the users to begin with
- ✔ Ease of use is a high-priority design goal for the GUI

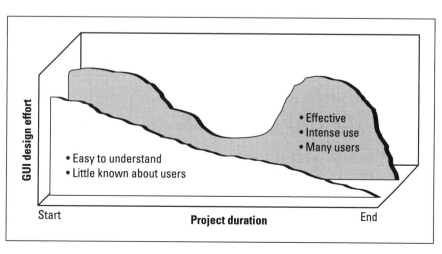

Figure 3-2: Two common patterns for interface design efforts.

In either of the preceding situations the most intensive part of the design effort comes at the beginning of the development project. You need to learn about the users and the tasks, and to prototype and test design ideas. Later the design effort will taper off. Because you can make and test a prototype and find out whether a program will be easy to use early in the development project, this type of project needs fewer last-minute adjustments to the interface.

Of course if the design has to be both effective and easy to use, if you know little about the users and there are many, many of them — in short if your project meets both sets of conditions described above — then you should expect a design workflow that charts like a very tall camel sitting down, as in Figure 3-3.

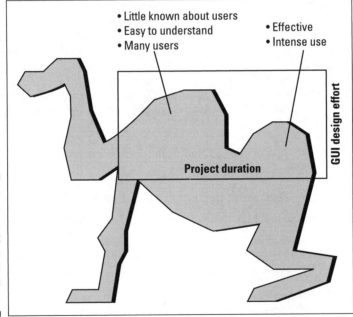

- Little known about users
- Easy to understand
- Many users

- Effective
- Intense use

GUI design effort

Project duration

Figure 3-3:
The design effort in a project where overall usability is critical.

Planning the GUI Design Work

If you're required to make a plan for the GUI Design efforts, use Table 3-1 as a guide. Some activities may not be relevant for your working situation, but all the activities are described in certain chapters of *GUI Design For Dummies*.

Notice especially that design and reality checks (evaluation or testing) go together hand in glove, in an iterative progression: Design a piece of the interface, check out how your design works in real life, apply what you've learned, design a new piece, and so on.

Table 3-1	What to Put in Your Plan
Activity	**Where to Find It in This Book**
Define design goals	Chapter 1
Learn about the users	Chapter 2
Learn the project architecture	Chapter 2
Learn the development tool	Chapter 2
Learn about tasks	Chapter 2
Learn about the users' environment and the project environment	Chapter 2
Document design considerations	Chapter 2
Organize your project	Chapter 3
Make a project plan	Chapter 4
Do some interviews	Chapter 8
Do some site visits	Chapter 19
Select the type of interface	Chapter 4
Select the main windows structure	Chapter 4
Draw the conceptual model(s)	Chapter 5
Try out the conceptual model(s)	Chapter 17
Understand the tasks	Chapters 8 and 9
Sketch out the navigation model	Chapters 6 and 9
Select top windows	Chapters 6 and 9
Create a paper prototype	Chapters 6 and 9
Review the design considerations	Chapter 2
Do some reality checks	Chapters 17–19
Design windows for critical tasks	Chapters 11–16
Design windows for frequent tasks	Chapters 11–16
Design windows for detested tasks	Chapters 11–16
Do some reality checks	Chapters 17–19
Complete the project GUI Standard	Chapter 7
Supervise design of remaining windows	Chapter 7
Do some reality checks	Chapters 17–19

Part II
Surviving the Early Design Stage

The 5th Wave   By Rich Tennant

"...AND TO ACCESS THE PROGRAM'S 'HOT KEY,' YOU JUST DEPRESS
THESE ELEVEN KEYS SIMULTANEOUSLY. HERB OVER THERE HAS A
KNACK FOR DOING THIS THAT I THINK YOU'LL ENJOY—HERB! GOT
A MINUTE?"

In this part . . .

You know you're in the early design stage when:

✔ You repeatedly take a fresh piece of paper and sketch a rectangle, and then . . . nothing happens.

✔ You start to read the section on "window types" in the development tool manual and get bogged down in terms such as "primary modeless application dialog window."

✔ The coffee-break discussion of the week is whether your program should have a File menu when it doesn't really work with files.

This part guides you through the decisions, chaos, and creative efforts of the early design phase.

Chapter 4

Choosing Type and Structure

● ●

In This Chapter

▶ Choosing among Almost GUIs, Standard GUIs, and One-time GUIs

▶ Meeting multiwindow, multidocument (MDI), and multiframe structures

▶ Choosing the right window structure

● ●

*I*f you want to know about water, don't ask a fish. A fish takes water for granted because water is always around. In a software development project, the development tool is always around. That's why some developers go into zombie mode and churn out programs that look just like their development tools. Programs created with Horrible Forms Version 4.0 look just like Horrible Forms Version 4.0, programs created with Multimedia Zap++ look Zapped, and so on.

It doesn't have to be that way. You have a lot of choices that you may not have considered. This chapter gives the information you need to make decisions about which type of interface and which basic window structures are best suited to your project.

Choosing from a Wide Range of UI Types

You have a whole spectrum of possible user interfaces to choose from, as shown in Figure 4-1. At the left end of the spectrum are the oldest forms of communication between computer and user — the bad old days of punch cards, when people had to bend over backwards to communicate in ways that computers could understand.

At the right end of the spectrum are the interfaces where tremendous development resources are invested so that people can interact with the computer as they would with the physical world — through hand gestures and even eye movements. New technology will eventually allow developers to implement *human metaphor* systems in which users can communicate with their computers as if they were interacting with other people — through speech, facial expression, and body language.

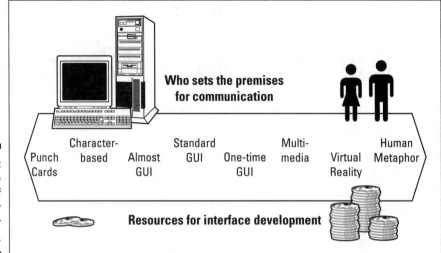

Figure 4-1:
A wide
spectrum of
choices for
a user
interface.

Moving from left to right along the spectrum of user interface styles, you can see a clear trend: More and more development and computer resources are being devoted to user interaction so that users can devote less and less effort to communicating with the computer.

Almost GUIs

At one end of the GUI part of the spectrum are the good, character-based designs that have been ported into a GUI environment with a minimum of changes. I call these *Almost GUI* solutions. Custom-made database systems tend to fall into the Almost GUI category, and so do some World Wide Web applications that support search and simple transactions.

Almost GUIs are usually associated with databases rather than with documents. They have lots of text fields and few interactive widgets such as sliders or list boxes. Graphics are used sparingly. The user must typically complete an entire transaction or abandon partially entered work. Because Almost GUIs are tailored for specific business or organizational needs, users may need specialized knowledge in order to use them. Figure 4-2 shows a window from an Almost GUI.

Like the character-based systems from which they are descended, Almost GUIs typically have oodles of full-screen windows. Getting all those windows organized and allowing the right degree of flexibility is a big challenge for the designer. If you make a large Almost GUI totally flexible, then users have

Figure 4-2:
Almost
GUIs have
lots of text
fields (from
a Lotus
Approach
97 sample
database).

to take responsibility for the process to follow when a business task must be solved by accessing several different windows. Worse, a new Almost GUI computer program is frequently associated with changed routines and new processes, so the users don't have a strong mental model of the task they are asked to perform. Training and support costs skyrocket.

On the other hand, if you make an Almost GUI inflexible, users feel "locked in," experienced users have no way to become more effective, users can't find new ways to work as business processes change, and the budget for maintenance and changes goes through the roof instead.

Standard GUIs

Smack in the middle of the user interface spectrum are the personal productivity tools that popularized GUIs in the first place: word processors, spreadsheets, and graphics programs.

These days, Web browsers may be included in the Standard GUI category. Microsoft Office 97 shows clear symptoms that the Web browser interface is beginning to leak into the more traditional office automation products. Instead of buttons, the toolbar now has clickable graphics (as shown in Figure 4-3).

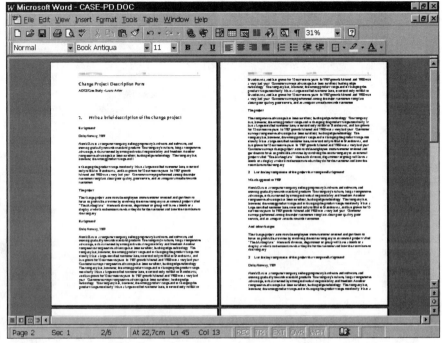

Figure 4-3:
Standard
GUIs are
often
document-
centered,
like
Microsoft
Word 97.

Standard GUIs typically use more graphics and a greater variety of widgets than Almost GUIs. Because they are based on documents rather than databases, Standard GUIs are easier to make flexible and user-driven. Standard GUIs are copycats. By copying each other and sticking very close to platform norms, Standard GUIs profit from the "learn one, you've learned them all" syndrome.

It is difficult (but not impossible) to design a database system in Standard GUI style. Just be prepared for a real design challenge: Users are rarely familiar with a relational database in the way that they are familiar with documents they can print out and hold. You need to understand very clearly how *the users* understand and use the data in the database in order to create an interface that centers around the users' work as a Standard GUI should. (See Chapter 5 on conceptual models for more about this subject.)

One-time GUIs

One-time GUI is my name for executive information systems, self-service applications, games, and any other interfaces that make heavy use of graphics and pointing, while making no attempt to conform to platform standards. Users may only use one of these GUIs a single time; what users learn about the interface is also "one-time" knowledge, because that knowledge can't be applied to other standard interfaces.

Like Almost GUIs, One-time GUIs are created to do very specific tasks. One-time GUIs are not usually especially flexible or efficient to use, but they tend to be designed so that they are easy to learn — perhaps even instantly understood. Figure 4-4 shows a screen from a One-time GUI — a touch-screen system for airline passengers who would rather check themselves in than wait in line.

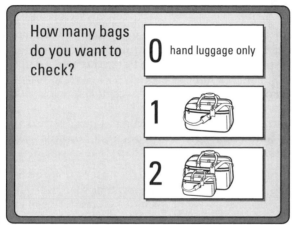

How many bags do you want to check?

0 hand luggage only

1

2

Figure 4-4:
A touch-screen system for checking in at the airport is an example of a One-time GUI.

Consider designing a One-time GUI when the user group experiences a high turnover rate or when ease of learning or ease of use is the top design priority. (See Chapter 1 about choosing design goals.) Consider designing a One-time GUI when users have little or no previous computer experience or no experience with GUIs. Finally, consider a One-time GUI when just about everybody is a user, which is the case with systems placed in supermarkets, malls, airports, and other public places.

Computer games have to please and interest their users instantly. People buy them and play them for fun, and are rarely willing to spend time reading handbooks. If you need inspiration for how to make something easy to understand or motivating and satisfying to use, try out a few games. Whether or not you find anything useful for your design project, at least you'll have a plausible excuse for playing the latest games during working hours!

Hybrid GUIs

The three GUI categories aren't chiseled in stone. You'll run across programs that seem to lie in between the categories — it may be that an in-between solution is the right one for your project, too.

For example, take a look at Time/system Activity Map shown in Figure 4-5. Activity Map is like a Standard GUI in its document-centric structure. The menu bar looks very familiar to word processor users. But the interaction in the Activity Map document is very visual, very simple, and based on direct manipulation. Here Activity Map comes pretty close to a One-time GUI.

Which type should you choose?

Chapters 1 and 2 show you how to set design goals for your interface and how to analyze use patterns. Use this information about your project to figure out what type of interface you will design. Remember that the percentage of development resources devoted to the user interface tends to increase as you move to the right of the spectrum shown in Figure 4-1.

- ✔ If ease of learning is an important goal, or if turnover is high among the users, move to the right end of the spectrum, towards a One-time GUI or even multimedia.

- ✔ If tasks are frequently repeated by expert users, if speed is a goal, or if the interaction must be system-driven rather than user-driven, lean to the left, towards Almost GUI or even to a character-based interface.

- ✔ If users are already familiar with at least one Standard GUI, you've a lot to gain by sticking as close to Standard GUI as you can.

Figure 4-5:
Time/
system
Activity
Map is
somewhere
between a
Standard
GUI and a
One-time
GUI.

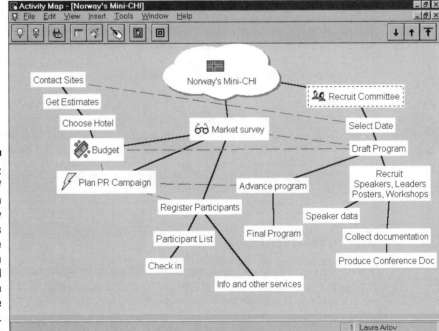

Recognizing Different Types of Windows

To talk about window structures, you and I need to agree on what to call the different kinds of windows, even though terminology varies in different operating systems and in different development tools. The list shows my names and informal definitions for the most common window types:

- ✔ **Main window:** A window that you can minimize into an icon. In Windows 95, a main window creates a button on the task bar. A main window may have (but doesn't have to have) its own pull-down menus. A main window may contain other windows, or data and widgets. A main window may launch other windows.

- ✔ **Child window:** Perhaps you already know this type of window under the name *document window*. A child window is always launched from a main window. A child window automatically folds away when you minimize its main window. Child windows are most common in multidocument interfaces (MDI) such as Microsoft Excel.

- ✔ **Dialog box:** Any window that asks for a response from the user. Dialog boxes usually contain at least one command button like OK or Cancel so the user can say, "I'm done responding!" Other names for dialog boxes are dialog windows, response windows, and pop-ups.

- ✔ **Modal dialog box or window:** Any window that insists on a user response by locking out other parts of the system. As long as a modal window is open, it is saying, "Me first, me first!" like a pesky brat. And who likes pesky brats? Don't use modal dialog boxes unless you have to. Particularly, don't use them to give feedback on progress.

  - **Application modal dialog box:** A modal dialog box that locks out the rest of its own application, for example the File⇨Open dialog box in most Windows applications.

  - **(Stinky) System modal dialog box:** An antisocial modal dialog box that locks up *everything* until it receives user input. Don't make one without a very good reason. The Shut-down dialog box in Windows 95 is a system modal dialog box used in an appropriate manner.

- ✔ **Nonmodal dialog box:** A dialog box that asks for a response from the user, but permits work to go on around it. Less intrusive than a modal dialog, but easier for the user to lose track of. Find-and-replace dialog boxes and spell-checker dialog boxes should be nonmodal.

Implementing Various Window Structures

Over the years, I've run across four basic ways to use windows. You'll find hybrids here and there, but these four structures show up again and again:

- ✔ **Multiwindow interfaces:** Examples are the IBM OS/2 operating system, most UNIX X-windows applications, and now Microsoft Windows 95

- ✔ **Multidocument interfaces (MDI):** For example, Microsoft Word or Excel

- ✔ **Multipane interfaces:** Microsoft Paint and Netscape Navigator are examples

- ✔ **Multiscreen interfaces:** Mostly found in One-time GUIs and wizards

I won't say that one particular structure is user-friendly and another is not, even if I do have some personal favorites. Each structure has its own characteristics. Whether these characteristics are strengths or weaknesses depends on your users and the users' working situation. Carefully examine the candidates in the following sections and pick yourself a sure winner.

Remember, no law says that your GUI has to look like the development tool you make it with. Choose the windows structure that supports your design goals and your user group, not just the one you're most accustomed to seeing.

The multiple window structure

If your application has more than one main window then the application has a *multiple windows* structure. I call it *multiwindow* for short.

A typical multiwindow application consists of many main windows, as illustrated in Figure 4-6. The main windows may launch dialog boxes, usually modal. Multiwindow applications are sometimes called *windows salad,* because that is what the display looks like when you're using them. If you happen to have your display set for neon colors at the same time, the correct term is *angry fruit salad.*

Each nonmodal window may have its own pull-down menu. The menus usually follow a pattern, with window-specific commands turning up in two or three predictable places. The menus may look exactly the same when they are closed, but different when they are opened.

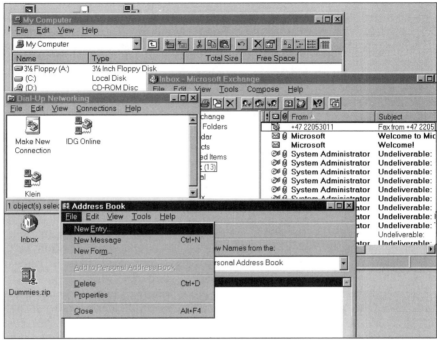

Figure 4-6:
Windows
salad
served up in
Windows 95.

Last time I looked, the IBM CUA (Common User Access) standard took this structure for granted, and it's very popular with the Object-Oriented User Interface movement as well. The structure is common in UNIX; the IBM OS/2 has a multiwindow structure, and Microsoft Windows 95 Desktop is developing multiwindow tendencies. Many development tools are multiwindow systems.

Multiwindows flex to the max

From a user perspective, the multiwindow structure has the following characteristics:

- ✔ A multiwindow structure allows maximum flexibility. The user can decide what information to view at any time and how much display area to devote to each window. The user can open and work with the different main windows in any order.

- ✔ Given two programs of similar extent in which one has a multiwindow structure, a user takes longer to become familiar with the multiwindow program. In a multiwindows system, program elements aren't always in the same place on the screen; the program has no stable working context for users to grasp.

- ✔ A multiwindow structure requires the most user effort for windows administration tasks such as opening, closing, stacking, and sizing windows.

When to choose multiwindow

Choose a multiwindow structure when the user's need for flexibility out-weighs the disadvantages of windows administration and complexity.

The multiwindow structure is a natural choice for the Windows Desktop. Obviously, most users need the flexibility to switch between tasks or independent objects at will. But what about within an application or a program? Do users still benefit from complete flexibility?

A multiwindow system is ideal for software development. Development requires creative thought processes and problem solving. Flexible multiwindow systems allow each user to structure development work according to her own thought process. The costs of extra windows administration tasks are small compared to the benefits of freedom and flexibility.

Consider developers as users: Developers are educated and paid to have their full attention on the system. They have extensive training in the development process; they can keep the process in their heads without any help from the system. They quickly become expert users. They have quiet working conditions with few interruptions, which means that it is easier for them to keep a mental overview of a complicated working situation.

If users of your design product are like developers and have similar working conditions and needs for flexibility, the multiwindows structure is an excellent choice. Unfortunately, multiwindow systems are often chosen because a completely flexible structure allows the development project to duck the question of "what are the users actually going to do with this system?"

Windows administration steals a lot of time and attention from the users of a multiwindow system, so multiwindow GUI is a poor choice whenever effectiveness is a high priority. To benefit from flexibility, users need over-view and initiative. A large multiwindow system can be very difficult to learn, especially for people who are new to window-based GUIs .

The multiple document interface (MDI)

If you've used a word processor or a spreadsheet in Windows any time during the past five years, it probably had an MDI or *multiple document interface*. See Figure 4-7 for an example.

MDI has one main window that displays one menu. The menu acts as a road map to the application. You get to keep the same map all the time, even if you open three different documents in three different child windows and switch around among them.

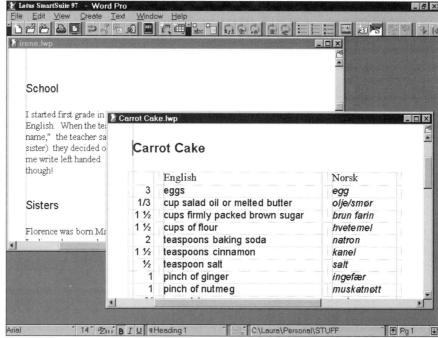

Figure 4-7:
Lotus Word
Pro 97
shows a
typical MDI
interface:
One main
window,
two child
windows.

Is MDI ready for the scrap heap?

I've heard the argument that File Manager in Windows 3.1 was MDI, and that was hard for novice users, so MDI must be bad and should be scrapped. Aside from the faulty logic in that proposition, File Manager was difficult because the *file system* is difficult, not because of its MDI structure.

Try teaching noncomputer people to use Windows. My novice users can master the concept that one child window equals one document, because they have one familiar concept to relate to one new idea. When it comes to File Manager, a lot of novices choke on the concept that one child window equals one directory. Many users never really figure out how to open two child windows to move or copy files between directories.

The real problem is not the MDI structure. The real problem is that documents are familiar, real objects in the physical world, and hierarchical directories aren't.

MDI offers a useful amount of flexibility for many users. I say that MDI should be kept around and used appropriately.

In theory, each child window is allowed to present its own version of the main menu: Microsoft Word documents with different templates may display special menu commands or tool buttons associated with the template, for example. In practice the main menu is rarely changed, maybe because a stable menu works better for the users, who often ignore changes.

The MDI main window takes responsibility for its children: The window menu helps users see which windows are open and allows users to go directly to any open window using the mouse or the keyboard. Close or minimize the main window, and the children get packed up and go along for the ride without being told.

MDI walks a fine line

The MDI structure offers *some* flexibility in information display. The user can decide to view two documents together or two different parts of the same document. The user avoids some windows administration tasks such as resizing and minimizing child windows, and others can be handled effectively through the windows menu.

The MDI structure offers a better overview of the working situation within the program than the multiwindow structure does, because MDI has a single, stable menu. Users can easily see which windows belong together in the application.

When to choose MDI

Choose — or at least give serious consideration to — a multidocument interface (MDI) in the following situations:

- ✔ If your design goals include both ease of use and flexibility
- ✔ If your application centers around documents
- ✔ If your users are already familiar with an MDI interface

While you can provide some hints about what to do next in an MDI interface, MDI is a poor choice when you just plain want to boss the user around. If your purpose requires you to maintain control of the interaction, think of something else. How about a series of modal dialog boxes such as those that the new wizards use?

Some of the advantages in MDI come from the practice of using a single, consistent menu that the users rapidly become familiar with. Roughly the same functions are available no matter which child window is open. In other words, the user can do the same things to all his documents.

If your application is going to fill up the child windows with forms or data tables that are wildly different from each other, you may find it difficult to fit your application into the MDI format.

If your user group includes people who don't use Windows, you need a structure that cuts windows administration even further. Consider moving to a multipane structure or even a multiscreen solution.

The multipane structure (frames)

What do you get if you divide a window into smaller rectangles? Window panes, of course. A *multipane interface* has a single main window divided into smaller rectangles or panes, like the Netscape News interface shown in Figure 4-8. Some of the panes boss the others around: When I choose a newsgroup from the upper-left pane, for example, the next pane gets an order to show the current discussion. When I select one discussion item, the lowest pane gets told to display the contents of the item.

Multipanes keep users from getting lost

Multipane interfaces sacrifice even more flexibility than MDI. The user can only view two pieces of information at the same time if the developer has planned things that way. In Figure 4-8, I can't compare two messages on-screen unless I open two instances of the application.

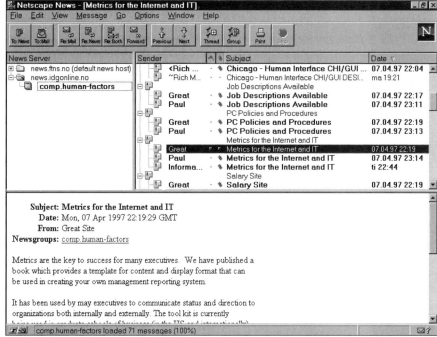

Figure 4-8:
A multipane interface is a window divided into smaller rectangles that may boss each other around.

In return for lost flexibility, a multipane interface gives the user security and a program that is simple to begin using. A multipane interface makes it easy for the user to keep track of what he is doing. The user sees what he chose in the "boss" pane, as well as which other choices he could have made. It is easy to go back and make a different choice. The screen changes with each choice, providing immediate response to each user action. As you see in Chapter 11, immediate response from the program helps the user to catch on quickly and painlessly to the cause/effect relationships in the interface.

When to choose a multipane structure

Multipane structures are easy to learn and can be efficient to use. They are only partly flexible. Users can perform their work processes within the program in any order, but users have less influence over how information is displayed. The designer makes that decision when selecting the number of panes and defining what each pane displays. Netscape News doesn't need to be quite as flexible as a word processor: The news-reading task is more predictable than word processing activities. Netscape News does need to be easier than the average word processor: The user group is broader, and users are typically engaging in a free-time activity — they won't want to have to attend a course or read a handbook in order to use the program.

Consider using a multipane interface in these situations:

- ✔ When ease of learning/ease of use is an important goal
- ✔ When you know enough about the user's task or purpose to be able to say which chunks of information must be visible at the same time
- ✔ When you need to present large amounts of information but do not want to risk your users getting lost
- ✔ When you don't care about, or can't predict, the order in which the user will work

Don't let your multipane interface get a mouse fixation. Users must be able to choose something from a pane by using the keyboard, especially if users will spend more than a few minutes at a time with the interface. Always provide keyboard alternatives. The opportunity to choose working style and to vary input devices helps your users guard against repetitive stress injury (such as carpal tunnel syndrome).

Multiscreen interfaces

What if you create a GUI where the user doesn't see any windows at all, such as the One-time GUI in Figure 4-4? Then you have a *multiscreen interface,* where you design the program to take all responsibility for changing the display, depending on the user's actions. If you do this without making the program take over the whole screen, the user will still see some windows and you end up with something like the new wizards. Figure 4-9 shows two successive screens from Microsoft Fax that guide the user through the process of sending a fax from the PC.

Figure 4-9:
The
Microsoft
Fax Wizard
is a
multiscreen
interface (in
miniature).

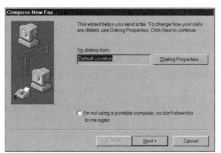 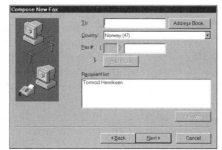

Multiscreen interfaces: GUIs with safety belts

A multiscreen interface takes over the whole display, protecting users from accidents like clicking outside the active window and getting an unwanted window on top — a common problem for inexperienced GUI users. Of course, it also "protects" users who know what they're doing. In a multiscreen interface you are rarely able to provide speedy, flexible short-cuts for experienced users.

Users can't choose in what order to perform tasks, and they can't choose to look at two different pieces of information at the same time — unless you specifically build a choice into the system. A multiscreen interface gives the developer strong control over the interaction, but with that control comes even more responsibility to ensure that the system is comfortable and effective for users. After all, the users of the program are locked into the steps that the designer defines.

When to choose a multiscreen interface

Choose a multiscreen interface when the task is short and consists of well-defined, serial steps. A multiscreen interface is suitable for airport check-in or sending a fax, but not for managing purchase orders or scheduling meetings.

A multiscreen interface can be constructed for maximum efficiency or for maximum error prevention. This type of interface is suited to the broadest user groups, but usually only for short-term use.

A multiscreen interface is often used on single-use computer systems to prevent unauthorized access to the computer outside of the multiscreen application. A multiscreen interface, for example, can be effective in an interface for a driving-directions machine at a car rental office.

Mix and match windows structures

Choose a windows structure for your program depending on users' needs for flexibility as opposed to overview and simplicity, but don't feel that an application is only permitted to use one structure.

In a multiwindow system, one of the main windows may have multiple panes, or there may be MDI windows within a multiwindow system.

An MDI child may be divided into panes, and MDI child windows can also have their own menus. I don't recommend it in principle, but your particular project may have a combination of needs that make this the best solution.

Figure 4-10 gives an overview of the characteristics of the different windows structures you can choose from.

Figure 4-10:
Each
window
structure
has its own
strengths
and
weaknesses.

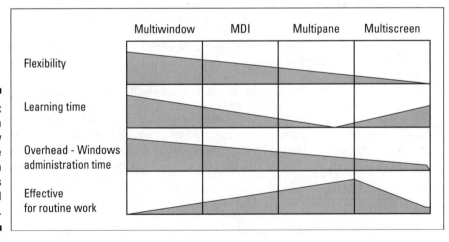

Chapter 5

Pin Up Those Super Models

● ●

In This Chapter

▶ Discovering mental models

▶ Understanding the role of mental and conceptual models in GUI design

▶ Drawing your own model — a recipe

▶ Build a model with me — a case study

▶ Using conceptual models in complex projects

▶ Designing windows with a model in mind

● ●

*I*f your users are already familiar with the basic ideas underlying your program, they will understand the program quickly and easily, and think that *you* are the cat's pajamas.

On the other hand, if the basic ideas underlying your program are foreign to your users, or if the ideas are so well hidden that your users don't realize that they're in familiar territory, they will instead revile you and your program. In situations like this, expect heavy support costs and lots of user errors.

This chapter shows how to figure out what ideas will already be familiar to the users, how to identify the underlying ideas of your own program, and how to use that knowledge to make a better design.

Understanding Mental and Conceptual Models

As a GUI designer, you have to guess what *mental models* your users bring to the program.

What we humans are already familiar with is stored in our brains, organized according to our mental models. The tricky thing about mental models is we don't usually know that we have them or that we are using them. With or without our knowledge, our mental models influence our behavior and also how we gather, interpret, and remember information. If our models are out of step with the real world, we make mistakes.

Watching a mental model in action

I am old enough that my mental model of the telephone system was originally something like the drawing in Figure 5-1. When I was a child, each home had one telephone in a fixed location. If I dialed the number correctly and heard someone pick up the phone, then I knew that I'd be speaking to a person at the location I dialed. I could call my girlfriend Janey who lived across from the park and ask if the schoolmate we both had a crush on was playing softball that night. I saw the telephone primarily as a simultaneous connection between two places, and I used it as such.

Figure 5-1:
My original mental model of the telephone system.

A few years ago, I gradually realized that I was making more and more "user errors" while on the phone. I was starting conversations with machines that weren't listening to me, and getting connected to people who weren't where I expected them to be.

Now my mental model of the telephone system looks more like the one shown in Figure 5-2. My behavior has changed accordingly. Since what is happening on the other end of the connection is a big question mark to me, I wait to speak until I know whom (or what) I am talking to. I know that communication may not be simultaneous. I call people who I know will not answer in order to leave messages. To a live person, I often begin with, "It's Laura, can you talk now?"

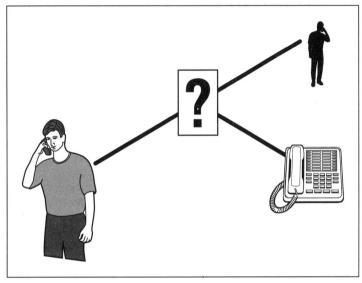

Figure 5-2:
My mental model of how a telephone works has changed, and so has my telephone behavior.

My mental model of the telephone system is still sketchy. A telecommunications engineer may point out that my model lacks all sorts of fascinating switches, networks, transmitters, receivers, fiber-optic cables, and satellites. For me, the telephone system is just something I use, not something I am interested in taking apart and putting together again — so my mental model stays simple.

From mental model to conceptual model

I currently have a mental model of the telephone system that is good enough to let me use the telephone effectively, even if it's not a clear representation of how the system is actually constructed. I have a good mental model of *how it works* for telephone users, not how it is built.

What is the simplest model of how your program works that your users can have and still use your program effectively? After you decide what this model is, draw your beliefs about, or *concepts* of, the user's simplest model. I call your model of the user's simple model your *conceptual model.* While mental models are usually unconscious thinking tools, a conceptual model is a tool that you know about. You create your model and modify it on purpose so that it is as helpful as possible.

Using the conceptual model in GUI design

The conceptual model for your program is the main message that your GUI has to communicate to the user, just as the thesis statement is the main message that your English essay goes on to support. My high school English teacher claimed that I couldn't write an essay worth a passing grade without including a thesis statement. In the same way, you need a conceptual model to design a GUI that passes muster with the users.

The role of the conceptual model in your design is shown in Figure 5-3 and is described in the following list.

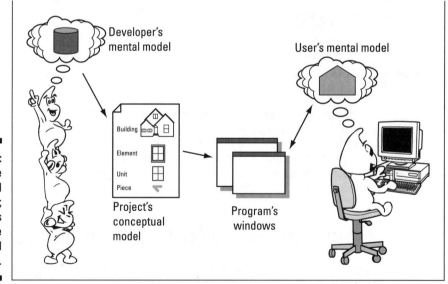

Figure 5-3:
We all have mental models; developers create conceptual models.

Developer's mental model

User's mental model

Building
Element
Unit
Piece

Project's conceptual model

Program's windows

✔ The users are going to use their mental models to interpret the conceptual model that you are trying to communicate. If you ask, "Do you want to store changes?" your user may think, "No, I don't want to send them away to storage, I'm still working on them." Your mental model tells you that the user is working on a *copy* of the data. The user's mental model, on the other hand, tells him that he is working on *the data itself.*

✔ If your communication succeeds, your users should have a new or slightly modified mental model that allows them to interpret your program correctly and use it successfully. In an example at the end of this chapter, you can see how a graphics program successfully "teaches" users what a template is while they create their first slide show.

✔ You and the other project members have your own mental models of the program, usually based on your experience of putting the program together. Don't assume that your mental model necessarily makes a great conceptual model; users don't share your experience and they want to use the program, not build one like it.

The closer you make the conceptual model to the user's original mental model, the easier your communication job should be. Don't fight gravity!

Drawing Your Conceptual Model — a Recipe

Start with this section of the chapter if you're ready to try your hand at drawing a conceptual model; if you're not sure, hop to the next section and I'll walk you through the process with an example from an e-mail program.

When you make a conceptual model, try to draw a one-page picture without too much detail. The most useful models that I have worked with have around five to ten items in the drawing, with a few text labels and some arrows thrown in for good measure. Follow these steps to draw your model:

1. **Ask yourself, "What are the main objects here, from the informed user's point of view?"**

   Draw the main objects. Try to draw and position the objects so as to communicate any important relationships between them. What comes first? What is part of something else? What depends on something else? What is unique? Do you need to show that there can be more than one of some object, like a customer?

2. **Ask yourself, "What are the main steps in the process here, from the informed user's point of view?"**

   Do you need to put the user in the picture? What starts the process? Did you remember to show the user's goal?

3. **Simplify and clarify the model.**

   Is there anything you can take out? Have you used order and positioning on the paper to support the order and relationships in the system?

   Your model shows the concepts, relationships, and steps that will be represented in a successful user's mental model of your product.

The next steps explain what to do with the conceptual model after you've drawn it:

1. **Sketch the mental model(s) that an uninformed user will be relying on the very first time he or she tries your product.**

   What experiences does the user have in the physical world that he or she will recall and build on when trying out your program for the first time?

2. **Compare the user's mental model to your conceptual model.**

   What's different about your conceptual model? These are the features, functions, or ideas that are going to be new and difficult for the user. Make sure your GUI communicates these things clearly, and test to see if the users understand.

Build a Model with Me — a Case Study

Suppose that I am going to design an e-mail program for a PC with a modem. I make a conceptual model for my program before I start drawing any windows.

Sketching the model

First I ask myself, "From the user's point of view, *what are the main objects involved?*"

When designing an e-mail program, objects such as *messages* or *letters* spring to mind first. Other objects may include the people *(recipients)* that users will send letters to, and e-mail *addresses.* Do I need to put both people and addresses in the model? If the user knows about the address, isn't that enough? Maybe not, because one person can have more than one address, or a person's address may change. And how about the mail server, the modem/telephone line, and the user's PC?

I begin my model by sketching the objects quickly and randomly on a piece of paper.

When I think about addresses, I also think about objects such as address books and distribution lists. I try to rearrange my drawing to represent the most important relationships between the objects. In Figure 5-4, you can see a typical drawing I might produce at this stage.

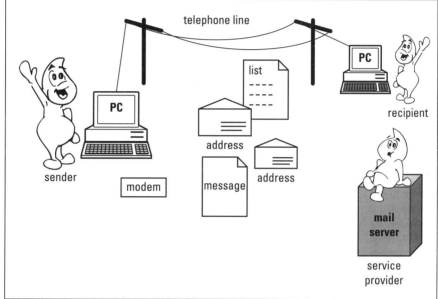

Figure 5-4:
Early sketch for the conceptual model of an e-mail system.

Now I ask, "*What are the main steps* in using an e-mail program to create and send a message? To receive and view a message?"

I identify the steps in sending a message as: Create a message, put a recipient name and address on the message, and send the message. The user will have to connect the e-mail program to a mail server through the modem in order to send or receive mail. Even with the connection open, the e-mail program will not send and/or receive continuously unless I design it to do so.

I notice that I have been using an envelope symbol for addresses, so I switch to another symbol, realizing that the user must know the difference between snail-mail addresses and e-mail addresses in order to use e-mail. I try to rearrange my drawing to represent the most important relationships between the objects. After some more fiddling, I end up with the sketch shown in Figure 5-5.

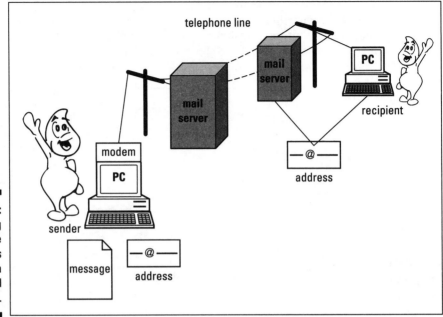

Figure 5-5:
Clarifying
the
relationships
in a
conceptual
model.

Comparing conceptual and mental models

For the time being, I assume that the user has a mail service provider and is capable of installing the e-mail program. Right now I am only interested in deciding what ideas the e-mail program needs to communicate when it is up and running, so I ask, "*Which of the ideas in my model will be unfamiliar* to a new user who is familiar only with snail-mail?"

Figure 5-6 shows my guess about what a non-techie living in Europe or North America might associate with the word "mail." Some users may associate "mail" with the internal mail distribution system at their office, which is also shown.

Comparing the two possible mental models with my model for the e-mail system, I see that the challenge is to help the user understand and remember to connect to the mail server. In the user's mental model, he doesn't have to make any effort to receive mail; letters and packages just arrive in his in-tray or mailbox. In his mental model, if he puts something in a mailbox or an out-tray, he's done his part of the job. So if I put in-tray and out-tray symbols on the screen, I know that the user's mental model gives him expectations about how those program elements will act.

I can see another problem looming around e-mail addresses and regular addresses. My program needs to show the user the difference between e-mail addresses and regular addresses. Tips or a wizard for finding e-mail addresses on the Net might be welcome, too.

Designing from the analysis of the models

On the basis of my conceptual model and my analysis of the mental models of non-techie users, my design for the e-mail program will include these features:

✔ Visible symbols or commands for message, recipient, address, address book, adding things to messages (enclosures or attachments), a place to get incoming mail, and a place to put outgoing mail. Each of these features ties into something the user already knows; if the feature has any "unexpected" characteristic — such as different elements in an e-mail address, compared to a regular mail address — then the program must be explicit about the differences. Differentiating addresses will be easy, since I can use leading texts and let the program give examples.

✔ When the program is opened it will automatically open communication to the mail server and will look for mail while telling the user what is happening.

✔ The program will actually send a message on the command "Send" or if the user places the message in an outbox or a mail slot. If no connection is open, "sending" mail will cause the e-mail program to open a connection.

> ✔ If a connection fails or mail that the user sent gets stuck on the way out, the program must inform the user and must show that the mail needs to be re-sent. In other words, the program will treat automatic transmission of mail as the normal situation.

Using Conceptual Models in Big Projects

If you're working in a medium-to-huge development project, you're not going to be able to get all of the essential ideas on one page. You need to create a set of related conceptual models. Think of them as a set of snapshots. This process is similar to your visiting Mount Rushmore to see the presidents' faces carved in the mountain; you take your first picture from several hundred yards away to capture all of the faces, and then you zoom in closer to take a series of pictures, each focusing on one president's face.

Figure 5-7 shows which conceptual models you may create for an integrated customer relations system. The top-level conceptual model emphasizes that customer data (represented by a smiley face in the figure) will be shared by all the programs in the system, and that level also shows the programs which comprise the system. The overall conceptual model is the one you use to design the users' desktop, the application launching bar, or your main menu — whatever it is that your users will have as their starting point for work with the system.

In Figure 5-7, the second level is a set of conceptual models, each of which gives an overview of the work process supported by one program. The production part of the system is so extensive that it will consist of several programs; Figure 5-7 shows the third layer of conceptual models needed for the programs inside the production module.

Checking your models

You can do a reality check to make sure that your assumptions about users' mental models aren't too wild. Just take out any titles or give-away text labels and hand the picture to a typical user. Ask, "Please tell me what you think is happening in this picture."

You can check your conceptual model in a similar way. Hand someone the picture and ask them to explain it to you. If your conceptual model is close enough to an existing mental model, your test person will be able to make some accurate comments about the picture.

Want more ideas? Read more about doing reality checks in Chapter 17.

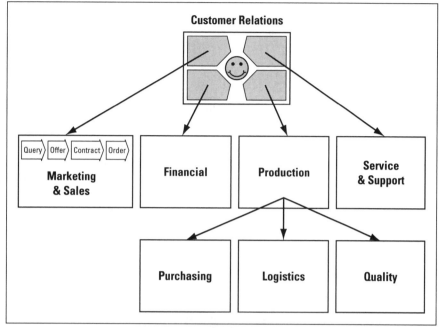

Figure 5-7:
A hierarchy
of
conceptual
models for
a large in-
house
system
development
project.

Putting Models to Work in Your Windows

Remember, a conceptual model is a picture of the basic ideas underlying your system. It is the minimum understanding you think that the user will need in order to work successfully.

You need to design the GUI so that it communicates your conceptual model to the user, especially if the model contains unfamiliar ideas. In this section, you see how two different programs with the same conceptual model went about the communication job.

Do you use a presentation graphics package? Several of the simple programs that produce an on-screen slide show use the conceptual model shown in Figure 5-8. The appearance of a slide results from what happens in three different parts of the program:

  ✔ The background and fixed graphics get copied from a *template*.

  ✔ The placement and some attributes of user text and graphics are determined by choosing a *layout*.

  ✔ The user adds the *content* by typing text or adding graphics.

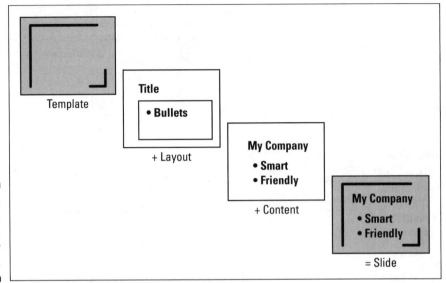

Figure 5-8:
Conceptual
model for a
slide show
package.

This interface keeps the model secret

A few years ago, I had the opportunity to observe people using two different slide show programs that both had the conceptual model shown in Figure 5-8. Program A was the strong, silent type. When users started Program A, they saw something like the interface shown in Figure 5-9. The program was set to default to a simple company standard template with a logo in one corner. The visual communication says, "Here is a piece of paper, do with it what you will." This interface activated the users' mental models of paper.

The layout didn't become visible until users started typing in a certain place. If users typed somewhere other than the certain place, the layout feature didn't kick in at all. When the layout feature did kick in, users thought they had made a mistake; they typed "A" but the result was a bullet symbol and an A. If the default layout didn't suit the users, they didn't know that they could choose another layout. They didn't even realize that they had a layout or what the function of a layout was. Their mental model of paper didn't have an interactive layout object in it.

What do you think users did when they wanted to remove the logo? Because their mental model of paper didn't include the idea of *template,* they thought that the logo was on the slide. So they tried to select the logo and erase it. But the logo couldn't be selected because it didn't live on the slide; it lived on the template. I saw one creative user drawing solid white shapes to cover up the unwanted logo on each slide.

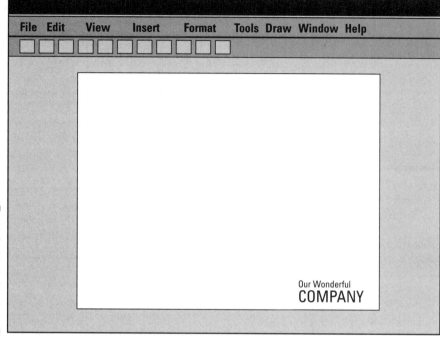

Figure 5-9:
User
interface
for Program
A, the
strong,
silent type.

So Program A had a conceptual model but did not communicate it to the users. Oh, users could have learned the conceptual model from reading the handbook or by attending a course — but they didn't do either of those things first. The users first tried to use the program and got frustrated and called the program names. I don't think they recommended Program A to all of their friends and acquaintances, either.

This interface puts the model up front

Program B was a lot more outgoing. The initial screens for Program B looked something like the ones shown in Figure 5-10.

When Program B started for the first time, it invited the user to choose a template. A thumbnail of the selected template communicated what a template does to a slide show: It determines the background color and fixed graphics. Users absorbed this knowledge unconsciously. If they didn't register the word *template,* they at least remembered where they had originally seen the slide background.

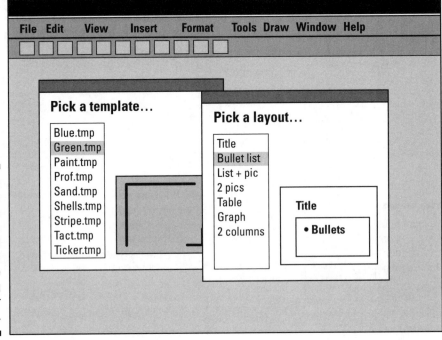

Figure 5-10:
Program B
has the
same
conceptual
model, but a
more
outgoing
user
interface.

The next window offered the layout choices. The mere act of choosing from the list showed users that they had a finite number of options. Those who later wanted a different layout realized that they needed to find a command to change the layout.

When the empty slide appeared, the layout elements displayed concise directions such as "Click here" and "Type here."

Program B successfully communicated the elements from the conceptual model — template, layout, and content — to its first-time users. The users that I observed reacted with pleasure and surprise at how easily they were able to create good-looking slides.

If you consider only how easy the program is for first-time users, Program B is by far the best.

Putting your own model up front

Think about how you use a new program. After the program is installed on your computer, you start the program and take a look at the first screen (or at least the first screen after the splash screen with the maker's logo, or a log-in screen).

You take a quick look around: You look at the menu headings, and any buttons, fields, or graphics that are immediately evident — to orient yourself in the program.

Putting the conceptual model up front in the GUI that you design means making sure that your program takes advantage of this golden moment with the user. *Whatever the user sees first* in your program should reflect your conceptual model. Depending on your application, the model may show up in various ways, such as:

- ✔ **The elements from the model show up as the titles of pull-down menus.** Consider a contact management program for salespeople. Pull-down menus could be titled Contacts, Organizations, and Appointments. The menu titles convey the idea that the user can probably find information and work with it from any of the three viewpoints. Would you expect to be able to find the current price of Brand X Whiffle-woofers? Perhaps not, because the program has no pull-down menu called Products. You may assume that the program cannot produce such a list, because the menu titles communicated that only Contacts, Organizations, and Appointments are important here. The first screen had nothing about Sales or Products.

- ✔ **The program begins with a dialog box that tells the user how to begin a task or even guides the user through a task.** Slide-show Program B from the prior section in this chapter is an example. That program opens with modal dialog windows that teach the user the steps in creating a slide show. Consider this solution when the user can perform only a few tasks. In Program B, the user must either create a new slide show or open an existing one in order to work with the program.

- ✔ **The first window provides an interactive map of the program.** You can choose to open your program with a flow chart or map of the whole program, with hot spots (places the user can click) that allow the user to navigate to any part of the program. I've seen this solution used successfully in multimedia training programs and executive information systems.

- ✔ **The program uses opening graphics to communicate important functions.** When the conceptual model is very close to some familiar object or system from the physical world, parts of the GUI may be drawn to look like the physical objects that they act like. A time management program might have a large picture of a calendar, for example. In this case the designer is using an *analogy* to convey the conceptual model. You can read more about analogies in Chapter 11.

The preceding list is just for starters. No two programs communicate the conceptual model in exactly the same way.

Unfortunately, some designers don't bother to work out a conceptual model. If you find a program to be difficult to understand — especially if you can never predict where various commands will turn up — you can safely bet that the program was designed on the basis of semiconscious mental models, rather than a well-thought-out conceptual model.

Chapter 6

How Users Get Around: Navigation Models

*D*id you ever try one of the early, text-based adventure games? You explored an imaginary cave by typing in commands. Sometimes you just had to cross your fingers and hope as you typed, **Go treasure** or **Go main entrance**. And usually the answer was, You can't get there from here. An angry green goblin confronts you.

In the adventure games, players used trial and error to become familiar with the different rooms in the cave and find the pathways for moving between them. In the same way, sooner or later the users will remember where most of the functions in your application are located. If you'd like it to be sooner, your interface needs a *navigation model* — a kind of a map — to make getting around predictable.

In this chapter, I show you how to figure out an appropriate navigation model for your program. You'll find it easiest to create your navigation model if you have already selected your basic windows structure (Chapter 4) and drawn a conceptual model (Chapter 5). You should also know roughly which tasks and which functionality your GUI is going to support (Chapters 2 and 9).

After you settle on a navigation model, you are ready to implement and test your design with a *paper prototype:* drawings of the important windows in your program. At this stage the drawings may not be especially detailed, but they will show the title and purpose of each window, and the commands or widgets needed to move (navigate) between the windows. This chapter tells you how to create a paper prototype. Chapter 17 describes how to test a design using a paper prototype.

Navigation Model: Better than a Map

A *navigation model* is a simplified, predictable map of the windows in your application. You create the model and then fit the windows into it. Later, when the user works with your program, she perceives the navigation possibilities from the visual clues you included in the interface. She learns her way around the interface quickly because she finds a regular, predictable pattern.

What if you neglect to make a simplified, predictable map — a navigation model? Many projects fall into this error. Walk into any big database-oriented project and you see the kind of wallpaper shown in Figure 6-1: large diagrams of the data model, and maps of all the windows in the system with lines showing which windows are connected. Now I ask you, if the developers who invent this system and live with it for months need to hang up the maps on the wall to keep track of where things are, how do they expect the users to manage?

Think about maps for a moment. If you have to learn your way around in a new city, is it easier to master a regular rectangular pattern of roads, or a tangle of switchbacks, blind alleys, and one-way streets? A nice, conspicuous mountain or some other landmark helps you stay oriented, too.

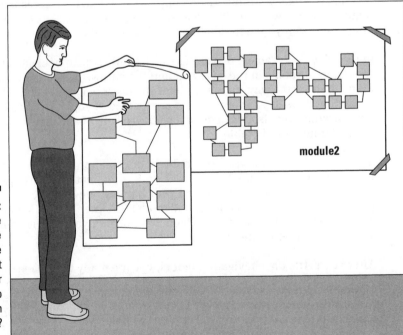

module2

Figure 6-1:
If you have to put the map on the wall, what will your users do to keep from getting lost?

When you give your project a navigation model, you impose some regularity or some organization principle on your program's map. You make the map memorable and predictable for your users. When you choose a top window, a central window, or a main window to be your "landmark," you make that window visually different from all the others so that it stands out. You provide navigation paths to the main window from all other windows so that your main window is always within reach.

To design the navigation model, decide which functions the different types of windows need to have, and how the user can get to each type of window. You don't need to decide actual window appearance now, but remember that the users need to be able to easily *see where they are* and *where they can go*.

Document-centric Daisy

Sometimes, it's easy to make a navigation model. Document-centric MDIs (multidocument interfaces, like Lotus WordPro or Microsoft Excel) typically have the daisy-style navigation model shown in Figure 6-2.

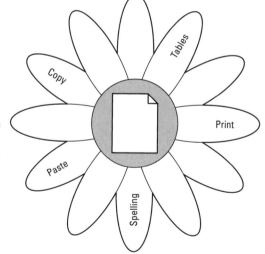

Figure 6-2: The daisy navigation model suits document-centric applications.

In interfaces that use the daisy-style navigation model, the document fills the middle of the window, and all the commands are arranged along the edges in the menu and toolbars. Commands lead to new, modal dialog windows, all of which apply to the active document in the center. Since document production is the main task, it makes sense that the document takes up the most space. The document provides the user with a *working context* — it serves as a continual reminder of what is going on.

Note that the user is the one who knows what's going on, not you, the developer. The task could be a thank-you letter for Aunt Ellen's elbow-warmers or a 150-page master's thesis on multimodal microbiology. The daisy model is well-suited to unpredictable, user-driven work because all the important commands are equally accessible and just about equidistant from the area where the user's attention is centered.

The daisy model works pretty well for documents, spreadsheets, presentations, and mail. The model can be used for simple utilities and "steering" progams where the PC, the disk, the network, or some other object to be controlled takes the central position of the document. But what if you don't have the luxury of a single object around which to center your navigation model? Then you're probably making a database-oriented application.

Navigation Models for Database Applications

In a database-oriented application, you generally have more data than you can present in a single view, document, or window. Instead, you present parts of the data in different ways through different windows or views, depending on which task or part of a task the window supports. Creating a good navigation model for a database application is more challenging than simply filling up a daisy; each database system has its own unique model.

In this section, I'll take you through examples of several different navigation models to illustrate how you follow these principles that lead to a user-friendly model:

- ✔ Make a predictable navigation model, not a complex, irregular model.
- ✔ Give your users only the flexibility they really need — and no more.
- ✔ Keep navigation paths stable and visible.
- ✔ Enable navigation in your application to reflect your conceptual model.

Turning a complex model into a simple model

Figure 6-3 shows the map for a small course-administration system using multiple windows. No need to start programming — you can see that this system is gong to be a pain to use just from looking at the irregular map.

Users will have trouble remembering how they can move from point A to point B. And they'll have to go through four windows before they can start working, if they happen to want to register a new course participant.

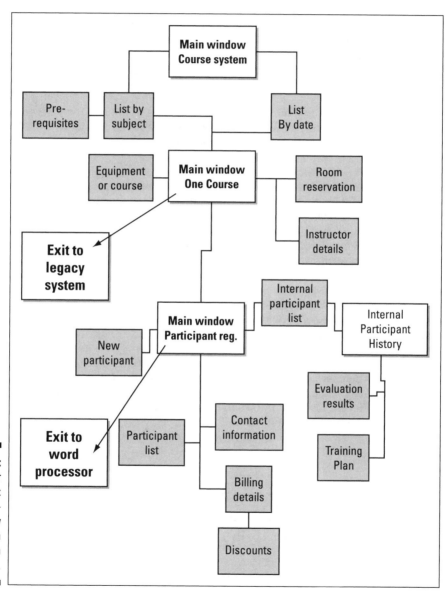

Figure 6-3:
Ripe for remodeling: a multi-window navigation model with problems.

So, how do you clean up? Figure 6-4 shows what happens when I apply the following guidelines:

- ✔ Define a home base or main window.

- ✔ Try looking for some way to organize or group your windows. Then you have a more general, memorable navigation model. If you end up making a true map — one square for every window — you've made a mistake.

- ✔ Feel free to put in lots of discreet shortcuts — expert users will discover them and rejoice — but keep the main routes open and clear.

- ✔ Use modal windows where you need to control the interaction, but don't force the user to go through more than one window, just to get to another one. Aim for a broad, shallow map rather than one that is narrow and deep.

Figure 6-4 shows what happens when I apply these guidelines to the course administration example. The main objects that the user seems to be dealing with are *courses* and *participants*. If I use a pair of tabs to present both the *course list* and *participant list* in the first window, the user can then immediately select the course or person that is of interest. These tabs reside in a main window that becomes the *landmark* or central point to which the user returns.

The modal windows holding the details about each person can "cluster" around the main window, accessible by both command buttons and menu commands. Thus I have a broad and shallow "map" with all navigation routes visible.

If the users can typically complete a task with the help of the main window and a single modal window, I've done a good job. If users have to visit three different modal windows in order to complete a task, then I'll need to do some further design work.

Figure 6-4:
Sketch for a wide and shallow navigation model for the course system.

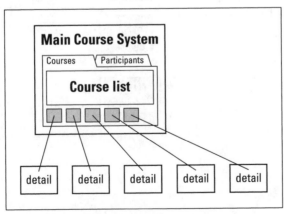

Getting flexibility right

Flexibility in GUIs comes in many different flavors. You can offer users alternative ways to do the same thing, for example with the mouse or the keyboard; this type of flexibility has nothing to do with the navigation model. But consider these other types of flexibility, which do depend on the navigation model: You can allow users to work in any order they wish, selecting windows or commands at will. You can allow users to switch between tasks at will, without necessarily completing one task before proceeding. You can provide alternate paths to the same destination.

Adding flexibility to the navigation in your program tends to add complexity.

When you design the navigation model, you make some choices that will influence how much flexibility is available to your users. You need to decide what kind of flexibility your users need, and where they need it. If your users are completely unpredictable, and at the same time very experienced, you probably *do* want to build a completely flexible system based with an independent, multiwindow structure.

Otherwise, consider these points on potential flexibility:

✔ As long as your program will run in a graphical user environment, the users will have flexibility on the *program* level. That is, they will be able to switch in and out of your program as needed.

✔ If your users need the capability to start several tasks in your application and switch between them freely, you need to associate tasks with individual main windows, MDI document windows, or nonmodal dialog windows. For example, in Microsoft Word a task is equated to working with one document. A user can choose to open and edit two or more documents and switch around to each at will.

✔ If your users need to be able to solve one individual task in different ways, you should avoid designing tasks as a chained series of modal dialog boxes. For example, student records will sometimes be updated for all the students taking a certain class, but at other times the registrar needs to access and change individual student records. Don't force the registrar to navigate through a "class selection" dialog box in the second case.

✔ If your users need freedom to compare information from different parts of the program in ways you may not have foreseen, most information should be presented in individual main windows, MDI child windows, or nonmodal dialog boxes. This way the user is free to open different windows and compare them.

A modal dialog box "locks out" other windows until it has received the attention it wants. (See Chapter 4 for more detail on windows types.)

Compare the analysis of users' needs for flexibility and the resulting navigation model in this example of a case-handling system for a social services agency, shown in Figure 6-5.

Caseworkers need to be able to switch easily between cases as they respond to telephone calls or deal with correspondence or interviews. They need flexibility on the case level, so each case must be in an independent window. On the other hand, the information within each case needs to be organized in a predictable way so that caseworkers can find information quickly. They need flexibility to choose what information to view, but no flexibility in where information is located. Finally, users should have no doubt about which information belongs to which case, so the navigation model must ensure that there are no independent windows *within* a case.

A navigation model that meets the flexibility requirements for the case-handling system is shown in Figure 6-5. This example is a multiwindow system, but complexity is limited because only two kinds of main window are included in the interface. A single main window provides a listing of cases and an overview of the case load. From the case list, users may launch one additional main window for each case. Only the case ID in the title field and the data contents of each window are different. All case windows have the same menus and buttons. Most information in a case is presented with the help of multiple panes or tab controls. This interface displays few modal dialog boxes; within the active case window, only one can be open at a time.

Keeping navigation paths stable and visible

Suppose that you are trying to find your way around in a new place. On most street corners, you find a map, but each map is different. Do you think you could find your destination? How would you feel?

It wouldn't happen in the real world, but computer programs have been known to do the equivalent by putting new commands into the menus for each window.

Look at the menus for a large program using an MDI window structure, shown in Figure 6-6. In this example, each child window is allowed to replace the main pull-down menu with its own menu. Basically, any time you make a menu choice that opens a new child window (for example, child window 2-2), the contents of the pull-down menu changes. What you have here is an old-fashioned hierarchical menu system masquerading as GUI menu.

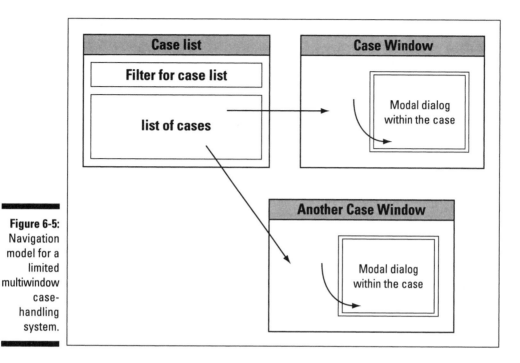

Figure 6-5:
Navigation
model for a
limited
multiwindow
case-
handling
system.

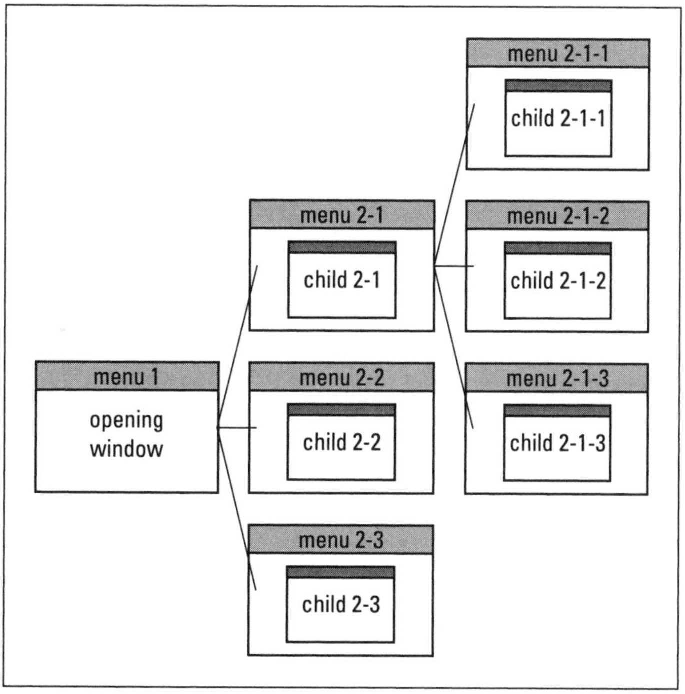

Figure 6-6:
If you want
your users
to get lost
and stay
lost, show
the
navigation
possibilities
in a
dynamic set
of menus.

The menu is always in the same place. It changes when you switch to a new child window, but you may not have been watching. Then you go to the menu for some reason, and "Hey, wait a minute, it didn't look like this before . . . or did it?" Users must learn which commands are available from each window. They end up saying things like, "I know there's a command for this, but which window do I have to go to in order to see it?"

Does it surprise you that new users of a system like this one develop a raging case of insecurity? Avoid this *dynamic menu* navigation model!

Making navigation and conceptual models visible

People don't walk through walls. Neither do users. If you want your users to *use* the windows in your application, remember to provide doors with handles: menu commands, buttons, list items, or graphics that remind the user that "there is something here you can go to." If you don't provide a visible entrance point, you're asking your users to remember where they can walk through the wall. The more visible your handles, the more likely the users are to use the windows. Compare the two lists in Figure 6-7. In both cases, the users can double-click on a lit item to see details. By adding an icon to each item, the programmer has made the right-hand list provide a visual reminder that the list is a navigation route as well as a list.

Figure 6-7: Provide visible reminders of windows and functions. In which list would you be more likely to double-click?

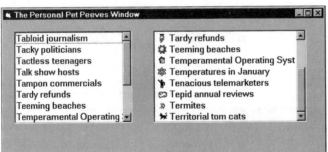

Your application also needs to communicate the conceptual model to the users. Because the conceptual model shows the main objects and the main steps that will be involved in the application, you ought to be able to see where these items are going to show up in your navigation model.

Figure 6-8 shows a conceptual model for a system that lets users view detailed building specifications. This figure also shows the navigation model used to display the information: a *multipane structure,* with panes for each level of the information structure.

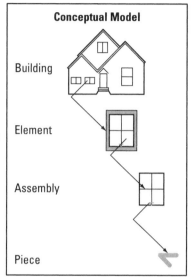

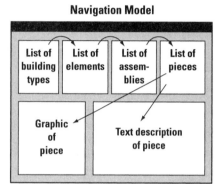

Figure 6-8: Conceptual model and navigation model for a building specification system.

Notice how the four levels of the conceptual model are represented by the four panes in the top row of the navigation model. The left-to-right positioning reflects the hierarchical relationship among the four levels: A building is made up of elements, an element has one or more assemblies, an assembly has one or more pieces.

This example is an excellent navigation model that allows the user to move freely in a large amount of information without getting lost or stuck. If the user's mental model of the construction trade includes the four levels — building, element, assembly, and piece — navigation will be intuitive.

Create a Paper Prototype to Test

After you select a navigation model and an overview of the important tasks the system needs to perform, you should make a paper *prototype:* a simulation of your whole program at the window level. That is, you can make paper windows and draw the buttons and menu choices needed to move from window to window. The windows may not have much in them yet, but you know which ones you need now.

Why prototype so early?

It depends on your approach to life. I figure that if you were the "ignorance is bliss" type, you wouldn't be reading this book at all.

Wouldn't it be great if you could be sure that users would be able to understand your opening windows? If you knew for a fact that users would be able to find those new functions when they need them? If you could demonstrate that users will be able to perform common tasks without chasing through too many different windows? With a prototype, you can do all of these, and more. You can discover and repair design problems *before* the program is implemented in code.

As described in the Introduction, to produce a good design you must alternate between creation and evaluation. A paper prototype documents your creation, and provides a basis for evaluation, discussion, and reality checks.

A prototype is a good basis for discussing your choice of interface type, window structure, conceptual model, and navigation model with user representatives, clients, and bosses.

You can perform all kinds of reality checks with a prototype. You can check menu structure, window flow, and task or function *findability*. You can check *leading texts* — the explanatory text in front of each field or widget. You can even use your prototype to collect samples of typical data. See Chapter 17 for more ideas, and for a discussion on how to do a test with users.

Creating a prototype forces you to answer design questions that you have ignored or put off. It takes you a giant step further in your design work. So the question isn't really should you make a prototype now, but can you afford not to?

Why prototype on paper?

Lots of good *Rapid Application Development* (RAD) tools are on the market, and more are coming all the time. Why should a real programmer mess around with something as low-tech as paper and pencils?

✔ Because they don't look real to users (or bosses), paper prototypes are not so likely to create unrealistic expectations: "But when you showed it to us last month, the response was instantaneous!" they complain. "Ah, uhm, that was just a prototype," you respond.

> ✔ You get more useful comments when you work with a paper prototype. Paper models tend to collect more comments about the design of the task, and fewer comments on how things look. As soon as you show people a "real-looking" on-screen prototype, they get more interested in commenting on the "easy" things like color, font, and 3-D effects.
>
> ✔ Keeping an open mind about a window you've only sketched is easier than keeping an open mind about one you've spent a lot of time programming.

Practical paper stuff

Have plenty of different sizes and thicknesses of paper on hand when you begin making a paper prototype. You'll probably also need scissors, tape, semi-sticky glue, and transparencies.

Here are a few tips for making your paper prototypes "work":

> ✔ You can draw your windows in the development tool or in a graphics editor such as CorelDRAW! and then print them out to create a paper prototype.
>
> ✔ Consider using an office copier to enlarge windows from letter size to a larger paper size: It's easier to write legibly on the larger buttons and windows.

Real programmers on paper prototypes

Most programmers that I've worked with are reluctant to do paper prototypes at first. However, the following comments illustrate what these programmers have to say after the first try:

 "When I use a prototyping tool, I have a large part of my energy and attention on using the tool — on figuring out how to do things. When I used paper, all of my attention was on the design."

"I thought it was nuts, but the HCI professional who held a week-long course for us told us to do it, so I sent a couple of guys over to the users' department with the window drawn on paper. They came back with much better input than we've ever gotten from those users before."

"The users grabbed it and started adding stuff onto it."

"There is no temptation to continue programming on a paper prototype. When we make a prototype on the computer we tend to go on and build further on the prototype, even though we know that we shouldn't."

 "We could afford to use it to try out several different designs."

✔ If you need to discuss your prototype with several people at once, consider creating it on flipover paper.

✔ A copier is also useful to make lots of copies of empty windows, or copies of fields and buttons to cut out and paste on windows. Use semi-sticky glue, rather than permanent glue.

✔ When you try out the paper prototype, place a sheet of overhead transparency film over the window to let users write in typical data or list contents.

✔ Cut up a colored plastic see-through binder to make rectangles for selection in lists or text.

✔ If you create a set of tab controls, tape them together at the bottom to keep them in order.

✔ Menus can "pull down" through small slits in the paper window below the menu bar. Fold the bottom edge of the list up a little and attach a tape "handle."

Sample prototype

There's a graphics file on the CD at the back of this book that you can print out to see what a paper prototype might look like.

Chapter 7

The GUI Standard

In This Chapter

▶ Deciding whether you need a GUI standard

▶ Considering a quick standard for small projects

▶ Using a standard to make development easier

▶ Using a standard to make your program easier to use

▶ Supporting a visual profile by using a GUI standard

▶ Thinking about what to put in a GUI standard

*I*f you have more than one developer in your project, you need to agree about how things are to look and how you want to use the different windows widgets such as frames, tabs, and command buttons — that is, you need a project GUI standard. Otherwise your users may someday feel that they're switching between universes instead of between windows.

Getting developers to agree to standards about GUI can be tough. A lot of creative pride is out there, along with a lot of individual opinions. After you decide on a standard, finding a practical way to get project members to stick to it is even tougher. You find tips about how to make the standards process work in this chapter.

If you get stuck writing the standard yourself, a good rule of thumb is to keep the standards document short. Put in examples rather than principles and leave out anything you can. At the end of this chapter, the section called "What to Write in Your Standard" gives you a boost. Better yet, the CD-ROM that comes with this book contains a draft standard that you can copy and edit to create your own standard.

Do You Need a GUI Standard?

When in Rome, do as the Romans do. When in Windows, do as Windows does. Unless you're making a One-time GUI (see Chapter 2), your application shouldn't hold too many surprises for the users. Following the platform standard is important — but that still leaves most of your design questions unanswered.

In a large project you may need to create your own *project GUI standard* (some people call it a *style guide*). Your standard doesn't replace the platform standard; you end up using both of them together. If your organization produces several products for the same users, you may want to create a common standard for all of the products.

A good GUI standard helps you pursue one or more of the following goals:

✔ To simplify the job of creating good GUIs

✔ To make an application that's easier for the users to work with by making things that look alike, act alike, and vice versa

✔ To reinforce firm or product identity through graphical design (often referred to as *brand identity*)

Notice that I said *pursue* these goals. Whether having your own standard helps you to achieve these goals is another question. Are you and your colleagues willing to expend the effort to create a good standard and to use it? Creating a standard is a bit like setting off to ski to the South Pole all by yourself. If you're in doubt about whether you're willing to give the task your best effort, don't bother.

Quick Standard for a Small Project

If you're working by yourself or in a *very* small group, you may not need to create an entire GUI design standard. In a very small project, the developers talk together often and see each other's work. You get "standardized" painlessly during the communication process.

To help keep the design consistent in a small project, you and the other developers should do the following together:

1. **Create a couple of typical windows.**

2. **Print out the window designs.**

3. **Make a list in the margin of each drawing, showing elements that you want to remember to copy throughout the application.**

4. **Hang the printouts near your monitor.**

I call these steps: Creating a quick-and-dirty standard. Figure 7-1 shows an example.

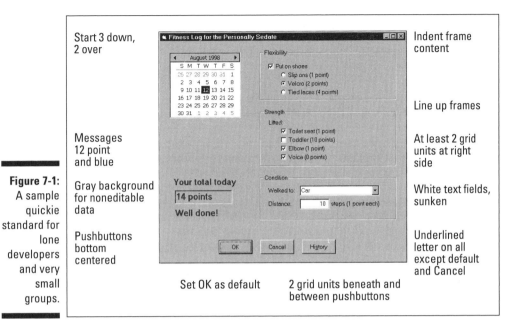

Start 3 down, 2 over

Messages 12 point and blue

Figure 7-1:
A sample
quickie
standard for
lone
developers
and very
small
groups.

Gray background for noneditable data

Pushbuttons bottom centered

Indent frame content

Line up frames

At least 2 grid units at right side

White text fields, sunken

Underlined letter on all except default and Cancel

Set OK as default

2 grid units beneath and between pushbuttons

Making Development Easier

Large projects often adopt standards in the belief that standards will make the GUI design more effective. The rationale sounds like this: "We won't have to make the same decisions over and over again, and it will be easier to check for consistency." However, to design windows with the help of a standard, you may need to make some changes in the way you and your colleagues work. The following sections describe some of the things you can do to increase your chances for success.

Involve other developers

Standards written by a single enthusiast often fail to take root in other people's work. Unless you're willing to make an absolute pest of yourself for a long time, you really can't develop and implement a standard single-handedly.

Making one person or a very small group responsible for writing the standard (or, better yet, making the pictures) does work, but try to get a larger reference group to discuss each section and reach a consensus about what rules the standard should contain.

People are more willing to change if they have a stake in the new requirements. To create ownership, you must listen to the other developers before making final decisions, and you must give away some control over the end result.

Make a developer-friendly standard

"What do we need to do to get you to follow the standard?" I asked a programmer one day. "Make the standard easy for me to follow and make deviating from it a lot of work," he replied.

He had an excellent point. Developers are going to use the standard, so you'd better treat them as users just this once. In creating the standard, follow these do's and don'ts to give developers something that makes their work easier:

- ✔ Do create a clear, concise standard with plenty of illustrations and examples.

- ✔ Do save time by including in your standard any points from the platform standard that aren't automatically covered by your development tool. (Looking for answers in one place is enough work for developers!)

- ✔ Do organize the standard from the developer's point of view, with main headings for window type, function type, and component type. If you use more than one development tool, add to the written standard some subheadings that give the specific rules for each tool. That is: "Radio Buttons: All tools" followed by "Special notes on radio buttons in Horrible Forms Version 4.0" and "Special notes on radio buttons in WinBricks 2.2."

- ✔ Do base the standard on the development tool you're using. Give measurements in the units used in your tool. Use the terminology used in the development tool.

- ✔ Do create an online repository of standard windows and components to copy.

- ✔ Do make a clear distinction between what developers *must* do, and what they are advised or allowed to do. Mark rules clearly as "required." Mark other recommendations as "optional."

- ✔ Don't write long sermons about design principles.

Living with a GUI standard

A GUI standard is a lot like a set of laws for a community: Laws that are made but not enforced are demoralizing for the citizens. Don't make GUI

standards without agreeing on how to ensure that they get followed —
whether you decide to have a committee review each window or just ask the
window's developer to sign a checklist.

GUI standards, like laws, sometimes need interpretation. And like laws, GUI
standards must sometimes be amended to keep in step with the changing
world around them. GUI standards have to reflect what works in practice,
not in theory. When a user test shows that the menu names in your GUI
standard don't work, fix the standard.

If you want a GUI standard that works, be prepared to follow the following
guidelines:

- ✔ Decide how you can make sure that the standard gets followed.

- ✔ Decide who has the job of answering questions, interpreting the
  standard, and making judgments about new situations.

- ✔ Decide how developers are to find out about changes.

- ✔ Decide whether changes can be applied retroactively: If a window has
  been approved and the standard changes, must the window be
  changed?

- ✔ Write down the routines and responsibilities in the GUI standard.

Give everybody a paper copy

Electronic standards have clear advantages: You can search in them, and
they're easy to update. Experience shows, however, that people must *also*
get the standard on paper if you really want them to use it. Maybe it seems
more real on paper. Maybe people prefer to read from paper. If copying and
distributing new versions of the standard seems like a lot of work, at least
you then have another good reason to keep the standard brief.

To be successful, standards work needs attention from development leaders
the same way that a houseplant needs water: in small doses at regular
intervals. If bosses make a big noise about needing a standard and then
forget about it for months, nothing much is going to happen.

Making the Program Easier to Use

A GUI standard helps to make your program easier to use if it makes the
program behave consistently. Things that look alike should act alike, and
vice versa.

A standard also helps your program behave like other programs with which the user is already familiar. On the other hand, such similarities don't help if your users don't actually use the other programs. A company that sells both a maintenance package and a health-care package should think twice before subjecting these products to the same GUI standard to make the users happy. How many users actually use both programs?

Understand that your real goal in following a standard is to meet user expectations, not to follow the standard. Users don't read standards; instead, their expectations are based on whatever programs they work with already. When you develop software for a single user group such as accountants or layout people, your best bet is to create a project standard that matches an existing, widely used program such as Microsoft Excel or QuarkXPress.

In the drive to standardize, the developers on a project can occasionally lose sight of why they made the standard in the first place. Consistency in your program's interface doesn't necessarily add value. Consistency is only there to make things easier for the user. Anytime consistency seems to be making things harder for the user, reconsider whether to apply the standard.

Figure 7-2 shows a dialog box from an e-mail program in which the project GUI standard must have said "Present parameters in alphabetical order." The option button group on the left obeys the standard. I see that group and wonder "Just how slow is Normal?" I would've preferred the group shown on the right, even if the order is inconsistent with parameter sets elsewhere in the program.

All properties dialog boxes in Windows 95 have a set of tabs. Some properties dialog boxes have very little information, so they have a single tab. To developers, creating a single-tabbed window is a simple case of consistency: This program element is a properties dialog box, so it has a tab set. A tab set with one tab is still a tab set. To the user, on the other hand, a single tab is like a doorknob on a wall: You can see what it is, but it doesn't do anything. The user asks "What does this thing do?" not "What category of windows does this window belong to?"

The e-mail parameters in Figure 7-2 and the properties dialog box both show that consistency, like beauty, is in the eyes of the beholder. Standards prescribe consistency by dividing design elements into categories; users take a more pragmatic view.

Users judge consistency on whether an individual window component behaves the way they expect it to. When users can successfully predict what will happen if they use the component, then users experience the interface as being consistent.

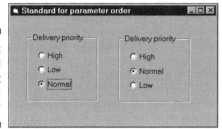

Figure 7-2:
Is Normal
the slowest
way to send
mail?

Supporting a Visual Identity

If the purpose of your GUI standard is to make sure that everybody can see how this program is a product of Our Wonderful Company, you need the help of a professional graphics designer to succeed. Visual identity is not a job for competent amateurs. Choose a designer who has experience in working with computer-based graphics on *your* development platform. You save time otherwise needed for converting files, and the designer and the development team can use the same drawing tools.

Get the graphic designer together with a team member who can explain the constraints of the development tool. The designer is going to be suggesting fonts, colors, and a layout grid. Try things out in the development tool so that you know the suggestions are feasible.

Ask the graphic designer to create sample windows for your standard. Request your graphic designer to create and comment on examples of good layout that you can include in your standard. Before-and-after pictures are always helpful, as are sets with "do this, not this" examples.

Remember that your designer is able to contribute more than just window layouts and icons for the toolbar. (If you have a marketing department, this problem may be their responsibility and not yours — but check anyway.) Have the designer look at all of the elements of the product: desktop icons, Help text designs, installation windows, splash screens, boxes, CD-ROM covers, documentation covers, and disk labels. Don't miss an opportunity to support brand identity.

Ask the graphic designer to cast a discriminating eye over all (theoretically) finalized windows. This step is especially important if many different developers create windows, because different developers all interpret the standard in their own way. Have a single, visually oriented person take the final look, and you're more likely to catch any fiddly little remaining inconsistencies.

What to Write in Your Standard

I can count all the people I know who like to write standards on my left thumb. For that reason, a draft standard is included on the CD-ROM that comes with this book, just in case you need to write a standard.

If you'd rather make all the decisions about a standard, this section shows what I'd suggest as a starting point for your project's GUI standard. Omit anything you can, especially items that are already covered by the defaults in your development tool.

Of course these suggestions are for an "average" project, and every real-life project is special. Expect to change them!

By the way, *widgets* refers to window components such as text fields, scroll bars, and the like. If any of the other terms used in this table seem mystifying, you find them explained in Chapter 16.

- ✔ **About the standard:** Answer questions about rules in this section. Who writes and updates the standard? How should developers use it? What are required items and optional items. Who gives permission for exceptions? What's the process for changing the standard? How does the developer find the newest version? Where does the developer find standard objects to copy?

- ✔ **Project design goals:** Put in the three top-priority design goals for the user interface, in order of priority.

- ✔ **Project navigation model:** Put in the navigation model, together with any decisions you've made about how to use various window types such as main windows, child windows, and modal dialog boxes.

- ✔ **Window types:** Show examples of each window type permitted in your project.

- ✔ **Window layout:** Define a layout grid that's measured in the same units as those used by your development tool (inches, pixels, millimeters, whatever). Show examples of how to use the grid. Define distances between the edges of windows and various widgets, and between groups of widgets. (Layout grids are explained in Chapter 13.)

- ✔ **Frames and lines:** If your design includes these graphic elements, specify when they may be used and give examples, including the distance to the nearest control/contents.

- ✔ **Pull-down menus:** Define standard menu items and rules for items that may vary from window to window or application to application. Define standard shortcut keys.

- ✔ **Pop-up menus:** Which elements of your design, if any, have menus that pop up on a right mouse click? What commands are included in the pop-up menu?

✔ **Toolbar:** Define standard toolbar icons and give recommendations for new icons and for tool tips.

✔ **Status line:** If your application has a status line, what appears on it? Are any sections of the status line variable? What are the guidelines for using these sections?

✔ **Pushbuttons:** Which types of windows may contain command buttons? Where should they be positioned? Are any buttons obligatory? What size should buttons be?

✔ **Text fields and leading text:** Define leading text alignment. Do you have colons after leading text? Do you indicate obligatory fields or fields with restricted (validated) entry in any way? Do you use title capitalization (initial caps on each word) or sentence capitalization (initial caps on the first word) in leading texts?

✔ **3-D effects:** Yes or no to 3-D? What depth? Which components are sunken and which are raised?

✔ **Option buttons:** Must option buttons be framed? Should the group be presented vertically or horizontally? What is the maximum number allowed in a group?

✔ **Check boxes:** Binary choices only? Do you allow interdependent check boxes?

✔ **List boxes:** What minimum number of lines must be displayed? How do you indicate multiple selection lists? Do you have a standard interaction style for moving items from a source list to a selected list? How does the user search or navigate in a long list? Do you allow horizontal scrolling in lists? (I certainly hope not, but it's your standard!)

✔ **Drop-down lists and combo boxes:** What are the maximum number of values recommended? How do you deal with lists containing both a code and a decode? How does the user search or navigate in a list?

✔ **Tabs:** Do you allow more than one row? What kinds of windows may contain tabs? What kind of data may be placed on tab controls?

✔ **Drag and drop objects:** How can the user identify draggable objects? How are acceptable destinations indicated?

✔ **Fonts:** Obey the user's font choice (all users won't make same choice) if possible. Otherwise, which font, size, font color, and background color are to be used on each control?

✔ **Icons:** Answer questions about the color palette used for icons, as well as the icons' dimensions in pixels and the general graphic style (formal, informal, degree of 3-D, shadow direction, and so forth). See Chapter 15 for more about icons.

✔ **Colors:** Respect the user's choices of color settings if the design tool permits this. Otherwise, define background color, font color, editable field color, and a single "attention-getting" color. (See Chapter 14.)

✔ **Messages:** Which types of messages does the system display in modal dialog boxes? What are the guidelines for wording these messages?

✔ **Pizza:** Should you eat a pizza slice beginning from the point or from the crust? Are anchovies optional or forbidden?

✔ **Access to Help:** Which shortcut keys and commands must be available in all windows?

✔ **Help structure:** What Help must be included: Field Help on status line, tool tips on icons, short tips for each window, full documentation for each window, frequently asked questions, a Help index?

✔ **Principles for good GUI design:** I leave these out of GUI standards because people don't seem to learn much from reading them. But if you want to put in some principles as a basis for discussion, see Chapter 21 for suggestions.

Part III
Designing GUIs that Work

In this part . . .

In this part I get to the heart of things: How do you design a program that is easy to understand and work with? First you need to find out how the users work, and tailor your program to fit their tasks. Then you make your program intuitive, and finally you make the users' work easier. Look in the next few chapters to discover a process for understanding the users' work, to find a collection of nifty methods for making your program more intuitive, and to see how you can make the users' work go like greased lightning.

Chapter 8

Learning How Users Work

· ·

· ·

Someday, I'll take part in the perfect GUI design project — one with a multidisciplinary team to design the GUI, and one of the members will be a functional expert. Oh joy! I'll have continual access to somebody who has actually *performed* the work for which I'm designing an interface. And while I'm at it, Santa, could I please have a social scientist or two to do the field study for me? (If you're wondering why I want a social scientist for this task, check out the section "Practicing the Science of Observation," later in this chapter.)

While I'm waiting for the perfect project to come along, I need to go out and scrounge around for the detailed information that I need about users and their work, and no doubt you need to do so, too. This chapter, therefore, tells you how to get in touch with your users as effectively as possible.

Deciding What Questions Need Answering

To make GUIs that work for the users, you need to know more about them and their work than you uncover in Part II, "Surviving the Early Design Stage." In order to create a GUI that is suited to the users' tasks, you need to be able to answer the following questions in detail:

✔ **What is the user's purpose and motivation in performing this work?**

For example, consider the work performed by an emergency services dispatcher. His work may consist of talking on the telephone and recording information on a computer. But his *purpose* is to help get the right personnel and equipment to the site of an emergency as quickly as possible. His *motivation* (or sense of satisfaction) with the work might come from the knowledge that help arrived at an accident in time to save a life — thanks, in part, to his intervention.

✔ **What information do users need to carry out their work?** Where does the information come from?

For example, the emergency dispatcher receives a description of the emergency and other information about the site from an *outside* source. This information may come in the form of a telephone call from a person in distress, from a witness to an accident, or perhaps from a police officer. The dispatcher must then use his *own knowledge* and *computer (and other) resources* to verify and locate the site and to evaluate the description. He needs to know the current locations and status of emergency services personnel and equipment, information that should come from the computer.

✔ **What information results from the work?** Who uses these results? What for? What form should this information take?

For example, the dispatcher takes the information that he gathers and produces *new information* — an assignment of an emergency crew to the incident, telling the crew where to go and what to prepare for. The dispatcher needs to send the message in a way that precludes misunderstanding. Eventually the dispatcher and the whole organization will want to know how they are performing, so the assignment and message must be saved and timed.

✔ **What is the work process?** What events set the work in motion? (How do the users know that they need to do something?) What are the steps involved? What decides the order in which users perform the steps? How do they know when a step is finished? How do they know when the work is finished? What are the possible outcomes?

For example, the dispatcher might identify the *telephone call* as the event that sets the task in motion. The steps that this initial event sets in motion might be collecting information from the caller, verifying the information and converting it into emergency services terms, checking resource availability, selecting a resource to assign, sending the message to the resource, getting confirmation that the message is understood, and getting estimated and actual arrival times. Then you would go into more detail about each step.

You might interpret this work process in one way if you discuss it with the dispatcher in a quiet interview room. However, you might interpret the work another way if you observe a busy operations center, with several dispatchers taking calls at the same time, where the steps in the task overlap due to time pressure, and dispatchers are receiving multiple calls about the same emergency. For some tips on how best to evaluate your observations about a user's work, see "Practicing the Science of Observation," later in this chapter.

If you already know the answers to these questions for your own users, you're ready to skip on to Chapter 9 on designing support for the users' tasks. If not, I suggest reading the rest of this chapter for ideas on how to *get* answers to these questions.

Getting Access to Users

Interviews with present or potential users of your GUI are a great source of factual information, and a good GUI designer guzzles facts the way Mom's '67 Cadillac guzzled gas.

Developers who tell me that they rarely interview users say, "I'm not sure I'm allowed to," or "I'm not sure how to go about it." Sound familiar? If so, this section is for you.

Talking to people who use your packaged software

In development projects for shrink-wrap software, bosses sometimes have the feeling that talking to users must be a job for sales or marketing people, not for techies, who could surely be more profitably employed behind (locked) doors in the R&D department. My most successful argument against this catastrophically shortsighted viewpoint is that developers who meet only other developers tend to make only developer-friendly products. If they want you to make user-friendly products instead, your bosses must let you meet potential users.

Perhaps you'd rather avoid an outright discussion with your boss about user interviews? You prefer the lay-up shot to the slam dunk? Try some of the following ideas to meet users (or potential users) of your interface:

✔ Volunteer to train course instructors or to provide technical support for your product at an exhibition. People who are already your customers can give you one angle, but you can also get interesting input from *potential* users.

✔ Try cruising the computer stores and striking up conversations with potential users there.

✔ Offer to visit an adult-education computing class to talk about your career and try to meet some novice users that way.

✔ Volunteer organizations may be willing to exchange user interviews in return for a little technical support. Be creative!

Because you're probably going to be working on several versions of the same application, spend some of your own time getting to know the field. Are you making a real-estate application? Study for your license. Are you creating an interface for a medical application? Volunteer at a hospital for a few months.

These activities are not only a great way to get to know potential users of your application, you can consider them an investment in your own technical competence. This *domain knowledge,* combined with your technical expertise and knowledge of your users, makes you a more valuable and versatile developer.

Talking to people who will use your custom software

In a custom development project, getting access to future users should be as easy as picking up the phone. After all, the people who will use your program either work for the same company you do, or they work for your client. In practice though, project leaders are often allergic to the idea of letting GUI designers speak with potential users: "It'll take too long." "It's too dangerous — we won't be able to afford to give them everything they'll ask for."

In dealing with your project leader's fears, focus on the need to eliminate uncertainty from the project design. Explain that you plan to study the users' work, not ask for their wish lists. Remind the project leader that early design changes are inexpensive compared to late design changes. Speak warmly of the security of basing decisions on the best possible data.

When your sensible, reassuring manner has almost won the day, expect one final feint. The project leader may ask, "Can't you just talk to the user representative?" The answer to that question should be that, of course you have already interviewed the user representative (in order to find out who *else* to interview to determine the needs of the custom interface).

A user representative is a real-live user, assigned part- or full-time to the development project. A user representative almost always gets picked for the job because he or she is exceptionally skilled at using the computer program you are replacing. Interviewing a user representative can be useful especially to determine what tasks a typical user needs to perform (as opposed to gathering information about general interface design preferences). However, a user representative rarely is a typical user, so don't stop with just one interview — try to interview a wide variety of people who will be using your custom interface.

When you receive permission from the project leader, call or write the department you want to visit. Explain the purpose of your proposed visit, *ask for permission* to interview, and suggest a couple of dates. Indicate that users are welcome to suggest an interview date that would suit them better. This low-key approach leaves the power of refusal in the hands of those to be interviewed — and so they rarely use it.

Should you meet with a refusal, you can express polite regret: "That's too bad, I was especially interested in you/your department/your group. Could you suggest someone else who has a similar degree of knowledge of this work (the work you want to know about)?" If that line doesn't cause your user to reconsider, at least you'll get another name or two of potential users to interview.

In practice, I find that most people are very pleased to be interviewed about their work, as long as I make it clear that I am there to learn about their needs, not to criticize or evaluate their work.

Practicing the Science of Observation

At the beginning of this chapter, I mention that my dream team for a GUI design project includes a social scientist, such as a social psychologist, an ethnographer, or an anthropologist. All these disciplines include formal training in observing and interviewing people in their own environments.

Observing people? Interviewing people? Is that so hard? Can't anybody do it? Well, yes, anybody *can* do it, but here are some of the pitfalls involved in the process:

✔ What people *say* is not always the same as what they *do*. They may simply be unconscious of their behavior, or they may be influenced by the expectations that you, the interviewer, unconsciously communicate to them.

✔ What people say and do in their normal working environment is not quite the same as what they say and do if you take them out of that environment or if you add a foreign element — you, the observer.

✔ You're not an inert substance. Your own opinions, your previous thoughts on the subject — even the very questions you choose to ask — all influence the people you're observing or talking with.

✔ You're not a recording device. You can't remember every single thing that you see and hear in a half-hour interview or during a day-long observation. You can't even pay attention to half of what you actually observe. What you select to notice and what you choose to recall are influenced by your own opinions, your previous thoughts on the subject, and the questions that lead you to conduct the interview or carry out the observation, to name just a few factors.

You don't need to be as rigorous as a scientist in your approach to an interview. Just keep in mind that you're conducting the interview to learn something new about the users' work. If you're too biased, you produce only the answers you expect to get, and the whole fact-finding expedition is a waste of time.

Preparing for User Interviews

To prepare for an interview, first determine the type of information that you need to find out (you can review the types of questions that you need to ask users in the "Deciding What Questions Need Answering" section, earlier in this chapter).

Make sure that the questions that you ask are concrete questions about the users' work. For example, "What tasks do you perform with your computer? In what order do you perform these tasks? What documents do you print out? Who do the documents come from?"

Perhaps you're considering asking people what they *would* do in a given situation or what they'd *like* to do with the interface you're designing. Don't bother! The answers you get from such questions are pure and unadulterated fiction. Ask an imaginary question — get an imaginary answer. Make sure that you ask users objective questions about the tasks that they need to perform. (Incidentally, a techie who reviewed this book says, "I can validate that point about hypothetical questions. I once asked a user, 'If a new system could do anything you wanted, what would it be?' She answered, 'It would be my paper and pencil!' ")

You're out there looking for facts, not answers to your own design questions. If you're interviewing as a way to take users' votes about how your interface should be designed, you're engaged in democracy, not design. Users are expert at their work, but they're far from expert at software design and it's a huge mistake to think otherwise.

Who to interview

Decide which users you want to interview. Ideally, you should talk with several people from each of your user groups. Interview people who are different from each other. For example, if your user group includes people aged 20 to 60, try to interview several people of different ages in that range.

In practice, however, you typically end up interviewing whoever is readily available. If you find reasons to believe that the people you interview are not typical of the users in general, you may just need to apply a mental fudge factor to what you learn — if your interview list does not include a diverse sampling of users, your results may lack significant statistical validity.

For example, suppose that you interview a 60-year-old male engineer who uses your project management application, which contains a simple calculation feature. Suppose that you ask this user whether he uses the calculator feature in the current program, and he pats a leather case hanging from his belt and answers, "No, I use my slide rule. It was good enough when I graduated from the U and it's good enough now." Should you conclude that users (in general) don't want or need the calculator feature on the basis of this interview? I don't think so! This man is probably more-than-usually comfortable with math. Keep this user's atypical technical proficiency in mind when you consider his answers to your other questions.

Interview checklist

Use this brief checklist to take you through the user interview process from start to finish:

- ✔ Define what you want to learn

- ✔ Ask permission; make appointments

- ✔ Decide how you will record answers; prepare any necessary recording equipment

- ✔ Practice asking neutral, concrete, and open-ended questions

- ✔ Write down your starting questions and the categories of information you want to gather

- ✔ Take consent forms with you and get them signed

- ✔ After the interview, write or call to thank the user for his or her time

If you schedule several interviews for the same day, you need some recovery time between them. And don't plan to spend more than an hour at a time interviewing a single person. You'll probably be concentrating so hard that you get tired and start to miss things after an hour. Your user may also get tired and want to get back to work, too.

Where to interview

Where's the best place to interview people about their work? Go to wherever they work. People on their home ground are more likely to use their own words and terms, which you need to learn. Users can show you the tools that they use in their own work environment, such as forms, equipment, or reference materials. Interviewing users in their own workspace gives you a chance to observe how users perform certain tasks (which the user might not mention otherwise).

For example, at one on-site interview, I noticed that one user continually referred to a large notebook by her desk. It turned out she had invented her own paper-based method, which duplicated the tasks she had been performing flawlessly on the new system. Although she registered data in the program as required, this user felt no confidence in the computer program's report function. Observing this user in her own work area yielded information that the user may not have mentioned in an interview process.

One thing you *don't* need to do ahead of time is to write down all your questions. If you're doing a good job at the interview, you're uncovering new information — things you didn't know before and thus didn't write down questions about. If you have too many questions written down, you may focus on getting your form filled out instead of on what your subject is actually saying.

Afraid you may get lost without questions? Try heading each sheet with one of the topics you're researching, such as "What information results from the work?" Then be prepared to formulate the actual questions at the interview, where you can put them into the user's own words: "After you're done working on the loan, what papers do you send to the securities depot?"

Consent forms

Prepare a standard *consent form* for each interview. Ask your interview subject to read the form, cross out any part with which they can't agree, and sign it.

Because I'm not a lawyer, I wouldn't dare to suggest the actual wording of a consent form, but yours should include the following points:

- ✔ A brief statement regarding what project the interview is about and what types of information you intend to ask for.
- ✔ A statement on how you plan to use the interview results.
- ✔ A list of who will have access to the interview results.
- ✔ An explanation of how answers are to be recorded during the interview (notes, tape, and so on) and whether the interview subject (and the subject's organization) will remain anonymous.
- ✔ A statement of the right of the respondent (and the respondent's organization) to protect private and/or proprietary information. You're not asking for such information to be revealed, and the respondent may refuse to answer any question.
- ✔ A statement on the order of "I understand and agree."
- ✔ Space for the respondent to sign and date the form.

To record or not to record

Using video or audio tape to record your user interviews involves certain pros and cons. The following list offers considerations to help you decide whether to tape your user interviews:

- ✔ **Pro:** Recording an interview — whether on audio tape or on video — frees you from taking notes. Unless you're experienced in speed-writing or stenography, you can never write fast enough anyway.

- ✔ **Con:** Subjects may not consent to being taped or may be uncomfortable being recorded. If a tape is running, most people take longer to begin speaking freely (which is why some warm-up chatter is a good idea, by the way).

- ✔ **Pro:** Recording enables you to later confirm exactly what people said. Recording your interviews makes up for the fact that you observe and remember selectively — the tape "remembers" more completely than you do.

- ✔ **Con:** If you just want to find certain quotes on the tape, you should expect to do a lot of fast forwarding and rewinding.

- ✔ **Pro:** Transcribing a tape isn't always necessary. You may, for example, simply replay the tape for other members of the design team and let them take their own notes.

- ✔ **Con:** If you decide to transcribe the tape, plan that the job will take one-and-a-half to two hours of transcription per 30 minutes of tape.

Tip: I recommend recording your interviews only on projects that are large enough to require a design *team* rather than a single designer. On a design team, you need more exact documentation, especially if other designers need to work with the results of your interview.

Conducting a Successful Interview

To make your user interviews most effective, your questions should encourage the user to talk about the things that you need to know more about in order to design your interface. Concrete questions produce interesting facts. Hypothetical questions produce hypothetical opinions.

You don't want too many questions that can simply be answered with a yes or a no. With yes-or-no questions you're doing most of the talking, and that's always a danger signal. If you're talking, the subject not only is *not* talking, but also is getting exposed to more and more of your thinking; increasing the risk that the subject will produce the answers he feels you expect.

Rather than asking yes-or-no questions, help your interview subject take center stage by asking *open-ended questions*. Be specific. Start with *What* and *When* questions and then go on to the *Hows*. Save the *Whys* for last, after you're both really warmed up.

You don't even need to lock yourself into specific questions. A simple encouraging comment like "That's interesting; please tell me more about that . . ." is a useful way to get users to open up. The following sections give you some ideas about good and bad questions to ask when interviewing users.

Good questions to ask users

When conducting the interview process, try asking questions that are similar to the following examples:

- ✔ **What do you save on your computer?** This question is a way of asking what work people do on the computer. They usually answer with the nouns that they use about their work: "Applications, proposals, letters, product descriptions." Then you're in business, because you've learned some of their words. If you start with *your* words for things, many subjects simply pick up your terms and use them for the duration of the interview.

- ✔ **What did you do yesterday?** Another way to ask this is, "How long did you use the computer yesterday?" Phrase questions about the user's time spent on the computer in a framework of how long they used the computer during the previous workday. People are better at remembering recent events than they are at estimating. Activate the user's memory first; then ask for the estimates.

✔ **Please show me how you'd print the document you have on-screen right now.** You'd like to know whether the user is left-handed or right-handed, whether they use the mouse or the keyboard. Watch them and then ask for confirmation of your observations *afterward*.

✔ **I'd like to be able to afford a $25,000 car in three years. How much would I have to start saving?** If you're trying to find how a customer advisor in a bank does calculations, slip in a tiny role-play (but don't call it that).

How to interview a user

Interviewer: What do you store on your computer?

User: Just about everything I do is on the computer. I write proposals, and I've got my calendar there, plus presentations and budgets and things.

Interviewer: I'm interested in how you go about writing a proposal.

User: Proposals? Well they usually start after one or more meetings with a client, where we're starting to get an idea, you know, of what they want and what we think we can offer. We have a team meeting to work out our approach and then we divide up the writing work. We tend to specialize about which parts we write. Then, at the end, we put it all together.

Interviewer: What proposals have you written this year?

User: Well, we did one for an analysis of a hotel site — we got that one and one for a new mall and a couple for the National Parks Service; we're still waiting for the outcome of all those.

Interviewer: Do you write new material each time or what?

User: Most of it is new, yes, because we need to write about that specific project. We do use descriptions of some parts of the work that we've written before. And, of course, the résumés and the reference project descriptions are the same.

Interviewer: I'd like to hear more about how you work when you get to those résumés and project descriptions.

User: Oh, we've got a great system for that. Everybody updates his own résumé and sends a copy to Mary Beth, and each project leader sends her a project description. She copies them onto a certain place on the main computer, and she's got a binder that we can borrow — it's all alphabetical. We just skim through until we find what we want — and the file name's on the bottom of the page — and we copy it into the proposal.

Remember: This interviewer asks concrete, open-ended questions about what the user does *now*. He bases new questions on the user's previous answers. This interview uncovers and collects new facts, which are a better basis for design decisions than users' opinions.

How *not* to interview a user: leading your witness

Interviewer: You have a lot of text stored on your computer — such things as proposals and presentations and reports made by your consulting company — don't you?

User: Yes, we have quite a lot of material.

Interviewer: Suppose you had a little window you could pop up that would enable you to find whatever you wanted from that stored text and bring it right in where you were working. Would you want that?

User: Well, I guess that would be useful, yes.

Interviewer: How would you want something like that to work? I mean, would you want a command integrated into your word processor, or would you prefer a separate little floating window?

User: I'm not quite sure what the difference would be?

Interviewer: Well, see, if you had an integrated command, it would be out of the way in the menu, but if you had a floating window, it would always be covering something else up. But then, of course, you could see that window all the time.

User: I think I'd rather have the command. I wouldn't use it all that often, so it'd work better for me if it was out of the way.

Interviewer: Yeah, that's probably the best idea. Now, what search criteria would be important ones for you?

User: I'm not sure what you mean. . . .

Remember: In this example, the interviewer has a pretty good idea of what she'd like to build. She thinks that she's collecting the user's opinions. Actually she's doing most of the talking herself and using some technical jargon that makes the user the weaker participant in the conversation. Her questions and explanations lead to the results that she's expecting. She's leading the witness and not learning much of anything new from the user.

Not-so-good questions to ask users

Use the following list as a guideline for questions *not* to ask during user interviews:

- ✔ **Do you do a lot of proposal work?** This query is a yes-no question, and it's so vague that you can't know for sure what the answer means anyway.

- ✔ **How much time do you usually spend on proposals?** People don't usually estimate averages correctly if the question comes out of the blue. You can ask, "Which proposals did you work on in January and February?" and then, after they've described the work, ask, "Which month was more typical?"

- ✔ **Would you use an integrated text search function?** This question is a hypothetical (would you?) question. It describes the proposed function in techie terms. Compare it to the more concrete "How do you find text that you've written before and now want to reuse?"

Who's doing the talking?

If you're doing a good job with your interview, you're busy writing and you aren't doing much talking. This interview game is all about getting the *other* person to talk, after all.

Your attention to what your subject is saying is the most effective tool you have for getting the other person to talk. If your subject can see that your mind's drifting, the flood of information dries up to a pitiful dribble. Depending on your natural conversational style, you may show that you're listening by nodding, by making little encouraging noises, or with a facial expression of alert interest. Your hectic note-taking is a good indication to the other person, too, that he's saying something that interests you.

Pay attention to the cues that the other person sends you. Some people are happy to speak on and on with little response from you; others prefer more conversational give and take. If your subject is using short sentences and keeps stopping and looking at you, you need to provide more encouragement: "This information is very helpful; please, go on." Or you can simply repeat the last few words in a gently inquiring tone, "The reports come every month?"

Using the subject's own words in your next question not only shows that you've been listening, but doing so also helps you hold the interview in the user's language rather than in your own.

Organizing Your Findings

Review your notes or tapes as soon as possible after the interview, while the material is fresh in your mind.

If you're working in a larger project, you need to document your findings and present them in a way that can help others get as much information as possible out of what you've gathered.

Here's a not-too-time-consuming way to report on a group of interviews:

1. **Run through your notes or tapes and jot down on big yellow stickies any actual quotes that reveal important facts.**

   Keep the quotes in the user's own words; they're more effective that way. Don't worry if you've got some quotes that contradict each other; that's evidence, too.

2. **Put the stickies up on the wall and sort them into groups or categories.**

3. **Name the categories.**

4. **Type up (or, if you're lucky, get somebody else to type up) the raw data in this form, with category names and a list of quotes under each category.**

5. **Write a brief summary of your conclusions/findings on the basis of the raw data, attach the raw data to your summary, and circulate your report.**

Beyond Interviews — Getting Some On-the-Job Training

You don't need to conduct interviews to get interesting information. One of the very best ways to learn about work is to perform it.

Ask for a week's worth of on-the-job training at a user site. You'll spend about the same amount of time that you would arranging, conducting, and analyzing a half dozen interviews — and you may enjoy the training a lot more than you would the interviewing. With a little bit of luck and, of course, your modest, unassuming charm and helpful attitude, you may even become "one of the gang."

A technique halfway between interviewing and on-the-job training is *site observation*. To do a site observation, visit the users where they work and pretend to be a fly on the wall. After you've observed users for most of the day, wind up with an interview. This method not only is a good way to gather information before you design, but it's also a great way to study your work after the first version's released — when you're ready to start thinking about a bigger and better version two. I describe site observation in Chapter 19, along with other ways to check out a design or a completed interface.

Chapter 9
Task-Oriented Application Design

. . . .

. . . .

*W*ay up in the North American forests was a little college town that had a new highway coming through. One day, the following notice was tacked up on the college bulletin board: "Part-time job: Duties consist of following an opinionated, illiterate road gang supervisor around and doing his paperwork. This man is too stubborn to teach and too useful to lose. You should be big, mean and ugly. Be prepared to spend considerable amounts of time in smoke-filled bars."

The ad has a lot in common with a good task description: It's realistic and has just enough detail. As you see in this chapter, a good *task description* helps you to flesh out your GUI design and helps you to heed that favorite admonition of GUI design experts: "Make the program well-suited to the user's task."

Figuring out exactly what an application should *do* is hard mental labor. Fortunately, task analysis makes the process of producing good results from all that skull sweat much easier. Many formal methods of task analysis are possible, but I find that people are most likely to master and use a simple, informal technique such as the one described in this chapter.

This chapter covers task analysis that takes place early in a project, as you're figuring out which windows to make and how to put them together. Chapter 10 shows you how to use task analysis to figure out how to make a single window perform its specific function.

Focusing on the Users' Tasks

Understanding the users' work is essential. You're going to have a tough time making a user-friendly interface if you base your understanding of the user's work only on the data model or even on the functional specification. You can't even rely on the users' own description of what they want, because a lot of their knowledge — like your own — is unconscious or implicit.

Here's a little example from my friend and fellow interface designer, Gautam Ghosh. Gautam asked, "What are the user's requirements for a tool for pounding in nails?" Here are some of the most specific answers he received:

- ✔ The tool should have a handle that feels good to hold — wood, for example.
- ✔ The tool should be about a foot long.
- ✔ The tool should have a small metal striking surface.

Gautam went out to his workshop and found an old wooden cutting board with a cutout handle. He snipped up a tin can, folded it around one edge of the cutting board, and fastened it with heavy staples. Gautam's "user-specified hammer" is shown in Figure 9-1. This device meets the specifications, and you can — just barely — use it to pound in nails. But it's far from well-suited to the task, as anyone who's ever hammered nails can tell you.

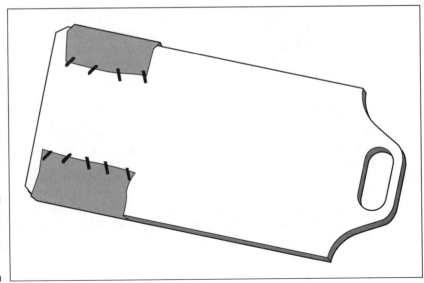

Figure 9-1:
The user-specified hammer.

Users are expert at performing their own work; they are the best source of information about the work. However, you can be expert at doing something without having *meta-knowledge* of your task (that is, being able to explain *what* is happening and *why* it happens). If I ask someone who occasionally hammers nails and who has some knowledge of physics to "specify the hammer," she might remind me to look at aspects like angles, point of balance, and concentrating and maximizing force at the striking surface.

All too often, software developers build user-specified "hammers" for tasks that they've never performed themselves — or even *seen* performed. You have nothing to lose and much to gain from doing a *task analysis,* which can help you to develop meta-knowledge of the task.

You need at least two different viewpoints for the task analysis. Conduct your analysis with the help of users or user representatives if you can. If you can't get "real users," find at least one discussion partner who is not another developer.

Discovering a Simple Method for Task Analysis

Briefly, *task analysis* involves looking closely at the user's work to gain new insight into how to create the design. Follow these steps to conduct a typical task analysis:

1. **Choose a specific task.**

2. **Create a *task description.***

   Describe the task with just the right amount of detail for the current design stage. Don't describe the design itself yet — just the user's work.

3. **Tell a story about how the user would perform the task through the use of your design.**

   This story is called a *scenario.*

4. **Think about what you learned from describing the scenario and then adjust your *design* if necessary.**

Three important terms are mentioned in these steps: *task description, scenario,* and *design.* I explain exactly what I mean by these terms in the following sections.

Tasks stay the same

Tasks are the users' work. Tasks are independent of your design; that is, users need to perform their tasks even if your system is never installed. For example, cleaning up after a meal is a *task*. You may wash the dishes in the sink, stick them in the dishwasher, or toss the paper plates in the trash, but the task is the same. (Blaah!)

A *task description* describes one concrete, specific occurrence of a task. For example, a description of the task of "cleaning up after dinner" might look like this: "Clean up the kitchen, the good plates, and the glasses after all seven of us have had homemade spaghetti and meatballs for dinner."

Task descriptions like this one can be short at the beginning of the project. You just add enriching details and break the task descriptions into steps as you go along.

"Register a new member in the database" is not a useful task description. This description is general instead of specific, and it assumes that there must be a database, which is part of the design, not the task.

The following task description produces some useful insights, however: "Carlos Suarez of 2347 Littlefield Drive wants to join the Volunteer Corps as a Supporting Member. He wants to pay his $32.75 membership fee by personal check and to receive his monthly newsletter at his business address. Do everything necessary to see that he can do so."

You need to reference your task descriptions again and again throughout the design project; put them in a word-processing document that you can add to the descriptions frequently. In a large project, the task descriptions should be part of the design documentation that's easily accessible to all project members. I like to keep the outdated versions of the task descriptions on file, too, so that I can see how much progress we're making.

What if you're designing a revolutionary new application for a re-engineered business or one that's using such cutting-edge technology that the tasks haven't been thought of yet? The best advice I can offer is to call in some outsiders to help you, set up the most realistic working conditions you can, and then role-play doing the work.

Scenarios tell a story

You generate a *scenario* by taking a *task description* on one hand and a *design* on the other hand and squashing them together.

In a scenario, you describe what "performing the task" would be like when using a specific design. For example, if the task is "write a letter," part of a scenario for a new office automation program might sound like this: "When the user is done writing, he can save the letter by clicking on a minimize button to turn the letter into an icon and then use the mouse to drag the icon to the printer and the file cabinet."

Someone else in your project may create a *different* scenario for the same task because they have a different idea of how the design should be.

The more detail you put into the scenario, the more new things you realize that you still need to find about the task, and the more new insights you gain into your design.

One of the beauties of this technique is that you can create a scenario and then document it any way that fits in with your project organization. If you're working alone on a small project, you may simply talk out loud with someone and make a few hand sketches and notes. In a larger project with a more formal organization, you may choose to create a storyboard prototype (a series of annotated screen pictures showing each stage in the scenario). You may hold a meeting to go through the scenario and then write down new additions to the task descriptions and questions about the design as part of the minutes of the meeting.

You can see one way to document a scenario in the section "Can This Project Be Saved?" later in this chapter.

Designs change

For the purposes of task analysis, your *design* is the best description of the interface that you have at the current time. You may even have several competing designs that you want to analyze.

Like the task description, a design is specific. And like task descriptions, designs become more concrete and detailed throughout the project.

Making a task list

If you have a window that you plan to use for only one task, one task description may be all you need. If you're designing a larger application, you need a whole list of tasks. Here are a few tips for setting up your list:

✔ Your list should cover all frequently performed tasks, critical tasks, and tasks that users most detest. (See Chapter 2 for more about asking the right questions.)

✔ Your task list should take you through most of the functions in your application, but you don't need to cover all possible combinations of data and functions. If you put in a task that calls for registering a new customer address, for example, you may not need to analyze the task of registering a new supplier address. The GUI will include both functions, but the tasks are so similar that if you understand one, you probably understand the other.

✔ If your task descriptions are unrealistic, the task analysis will be wasted effort. So, try to involve one or more users in setting up typical task descriptions — or at least get your task descriptions checked by a user.

✔ If you have more than one user group, remember to list some typical tasks for each group. Different user groups can have completely different perspectives on the same task because they perform the task for different reasons and under different circumstances. For example, a desk clerk in a hotel and a reservation clerk at the hotel chain's national call center can both perform the task of "reserving your room for an additional night." However, the call center operator would have to begin by asking, "Which hotel are you staying in, please?" while the desk clerk would already know the answer to that question.

Implementing a Task Analysis

You can do *task analysis* anytime, anywhere, and with whatever people and materials you have at hand. (If you've designed a GUI before, think back a little and you can probably see that I've merely described something that you were doing all along.) If you haven't performed a task analysis, read on to discover how.

The term you use to describe *task analysis* really doesn't matter. What's important is to think of your *task descriptions,* your *scenario,* and your *design* as three separate items. Otherwise, you can all too easily muddle the task and the design together in your head, and that's when you may start thinking about the work in terms of whatever is most familiar to *you* — the data model or the development tool — instead of understanding the work the way your user does.

How can this design be improved?

After you have the three separate elements clear in your mind, think of them like the three points of a triangle, which you can use to add detail to your design (or to evaluate your design). I call this model the *Task Analysis Triangle*.

If you want to know if your design can be improved, work your way around the Task Analysis Triangle in the direction shown in Figure 9-2. Start with the most detailed version of the design that you have, describe the scenario for that design, and compare the scenario to the task. If the scenario and design seem to match up pretty well, the design is good. If the scenario departs from the task, go back and fix the design to better support the task.

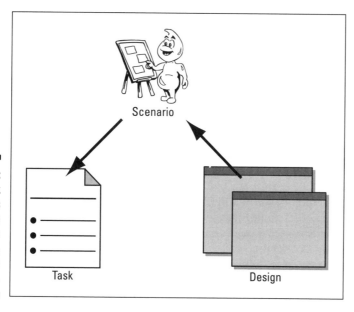

Figure 9-2:
The Task
Analysis
Triangle: To
check a
design,
start with
the design.

Scenario

Task

Design

The section "Can This Project Be Saved?" later in this chapter shows a case study that uses a task analysis in this way to figure out where the design goes wrong and how to change it to better support the task.

Making the design more concrete

If you just need help finishing your design, deciding what windows it needs, or determining what to put in the windows, you can start with the task and work your way around the Task Analysis Triangle in the opposite direction, as shown in Figure 9-3.

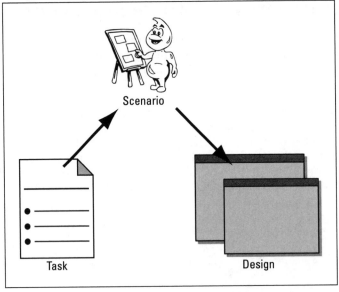

Start with the task description. Break the description down into steps and make it as detailed as you can. Then try to tell a story about how you'd perform the task by using a computer. You uncover the questions your design needs to answer by doing so, and you may even see your way clearly to the best answer.

The case study described in Chapter 10 shows you an example using task analysis to create a design.

How much detail is enough?

If you're doing a task analysis and you have a feeling that you're wasting your time, you're probably working with too much or too little detail. With too much detail, you feel bogged down — you're not making useful progress. With too little, you get the feeling that you're simply restating obvious points about the task or the design. To move to the most helpful level of detail, consider how far along you are in the design process:

✔ If you're close to the beginning of the project, work with few details. Stand back and see the big picture. At this point, you're deciding which windows you need to carry out tasks. You need a name, title, or "theme" for each window. You need to think about how the user is going to move from one to another. The case study in the following section is at this level of detail.

> ✔ If you're in the middle or near the end of your design project, move up
> close and pay attention to all the details you can. Now you're thinking
> about how to make the best possible window. You need enough detail
> in the task description to be able to determine exactly what data needs
> to appear in the window and what *widgets* (buttons, fields, lists, and so
> on) you need to include. The case study in Chapter 10 shows the single
> window level of detail.

Can This Project Be Saved?

Once upon a time, not so long ago, a software development project was
creating . . . oh, say, a customer service center application for a large
telecommunications company.

Originally, each customer service operator in the company was a specialist.
Some operators dealt with new customers, while others set up service
visits, moved accounts to new addresses, or added such services as call
waiting to existing accounts. If you consider cellular service, business
customers, special discounts, ISDN lines, and all the rest, you can appreciate
that, as a group, the service operators had a lot to keep track of.

Because the telephone company's customers didn't particularly enjoy being
shuffled from one operator to another in search of someone willing — and
able — to help them, the powers that be decided that in the future, each
operator must be able to solve any and all customer problems.

A wonderful new client/server system with an intuitive GUI was supposed to
give operators all the help they needed to carry out unfamiliar tasks efficiently. A GUI would free the operators having to memorize a lot of codes
and screen elements.

Time (and money) passed, and the designers sweated. They decided to use
a multiwindow system, because the situation obviously called for great
flexibility. They decided to use the popular object/action paradigm, because
that would ensure that the system was easy to use. Finally, they presented
the fruits of their efforts, only to be met with absolute disgust from the
users, who claimed that the system was completely unusable and unsuited
to the task.

I've set the scene — now try to imagine that *you* have been brought into this
project as a GUI designer to try to find a solution. The problem is to make
the design more user-friendly without making massive changes; hundreds of
windows have been designed and programming is already underway.

Take a look at the design and see what you think. I illustrate it for you in the following section in the form of a *scenario*. The scenario tells how to use the design to perform the following hypothetical task:

> Rudolph R. Deere calls and says that his cellular service bill for last month is wrong. Retrieve the billing data and check whether an error appears. If so, make an adjustment and ask the accounting department to send a replacement bill. Send a record of the adjustment to accounting and to Mr. Deere.

Scenario 1: The original design

In this scenario, I'm working at the application level. I want to see what windows I have and how they fit together, so I just draw each window with its name or purpose. I show very few details of window contents. The details I do show are the commands used for navigating to other windows.

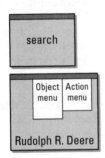

The user searches for the customer, Rudolph R. Deere, while Mr. Deere describes the problem: Correct his cellular bill.

Mr. Deere is found. The customer object window opens with his data. As in all object windows, you have an Object menu and an Action menu. The user now considers Mr. Deere's problem. The user asks himself, "Which object (window) do I have to go to in order to solve the problem?" The answer: the cellular bill object for last month. If he finds a one-to-one relationship between the customer object and the cellular bill, the user should go to the Action menu. If not, the user should go to the Object menu to move to a new object.

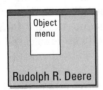

Because he has more than one cellular phone bill for each customer, the user chooses the Object menu. The cellular phone bill isn't in the Object menu, but Account is, so the user chooses Account in order to go to the cellular phone account — eventually.

The user sees a window that lists all of Mr. Deere's accounts. Deere has two phone lines as well as two cellular numbers. The user selects the correct cellular account.

cellular account

list
of bills

Action
menu

bill for last month

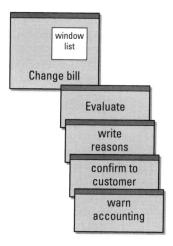

window
list

Change bill

Evaluate

write
reasons

confirm to
customer

warn
accounting

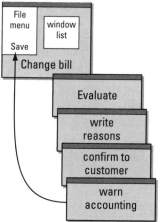

File
menu

window
list

Save

Change bill

Evaluate

write
reasons

confirm to
customer

warn
accounting

The cellular account object window appears. Because each account has more than one bill, the user goes to the Object menu. In the Object menu, the user finds and chooses Bills.

A list window opens and displays all of Mr. Deere's bills for this cellular account. The user selects the most recent bill.

The Bill object window opens, displaying the data for the most recent bill. The user evaluates the data and agrees with Mr. Deere that the bill needs to be reduced. Now the user is at the correct object, so he can go to the Action menu. In the Action menu, the user finds and chooses the Change Bill command.

The main Action window for bill adjustment opens. This window contains a list of the other windows that the user must complete. The user can access each window from the list by clicking the window name in the list. The secondary windows include one that sends information to the accounting department and one that sends a printout of the adjustment to Mr. Deere.

After the user completes each of the windows on the list, he must return to the main Action window and choose Save from the File menu. The user then says to Mr. Deere, "It's all taken care of; can I help you with anything else?"

This scenario shows why users were less than ecstatic about this design — users had to pass through too many windows before they could tackle the actual task of adjusting the customer's bill. Still, it isn't yet obvious how to solve the problem without a complete (and costly) redesign.

The next step is to compare the scenario to the task itself.

Comparing task to scenario

Review the user's task (described at the end of the "Can This Project Be Saved?" section) and divide the task into the following steps:

1. **Take Mr. Rudolph R. Deere's call, and find Mr. Deere's data to ensure that he is, in fact, a customer.**

2. **Find and look at the bill in question.**

3. **Make a decision.**

   Suppose that the decision goes in Mr. Deere's favor, just for fun.

4. **Do whatever is necessary to adjust the bill.**

5. **Assure Mr. Deere that everything is now in order.**

6. **Ask Mr. Deere whether you can do anything else for him.**

   Maybe a rechargeable nose battery?

Figure 9-4 compares the steps in the task with the steps in the scenario (on the right, I generalize the scenario steps a little). This simple flow chart shows the navigation pattern for all tasks with the customer service system.

What does the comparison tell you about the design? In trying to improve the design, where should you focus your efforts? What improvements do you suggest? I draw these conclusions:

✔ The interface users are forced to scurry around the data model like mice in a maze. No wonder they're cheesed off. I need to change the design so that the users can go as directly as possible to the main Action window for any task.

Suggestion: Bring all the Action menus together in one big cascading menu attached to the customer object, which should help.

✔ A second problem is unnecessary flexibility. Because the multiwindow design uses independent windows, the user must restack the windows in order to locate the main Action window in order to save the work. The multiwindow structure was probably a poor choice for this GUI,

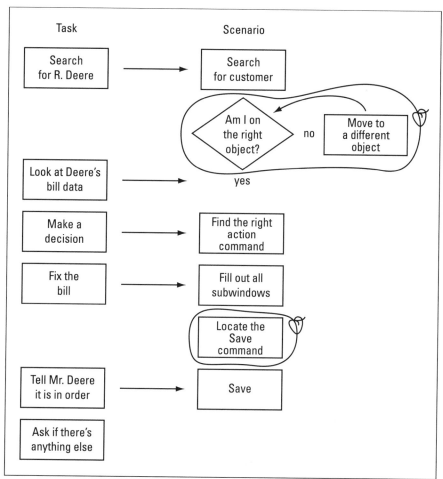

Figure 9-4:
Look for trouble where the scenario steps don't match the task.

but it's too late to do anything about that now. (See Chapter 4 for more information on choosing a window structure.)

Suggestion: Make the main Action windows stand out so that they're easier to find and constrain the subwindows so that their default behavior is to stack themselves. This solution doesn't *remove* any of the flexibility, but it does keep the flexibility out the way.

Scenario 2: After redesign

The following scenario shows how the new design carries out the same bill-adjustment task:

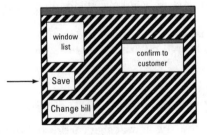

The user searches for Mr. Rudolph R. Deere.

The customer object window opens.

The user chooses Account/Cellular/ Adjust Bill from a huge three-level cascading menu containing all 180 possible actions or services. The cascading menu has the advantage that users can navigate by using either the keyboard or the mouse.

The system displays a list window containing all the cellular bills for Mr. Deere, and the user selects the bill to adjust. (Sorting puts the newest bills at the top, because these are the ones most likely to be under discussion.)

The main action window opens, and the subwindows automatically open and stack. Notice that the main Action window is now enlarged and has a distinctive background, while the secondary windows are arranged so that they don't obscure the window list or the Save command. The user can complete and close each secondary window.

After Mr. Deere's account is adjusted, the user clicks the Save command, which has moved from the menu to a nice, big button that remains visible throughout the task.

To end the story, the users, developers, and project leaders accept the redesign with mutual relief, although you have no way of telling whether they all live happily ever after.

Chapter 10

Task-Oriented Window Design

. . . .

In This Chapter

▶ Thinking tasks instead of data

▶ Reviewing the steps in task analysis

▶ Analyzing a task for the Straight Edge Associates case

▶ Building a task-oriented window for the case

▶ Examining a scenario for a database-oriented solution

▶ Doing an "instant" task analysis for a window

. . . .

*Y*ou're ready for this chapter if your interface has a lot of empty windows squawking to be filled up with good stuff like text fields and radio buttons and scroll bars and lists — *widgets*.

In this chapter, I show you how to use a simple *task analysis* to decide what widgets and data to put in a window.

If you're not sure what windows you want to make or what windows have to do with tasks, try reading Chapter 9 first. Take a look at Chapter 16 if you want to get up close and personal with the various standard widgets, from menus to drop-down lists.

Why Think About Tasks in a Window?

Task analysis at the window level helps you to get the right data together in one place. Task analysis helps you to see how the data should be arranged and presented to the user.

For most software developers, the alternative to *task-based thinking* is *implementation-based thinking*. In this section, I show you the difference in a little scrap of an example. Figure 10-1 shows two examples of a view window from a national registry of dog kennels. The user views kennel data in this window and refers to it while answering phone queries such as "Is there a kennel close to me that offers training and grooming services?"

Figure 10-1:
Who hasn't
paid dues?
You must
search for
the answer
in this
implemen-
tation-
oriented
solution.

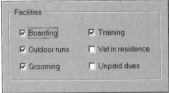 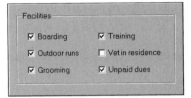

The check boxes all describe binary, either/or situations about a particular kennel, such as:

✔ The kennel either takes boarders, or it does not.

✔ It offers training, or it does not.

✔ The kennel's registered owners have paid this year's dues, or they have not.

What's wrong with this picture? The window is *implementation-oriented* because it presents and groups the information based on what kind of database field it comes from: "Ah, a binary (true/false) field. That means a check box. All the check boxes go here in neat rows."

Figure 10-2 shows a task-oriented presentation of the same window segment. Here the designer has considered how the information is used, rather than how it is stored in the database.

Some of the information in this window describes the attributes of a kennel as the user would describe the attributes to an inquiring dog owner. The annual dues information is different. For the registry secretary, unpaid dues serve as a warning that the kennel is not well-administered; though the information is not given out, it may affect the recommendation. Further-more, this information should stand out clearly when the secretary views the record for any reason.

Compare the right-hand views in Figures 10-1 and 10-2. Where would the user be most likely to overlook unpaid dues? Is overlooking unpaid dues a user error or a system-induced error?

Figure 10-2:
Which
kennel
would you
recommend?
The
designer of
this view
window has
considered
how
information
is used.

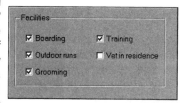 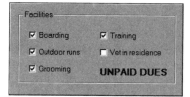

In designing a window, think "What is it that the user is trying to do?" rather than "What type of data is this?"

Task, Scenario, and Design

The task-analysis process uses three elements — tasks, design, and scenario. Chapter 9 explains task analysis thoroughly, but I can give you the basics here in a few sentences:

- *Tasks* are jobs that the user performs and are independent of the design of the computer system. Tasks should be specific and concrete. Task descriptions get more detailed as you get farther along in the project.

- The *scenario* is a story that tells how the user may perform a specific task using a specific design.

- The *design* is the GUI or a description of it. You may have text, sketches, a prototype, or finished windows. You can have several alternative designs if you want.

The following sections walk you through a task analysis to design a window. Figure 10-3 gives an overview of the process.

1. Start with the task. Break it into steps.

2. Tell a story about performing the task (the scenario). The scenario reveals how the window needs to support the task.

3. Use the results from the scenario to design the window.

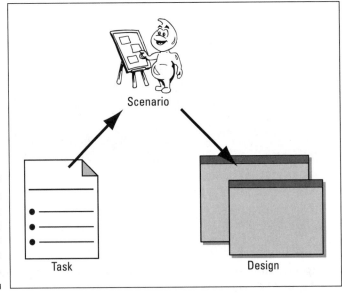

Figure 10-3:
Start with
the task
description
to design a
window.

Task

Scenario

Design

Analyzing the Case of Straight Edge Associates

Straight Edge Associates is a purely fictitious company providing consulting services in information technology. Straight Edge is growing quickly and has run out of private office spaces to assign to its 500 consultants. The president of Straight Edge has decided to solve the space problem by switching to an office hotel. The consultants will accept the new system if it meets their needs better, so the president has declared that the office manager will assign office space on the basis of need. The office manager will also resolve any conflicts that arise when the demand for desirable office space threatens to exceed the supply.

The development project has already designed an interface for the system, but the office manager tried out her task and then rejected the solution. The project needs a task-oriented design for the part of the interface that the office manager will use.

The task description

The following is the original *task description*. This description is not sufficiently detailed, but you can add to it during the task analysis:

Consultant Ahmad Bashir calls the office manager. Ahmad is having a meeting with two clients in a couple of weeks. He would like to reserve a private office or a small meeting room, but all the suitable spaces are already reserved by other consultants. The office manager has to find someone who can be moved to one of the spaces that are still available, change the old reservation to Ahmad, and make a new reservation for the unlucky person who gets bumped.

The scenario, with some task analysis

To create the scenario, you get together with a consultant and a secretary — the office manager is too busy to take part. Together you break a specific task into steps and use your imaginations about how the computer program could support each step. When your group thinks of something that needs to go in the office-assignment window, you jot the data element (or whatever) down on a yellow stick-on note. In the scenario text below, data elements are *italicized.* Your group comes up with the following scenario:

1. The problem arises.

   Ahmad tries to order a small meeting room or a private office for Tuesday, September 15. However, no space is available. Ahmad contacts the office manager. Ahmad is not going to be happy until the problem is solved, so you assume that he would prefer an immediate solution and will use the phone.

2. Ahmad calls the office manager.

   Ahmad gives his *name,* the *date* for which there is a conflict, and *what kind of office space* he wants (which is already fully booked) in his first sentence or two. He will very likely also explain what he *needs* the space for without prompting. The office manager needs to be able to capture this data immediately.

3. While Ahmad waits on the phone, the office manager checks the list of reservations for office spaces that can meet Ahmad's need.

   Ahmad is waiting, so this needs to be fast. The date and the type of space he wants have already been entered. Together these two pieces of information define which of the *reserved spaces to consider* giving to Ahmad, so the application should be able to display this list without further input from the office manager.

4. The office manager considers who can be bumped.

   In order to pick the unfortunate person, the office manager must be able to see the *needs of the people who may be moved* and compare them to the *spaces that are still available.* To follow the policy that offices are assigned on the basis of need, she must find someone whose need can be met with a less exclusive office space.

5. The office manager selects a consultant to move: Jill Bates.

   Jill is going to reorganize the hard disk on her laptop. Though Jill prefers to work in a private office, she can easily perform this task in a double office or a cubicle, which are the only categories of space still available.

   An unfortunate situation occurs if the same people get bumped all the time. Should we put in information about when they were last bumped? No, the policy states that offices are assigned on need alone.

6. The office manager transfers Jill's old reservation to Ahmad.

   Ahmad's name, date, and need have already been entered, so the manager has no reason to enter them again.

7. The manager makes a new reservation for Jill in one of the available spaces.

   If the application doesn't throw Jill's data away, that data won't need to be entered again. And by the way, this is a multiuser system. What if someone takes the last suitable space for Jill before the office manager's request is processed? The application must lock both reservations — Jill's old one (for Ahmad) and her new one — before making any changes. Even if the database views this as two operations, the office manager shouldn't need to enter duplicate data.

8. The office manager informs Ahmad of the reservation and sends a courteous explanation via e-mail to Jill so that she will know what to expect.

   The e-mail to Jill can be automated.

The initial window design

Talking through the scenario shows that the office manager's conflict resolution window should present the following data, in approximately the order shown in the following list:

✔ **Name of consultant who needs work space:** Selecting a name from a list is quickest, especially if the user can simply type the first characters of the name and a list scrolls to the closest match. Should you put first names or surnames first in the list? You take a quick look to determine whether first names or surnames exhibit more variation at Straight Edge Associates. Because surnames show more variation, you put the surname first — that way the user won't end up scrolling to the top of a group of 12 consultants named "David".

✔ **Date on which consultant needs space:** Should you use a calendar widget, a spin box, or a date field? The calendar widget will help the office manager verify that she has the correct date, but it is quite mouse-oriented. The user can select from the calendar widget with the arrow keys, but that, too, requires moving the hands out of typing position. Nevertheless, you decide that it is more important to help get the right date than to support speedy data entry, so you choose the calendar widget.

✔ **Type of meeting space that the consultant wants:** Does the office manager have to enter this? Can't the application just pick the appropriate type of space, based on what work consultants say they are going to do? No, because that would require a predefined — and likely extensive — list of the purposes for which consultants need space. Besides, whenever consultants reserve space, they will want the freedom to choose office types for themselves.

So should you use radio buttons for the type of office space? No, because in many cases more than one type will be acceptable. You decide to use check boxes so that the office manager can check more than one.

✔ **Reason for needing space:** The office manager must enter this information in order to create Ahmad's reservation (a text field). All reservations must contain the reason for needing space; otherwise, problems like Ahmad's cannot be resolved according to the "basis of need" policy.

✔ **List of reservations to consider changing:** The list should show only reservations for those consultants whose reservations might be changed; that is, reservations for the date in question and the type(s) of space needed. This list should include the description of need associated with the original reservation and the person's name.

✔ **List of available spaces on the date in question:** The office manager needs to find a consultant with a reservation who can use one of the office spaces that is still available. According to the policy, the consultant who gets bumped is also entitled to a space that meets his or her needs.

✔ **OK button:** This button locks both selected reservations and modifies them both before unlocking. The OK button also initiates an e-mail message to inform the consultant whose reservation has been changed.

✔ **Cancel button:** This button is standard operating equipment in case the office manager decides to break off the task without completing it.

No law says that you have to write down a task analysis in this degree of detail. I usually just discuss the scenario with a user or another designer.

(Okay, I'm a Gemini. When I'm really hard put, I'll even talk to myself.) While working through the scenario, I suggest that you write a yellow stick-on note for each widget that you think you may need in the window. Then arrange the yellow stick-on notes for a very, very rough window design. Finally, draw the window. The result of all this hard work is shown in Figure 10-4.

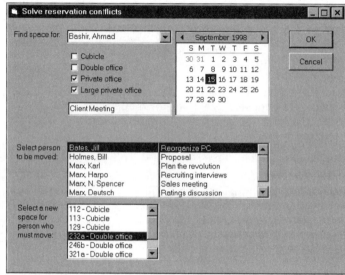

Figure 10-4:
Initial design for a window to resolve scheduling conflicts.

The window looks great to you now, because you just finished designing it. As soon as you feel a bit more objective, print out the window draft two times — with and without data in it — and blow it up to a larger size on the copy machine. Then you can trot along to the office manager, give her the blank window, and say to her, "Pretend I'm Ahmad Bashir, and I'm on the phone requesting you to find me a private office for a client meeting because everything is already reserved. Please show me if you can solve the problem with this window."

If you're like me, at this stage you can't see any usability problem in the window. On the basis of past experience, however, I can guarantee that the informal testing session with the office manager will reveal one or more ways to improve this window.

If you want to be a good designer, open yourself up to user feedback. It's the cheapest and best design education going. You can read more about getting user feedback in Part V, "Doing Reality Checks."

A database-oriented scenario (a gruesome sight)

You may want to compare the task-based window design described in the preceding sections with another solution proposed by another project member. I'd call it a generic database-oriented approach: One table in the database equals one window with a list in it, and one record in the database equals one window with a form on it.

The design described in the following scenario has one window to list all reservations and one window to display individual reservations. The windows merely offer a view on the contents of the database and the necessary commands to create and modify the records.

Start in the list window and adjust or filter the list to show what is still available on the day in question.

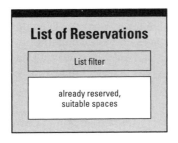

Now filter the list to show the reserved spaces of the relevant types for Ahmad on the relevant date.

Scan the list for a consultant whose need can be met by one of the other available spaces. (That's why you have to remember to look at what's available first.) Select a consultant to move and double-click to open the individual reservation.

In the individual reservation window, give the Modify command, which is protected from all users except the office manager and the reservation owner. Type in Ahmad's name and why he needs this reservation. Then save and close the reservation.

Go back to the list window, adjust the list to show the available spaces again, and select one for the unfortunate consultant who got moved. Click New for a new reservation.

The individual reservation window opens. Type in the consultant's name and need; then save and close the new reservation.

The weaknesses of a database-oriented approach are now glaringly obvious:

✔ The office manager has to make *four* one-way trips between the same two windows in order to complete one task. In the task-oriented design, she used one window.

✔ She needs to have the work process firmly in mind, because the windows don't give her any clues. If she forgets to check available space first, she won't be able to judge correctly which consultant will be least affected by getting bumped. She has to filter (or refilter) the list three times to complete one task. In the task-oriented design, each list contained only the information that she needed.

✔ She will have to remember Ahmad's name, the date he wants to use a room, and other data (she'll probably need to jot them down on paper) because he gives this information at the beginning of the conversation. After that point, she must evaluate the reservation list twice before she can move to a new window and enter Ahmad's data.

✔ She also needs to remember or jot down the name and need of the consultant who gets moved when she erases that data from the original reservation.

✔ In the database-oriented design, Jill's reservation is given to Ahmad and Jill is left without a reservation until several additional steps can be completed. What if somebody else nips in and reserves the last available space while the office manager is working on the reservation for Ahmad? In the task-oriented design, no changes are made until both reservations are selected and locked. In an office of 500 consultants, it is unlikely that several users will try to reserve the same space within a few moments; still, a designer should be in the habit of thinking about such possibilities.

Instant Task-Oriented Window Review

You can run a quick task-oriented check on just about any existing window design. For any given window, pretend to be the user. Ask yourself, "Why am I looking at this window?" Try to state your answer in the user's words and in just one or two sentences. Then look at the window to see if you can find a way to make it better support the user's purpose.

The analysis of a window listing stockroom inventory in a simple maintenance program may go like this:

1. **The user's reason for looking at the window:** I am looking at this inventory list to decide what stock items we need to reorder.

2. **The designer's question:** Can this window somehow make it easier to decide what to reorder?

   I should reorder when we are starting to run out of some item, which means that I have to guess how quickly we are using up each different item. Will 24 packages of paper towels last us for one month or three? How quickly do we use up copier paper?

3. **A possible improvement:** In the inventory list window, add a column that shows what the inventory will be one month from now (assuming that inventory gets used up at the same rate as it has been during the past month). Have the application highlight all items that will run out within the coming period (number of weeks?) determined by the user, provided consumption continues at the present rate.

Chapter 11

Making Your GUI Easy to Understand

Sometimes, even an expert loses sight of what is "obvious." For example, a certain mathematics professor finished filling a chalkboard with equations, and then began writing at the top of a second board. "So, it is obvious that . . ." His voice trailed away; he cocked his head and looked searchingly at the first chalkboard for several minutes. Then he shook himself like a wet dog before continuing in a relieved tone, "Yes, it is *obvious* that *X* must be the missing variable."

What's obvious (or what's *intuitive*) to whom, and why, often seems pretty mysterious. Users expect a GUI to be intuitive, but what steps can you actually take to *make* something intuitive?

Fortunately for us GUI designers, cognitive psychology studies how people think and how they solve problems. In this chapter, I show you some of the mechanisms of human thought and how you can use them to make your interface easier to understand.

You find additional tips for making your program easy to understand in Chapter 13, which deals with visual communication, and Chapter 5, which covers mental models.

Giving Feedback

Humans have a strong preference for cause-and-effect relationships. In fact, give us an effect — any effect — and we assign a cause to it. Usually just one, because that makes everything so neat and tidy. Your hard disk crashed? Must be because you smoked in your office. Kitty just streaked past the picture window? Must be the neighbor's dog chasing her. Windows 95 is selling millions? Bill Gates must be a genius.

If you provide good feedback — noticeable, appropriate, and immediate "effects" as a result of user actions — the penchant for cause-and-effect relationships works in your favor. Users quickly grasp the logic of your interface. They find it easy to understand.

 Good feedback is one reason that WYSIWYG (pronounced *wizzy-wig*, means What You See Is What You Get) word processing is easier for people to learn than the older word processors that relied on formatting codes. Now I click the Bold button, and I see that the button appears to be pressed in. I type a new character, and I can see that it's darker than the preceding regular characters. I know right away that I did what I intended, and my perception of the relationship between what I wanted (bold text) and what I did to get it (clicking the Bold button) is reinforced.

The user's desire for neat cause-and-effect relationships can also work against you.

If you don't bother to provide feedback, users may get into difficulties even if they do the right thing several times (on the old *just-talk-louder-and-they'll-understand-you* principle). Surely you've seen a novice user accidentally start several copies of a Windows program: The user double-clicks, and then, from the user's point of view, nothing happens, so she repeats the double-click. The program was so busy getting its act together that it neglected the elementary courtesy of feedback — to provide some signal that the user can interpret to mean, "Yes, I heard you; I'm coming."

Users may also have problems if the interface feedback is so subtle that the user doesn't notice it. The *drag-and-drop* capabilities in many current word processing programs can provide an example. A user who's just a bit shaky with the mouse may accidentally drag and drop words around, when all he intended was to drag the pointer across the words to select them. The sequence of events goes something like the ones shown in the following steps:

1. User drags to select text (perceived cause).

2. User briefly (accidentally) releases the mouse button and then presses the mouse button again (unnoticed cause).

Kinks in keycard feedback

Misleading *feedback* can stop many hotel guests cold at the room door. For example, a common keycard lock for hotel room doors works like this: After you insert the keycard, a green light comes on. However, with this simple design, the feedback (the green light) doesn't actually mean that you can go in now — it only means that the card reader has read the card and accepts the card as "valid for this room." However, you must actually wait a few *more* seconds for the lock to make a clicking noise, which is your signal to open the door. If you try to open the door *before* the lock clicks, you must remove the keycard and begin again. Pretty confusing.

This keycard lock design has a couple of problems:

✔ Because the green light is a widely accepted signal to proceed (just think of all those traffic lights!), the lock's green light is misleading — several seconds must elapse between the time the green light comes on and when the guest can actually open the door.

✔ Also, even if the designer added an audible signal to overcome the confusion caused by this misleading green light, the design would still be useless to hearing-impaired guests (who wouldn't be able to hear an audible signal) and to vision-impaired guests (who wouldn't be able to see the green light).

This designer erred by creating a two-step process: green light means "card accepted" and a click means "enter." For this simple interface, the user needs feedback *only* when the lock releases and he can open the door. If the designer improves this interface by synchronizing the green light with the lock release, the door lock can be more intuitive — and easier to understand for a broader range of users.

3. The mode switches to drag mode (undesired effect), signaled by a discreet gray rectangle below the mouse pointer (unnoticed feedback).

4. The selected text moves (perceived feedback and effect).

Because the user doesn't notice the subtle feedback on the pointer, he's unlikely to realize that he let the mouse button slip up for a fraction of a second. The situation gets worse. Because the user slips up with the mouse button only occasionally, he sees the situation this way: "As I drag to select text, sometimes the text gets selected, and sometimes I end up moving the text. I hate computers."

When everything goes well, a GUI gives the user visual feedback through dynamic widgets. When a problem arises, GUIs give feedback in modal dialog boxes — error messages. You can read more about both forms of feedback in the following sections.

The striptease method

Many GUI widgets provide visual feedback: for example, when you click a button, it looks as if it is being *pressed;* a list *drops down;* or selected text in a field *changes color.* Once in a while, you may need to help the user understand what is going on by carrying visual feedback to the extreme with the *striptease method.*

With the striptease method you simply reveal the window contents step-by-step in response to user actions. You can use the striptease method to help the user understand the relationships between the different pieces of information.

Because you reveal new information only after the user does something, the user connects his action with the new information. Trust me — this approach is easier than it sounds.

Figure 11-1 shows two versions of the Find-a-home window, with various selection criteria displayed. Because users may not be familiar with the idea of filtering or selecting from a database, the program doesn't put all its cards on the table at one time. The first window offers only one command button for the user to click. After the user clicks the Show Matching Listings button, the program reveals the goodies, as shown in the second window in the figure. The user connects the change in the display with the action that triggered it — clicking the button — and understands "intuitively" that clicking this button produces the additional information.

By giving dramatic feedback on the first selection, I help users notice and understand the relationship between the top of the window and the resulting list. This way, users catch on to the idea that they can change the top of the window and then click the button a second time if they want.

Error messages are feedback

Feedback can be subtle. Sometimes you may not notice that your program is giving feedback to the user, but that shouldn't be a problem with error messages. After all, error messages are such vital feedback that you force the user to look at them. A message window takes a stranglehold on the application and doesn't let go until the user says "OK." Right?

Seen in that light, maybe GUI developers ought to try to write fewer error messages, as well as writing better ones. Yes, I said *better ones.* Error messages are a great place to look if you want to give other software developers a hard time. Here are some real-life examples of some poor error messages that I have run across:

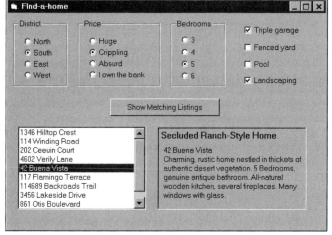

Figure 11-1: Click "Show Matching Listings" to see the rest — gradual disclosure supports the user's understanding of the data.

✔ If "Some" is explicitly selected, something must be selected in the "Some" window. This error message is cryptic and confusing.

✔ Divided by Zero. OK? This error message is worded from the program's viewpoint instead of the user's.

✔ This error message does not occur. Call Dan Developer at 555-5555. Don't include error messages that you plan to remove later (Dan actually put his own surname and phone number here, but I won't).

✔ Panic. Required data not found. I have to crash. This message is likely to frighten the user.

Many error messages sound as though the program is talking to itself. The user, however, wants to know what *she* is supposed to do now. Consider the difference between the following two error messages:

✔ Invalid format

✔ Type a date like this: mm/dd/yy. For example July 4 1998 is 07/04/98.

The first error message just tells the user what he did was wrong with no clue as to what to do right. On the other hand, the second message contains concrete information and instructions, including an example.

 Remember that the user needs to click OK to get rid of the message. Read your proposed error message to yourself and ask, "Could *I* answer OK to this message without wanting to snort?" Ask your technical writer or documentation person to review your error messages before you send out a beta test.

Taking Advantage of Affordances

By the time we're old enough to use computers, we've already seen, handled, and used hundreds of physical objects in the physical world. We've developed strategies about how to approach new things, based on our experiences.

Often, our strategies are based on the *affordances* of the new object: Affordances are the visible characteristics of an object that tell you what you can do with that object. An object that lacks *affordance* is difficult to figure out; and a GUI designer would say that a command button *affords* being clicked.

For example, a needle or a pin is sharp. You can poke it through some things. Not through a table, however, which has a hard, flat surface that affords support to other objects: a glass jar or a vase of flowers, for example. The vase has an opening in the top of an enclosed space; it affords being filled. The shape of the lid on a glass jar tips you off. Some objects afford prying off, and others beg to be twisted.

Using affordances

Within the world of GUI, you can use affordances to tell any slightly experienced user what actions are possible. In fact, the GUI user has a strictly limited group of actions from which to choose. Your user can point, click, drag, double-click, or type. Use affordances to provide consistent visual cues as to which of these actions are appropriate.

In Figure 11-2, for example, suppose that you click at the spot marked *X*. Do you think that you can type new letters here?

Figure 11-2:
Can you
type at the
spot
marked X?

CheckOut	☒
All files will be extracted to the specified folder, and a program group will be built.	OK
Folder: **X** [C:\Laura\Demozip]	Cancel
Group Name: [Demozip]	Help
Maximum Icons: [20]	
☑ Create Icons For Programs And Documents Only	
☐ Run Virus Scanner	

Most people say, "No, of course not." You don't really know that you can't, however. But all your experience with GUIs tells you that any text "on the background" of a dialog box (without a rectangle around it) is not editable text. So you feel quite confident that your answer is right, just as you should.

In Microsoft Windows 95, for example, the following visual signals are affordances. Take advantage of them to help your users experience that nice, secure feeling that they know what they're supposed to do — and actually can do — with each part of your window.

- ✔ White or light-colored rectangles indicate a place for the user to type or click to input data.

- ✔ Items with well-defined edges (buttons, fields, scrollbars, title bars, and the like) invite the user to click on the item.

- ✔ When the window background color is used behind text, data, or a symbol, it means the user cannot change the text, data, or symbol.

Although affordances in the physical world don't change very fast, GUI affordances are part of a more dynamic reality. Software released this year exhibited more items that users could drag than did software released last year. So far, however, the industry is unsure exactly what characterizes a draggable GUI item. I see different interfaces using one or more of the following conventions, also shown in Figure 11-3:

- ✔ An object that a user can drag has some degree of 3-D to make the item seem as though it's resting on the background rather than attached to it. The problem with this convention is that it is not exclusive to draggable items. All draggable things have some 3-D, but not all 3-D things are draggable.

- ✔ An object that a user can drag has little ridges similar to those that you find in the physical world to provide traction for a finger.

- ✔ Draggable items in a list may display icons to reinforce their "objectness."

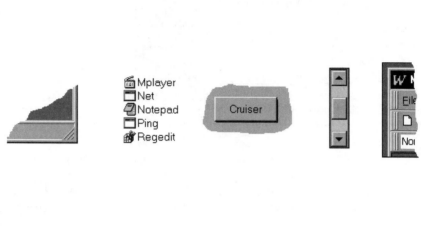

Figure 11-3:
GUIs lack a visual signal to say, "You can drag this." Finger ridges, object icons, extra shadows, or placing object in a "groove" can help.

Many software developers are active World Wide Web users, and Web pages are a special category of GUI. I note with interest (though not necessarily with enthusiasm) that the Web convention that "many graphics are clickable" leaked into Microsoft Office 97. Compare the Microsoft Office 97 toolbar with the Lotus SmartSuite 97 toolbar in Figure 11-4. Do you think that one looks more clickable than the other? Does one look more draggable to you?

Figure 11-4:
Office 97 (top) and SmartSuite 97 toolbars: Which buttons and toolbars offer more compelling affordances?

Watch out for invisible affordances

Sometimes the design of a cabinet door, a Thermos flask, or a remote control is so minimalist that all affordances are removed or concealed. If you find yourself asking, "How do I open this thing?" or "How do I turn this thing on?" or, even worse, "What *is* this thing?" the problem is usually a lack of visible affordances. GUI designers can also fall into this error.

Did you know about the selection bar in Microsoft Word? That's the (invisible) area in the left margin, where you can point and click if you want to select a whole line of text. It's been there for years but no one has ever seen it, so very few users know about it. Interestingly, some people use it occasionally without consciously knowing that it exists. Because selecting one whole line of continuous text is not a vital function, the fact that the selection bar is invisible rarely causes a problem.

The pop-up menu that you can open by clicking the right mouse button is great for users who know it's there. Because the pop-up menu has no visible affordance, however, lots of people who theoretically know that it's there forget to use it. Maybe we need another acronym, WTSIWTR (pronounced *what-see-water,* meaning What They See Is What They Remember). Go ahead and provide shortcuts for the experienced user by way of the right mouse button, but make sure that anything you put there is also in the main menu, accessible — and at least occasionally visible — for tyros.

Where would you click for help in the window shown in Figure 11-5? If you should happen to pass the pointer over the company logo corner at a time when you were desperately looking for help, and if you happened to notice that the pointer changed into a little hand, the thought may occur to you that, yes, of course, I click the company logo for help in this window. On the other hand, if the window had a Help menu or even a Help button, more users may discover the help they need.

Figure 11-5:
Where do
you click
to get help
in this
window?

Making the Most of Your GUI by Mapping

Mapping is representing a big piece of terrain on a much smaller piece of paper, right? Well, almost. If you're talking about usable GUI designs, mapping refers to the relationship between the problem and the design or between the user's task and the user interface. Good mapping results in an easy-to-use interface; poor mapping gives users a difficult interface.

A foolproof safety measure fails

A certain Norwegian city has a trolley system. Although most of the trolley tracks are double, enabling trolleys going in opposite directions to pass, one stretch of single track winds along a forested hillside. A trolley may enter the single track only if its driver is in possession of a gaudy relay baton picked up from the driver going in the opposite direction. "The system is foolproof," a company official said. "They have only one baton. If a driver doesn't have the baton, his trolley can't be on the track, so he can't have a collision."

Foolproof maybe, but not forget-proof. Early in 1997, somebody forgot the baton and a head-on collision occurred, fortunately with no serious injuries. The trolley company then planned to install traffic lights at each end of the stretch.

Don't assume that your user has a perfect memory. Give your program visible reminders instead!

You have good mapping if you have a natural, one-to-one relationship between the user interface and the user's task. For example, digital wrist-watches often suffer from poor mapping: These watches often have 17 different functions — but only three arbitrarily-placed buttons that mean something different each time you press them.

Figure 11-6 shows an example of unnatural mapping — an elegant light control panel that my business partner ran across in Sweden. The panel enables you to set the light at four different levels. The bottom switch turns the light off. Ah, but which control do you press for the brightest light? Not P4, which would be a natural mapping, but P1!

The following example describes a problem interface that was improved by applying the principles of good mapping. A shipping firm received the specifications for each shipment from its customers via EDI (Electronic Data Interchange). Gate clerks at the shipping yard needed to make sure that the customer-submitted data matched the actual shipments, and then record their findings in a computer program. Each shipment was checked three times, as follows:

1. Before admitting any truck to the shipping yard, the gate clerk checked to make sure that an EDI form was received for the shipment.

2. Each shipment then needed to pass the scales, where weights and numbers of packages were automatically registered on a separate system.

3. The gate clerk compared the scale results with the EDI form and okayed the shipment for further handling if the numbers matched up.

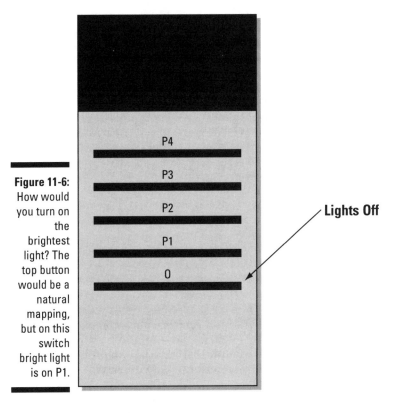

The clerks then need to clear up any discrepancies by telephoning the customers and asking them to send for new, correct EDI forms.

A slice of the original window where the clerks recorded their findings is shown on the left in Figure 11-7. Although this inefficient process involved three steps, only two columns were set up for it in the window. The clerks had to enter different values in the columns to distinguish different steps: Gate: OK means the first gate check was all right; Approved: Gate means the final gate check was all right. By the end of the day, each clerk may have needed to scroll through 300 entries to spot the ones that still needed attention.

A slice of the improved window is shown at the right of Figure 11-7. In this window, you have three steps and three columns in the same order. At each step are three possible conditions: Nothing has happened yet (blank), everything is smooth sailing (-), or something is wrong (×). The natural, one-to-one mapping between the checking steps and the new design made the process of entering data and scanning for problem shipments simpler for the clerks.

Figure 11-7:
In the
original
window on
the left, the
three-step
process is
concealed
in two
columns.
On the right,
each step
maps to one
column, and
symbols
require less
interpretation.

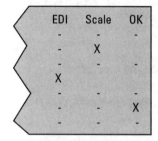

By the way, one line in the left-hand window represents a completely okay shipment. Can you spot it? (The line with `Approved: Gate`.) Now find the three shipments in the right-hand window that have known problems. (The three lines with ×.) Which task did you perform more quickly?

Because good mapping helps to make interfaces more intuitive, you should usually consider the following guidelines in your designs:

✔ Have one control or widget for each function.

✔ Call the same things by the same name all the time.

✔ Look to the user's task to discover the best arrangement for widgets and fields.

✔ Look for a spatial arrangement in the window that's meaningful to the user.

✔ Remember that the GUI is the map. And as hikers say, "If the map doesn't match the terrain, the terrain is rarely at fault."

Making GUIs Intuitive with Familiar Analogies

You make an *analogy* if you draw attention to the similarity between two things by using a familiar concept to explain an unfamiliar one, as in the following examples:

> ✔ Look, Junior, the earth is like your softball, and we live just about here.
>
> ✔ The cell membrane sometimes acts like a wall and sometimes like a gate.
>
> ✔ A directory is like a file folder; you can put things in it.
>
> ✔ What does an interface designer do? Well, I'm kind of a Miss Manners for computer programs.

Analogies work best if your listener recognizes the familiar concept and thinks of the same things you do in connection with it. I think of Miss Manners as "someone who helps people get along with each other smoothly." If someone else, on the other hand, thinks of her negatively, such as "a newspaper columnist who is a pedantic prude" (how unfair!), the analogy doesn't communicate the meaning that I intended.

If you explicitly put a word or a picture into your GUI to tell the user, "This program or command works like that familiar thing from the physical world," you're using an analogy in your interface. (Many of my colleagues would say that you're actually using a metaphor, but in the section "Metaphors Are Invisible" I tell you why you're not.)

A successful analogy makes your GUI feel intuitive to the user. Figure 11-8 shows some successful analogies that are already used in GUIs.

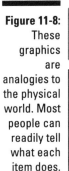

Figure 11-8: These graphics are analogies to the physical world. Most people can readily tell what each item does.

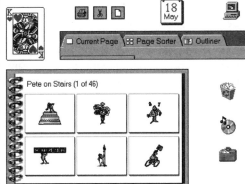

If you try to create an entire application that behaves like something in the physical world, you're using a *controlling analogy*. A controlling analogy organizes the entire application; an analogy for a single function may show up only on the toolbar button. The Microsoft Windows Calculator program and the IBM Virtual Telephone all are examples of this type of analogy. Computer games often use controlling analogies, too. Figure 11-9 shows Lotus Organizer, yet another well-known example of a controlling analogy — the interface resembles a "day planner," which many people already use and are familiar with.

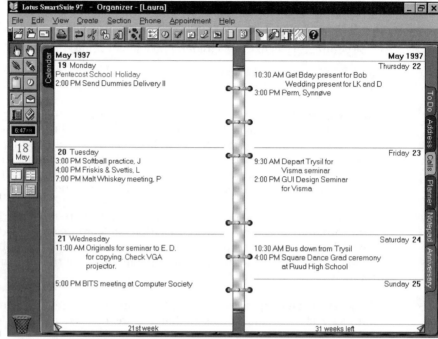

Figure 11-9:
Lotus
Organizer.
The
notebook
expresses a
controlling
analogy.

Pitfalls around analogies

Whenever you choose a controlling analogy, you're bringing the limitations of the physical world onto the computer along with your analogy. The limitations may be in your mind — you plan to make it like the real-world object, and this decision limits your creativity — or they may be in the user's mind. You may have put in extra features that the user doesn't notice, for example, because your analogy has him convinced that this computer thing works just like the real thing.

Take the Microsoft Calculator accessory, as shown on the left in Figure 11-10. I know how to use a calculator, so this one in Windows is immediately familiar and useable — hurrah for analogy! But my most common problem in using a calculator is that I mistype the numbers. The calculator could easily show me what numbers I've typed, even if a real calculator doesn't. The analogy seems to have limited the designer's approach to the problem. I manipulated the picture to create the calculator shown on the right in the figure, which is one I would prefer to use.

Another problem with analogy is *noise,* or unintentional communication. The user may associate other properties with the analogy than you do.

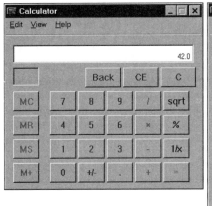
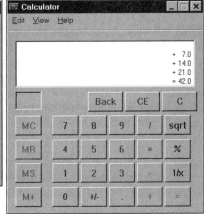

Figure 11-10: A controlling analogy limited the left-hand calculator's design.

 Some programs use a disk symbol for the Save button. And some users without 12 years of PC experience don't associate this symbol with the good old days of PC use, when all saving was done on disks (which didn't look like this one anyway). They figure "disk" means "disk." So they insert a disk in their disk drive, click the picture of the disk, and assume that they just saved the current document to the disk. I'd say that the analogy is at fault here rather than the user.

 Any user error begs the question, "What did my program do that encouraged the user to believe that this action was a right action?"

When is analogy a good idea?

 Use appropriate analogies for button or toolbar symbols in any program. Hold back on a controlling analogy until you are sure it will do more good than harm.

A *well-chosen* controlling analogy — one without any inappropriate associations — helps new users get started fast. For example, if users know how to use a piano keyboard and they recognize the keyboard in your music editor, nothing could be better. On the other hand, controlling analogies bring unnecessary limitations from the physical world into the GUI. Mimicking the physical world is rarely the most efficient way to interact with the computer. Think back to the calculator: You can type numbers much more quickly than you can "click" them in with the mouse.

As an interface design mechanism, the strength of controlling analogy is that it makes a GUI easy to understand. The weakness of controlling analogy is that it frequently makes the GUI less effective, a weakness that is particularly noticeable for expert or experienced users. A controlling analogy is most likely to be helpful if your project falls into one of the following categories:

- ✔ Computer-based training programs
- ✔ Walk-up-and-use systems such as an information kiosk
- ✔ Information programs
- ✔ Computer games
- ✔ Demonstration programs

Picking a good analogy

The following list offers a recipe for selecting an analogy that can be most effective and intuitive for users:

1. **Are you trying to find a controlling analogy or an analogy for a single function?**

   A controlling analogy organizes the entire application; an analogy for a single function may show up only on the toolbar button.

2. **What important feature(s) of the program do you want the analogy to communicate to your users?**

   What does the user need to understand about your program or function to use it? What may be overlooked or misunderstood?

   Suppose that I want to design a GUI for Internet Relay Chat (IRC). An important feature of IRC (which may not be immediately obvious to the new Internet user) is that many people may be present in an IRC session without "speaking." A telephone analogy provides only weak support for the idea that many people are present: conference calls or chat lines are not the first things you think of when you see a telephone. A meeting room analogy better supports the central idea of IRC.

3. **Brainstorm a list of possible comparisons.**

   List as many different familiar, real-world items or situations as you can. Let yourself go wild. Party down. You need at least 10 different alternatives. Don't look for sensible right now, just jot down anything familiar that you can compare to those vital features in Step 2.

4. **Evaluate your alternatives.**

   This is where the kinky ideas help you out. As you analyze which analogies best support your critical features, the wild alternatives throw new light on some of your more sedate suggestions.

Be especially careful to consider what noise, or undesired associations, each analogy may have.

For example, I once tried out a game board analogy that I thought would guide users through a computer-based training program. Instead, the analogy got users thinking about strategy, winning, and losing. They began trying to outwit the program instead of learning from it. The undesired associations with the game board analogy outweighed its benefits. (Fortunately, I caught this blooper in an early user test. You can read more about it Chapter 18.)

5. **Choose the analogy that's the best illustration of what the user needs to understand without creating incorrect expectations.**

Now get a professional graphics person to render the illustration for you. Unrecognizable analogies don't do much good!

Implementing Unforgettable Idioms

When you talk, idioms are those colorful expressions that aren't meant to be taken literally. The following list offers a few examples of common idioms in English:

✔ "He's no *rocket scientist.*" (He's not especially bright.)

✔ "I don't need any comments from the *peanut gallery.*" (May have originated on the *Howdy Doody* show back in the '50s — my Dad used the term to mean "you kids in the back seat of the car.")

✔ "Don't get your *knickers in a twist.*" (Don't get upset. This one is a British idiom — knickers = underpants.)

You may not understand an idiom the very first time you hear it, but you can often figure out what it means from the context. And after you've assimilated an idiom, you don't usually forget what it means.

Lots of the symbols and widgets that make GUIs easy to use are idioms: scroll bars, drop-down lists, and many button symbols, for example. They aren't analogies because you don't find their equivalents in the physical world. Still, they're so distinctive and fitting that, after you've learned what they mean, you don't forget them. That's what makes a good idiom — it's *distinctive* and *appropriate*.

In Figure 11-11, compare the standard buttons for window administration as they appeared in Microsoft Windows 3.11 with their equivalents in Windows 95.

The first, old set is not especially distinctive; the second, new set displays more individual variation. The arrows of the old set (and the X of the new set) are abstract symbols. The first three symbols in the new set can be associated with the tool bar, small windows, and a large window. On the whole, the new buttons are more appropriate as well as more varied. The new set, therefore, is more idiomatic.

Figure 11-11:
The Windows 95 buttons on the right are better idioms than those used in Windows 3.11, on the left.

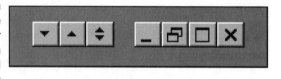

 If your GUI is going to be used by the same people over and over again, you should be prepared to rely more on idioms than on analogies. On the frequent occasions when making things self-explanatory is not effective, try to make the interface idiomatic — once learned, never forgotten — rather than self-explanatory.

Metaphors Are Invisible

Most people working within user interface design today use the word *metaphor* to talk about both metaphors and analogies. Being able to tell the difference between the two terms pays, however, because you need to do different things to use a metaphor well than to use a good analogy. Earlier in this chapter, I give you the lowdown on analogies. In this section, I show you how to use the mystical, magical, and menacing metaphor.

In speech and in the user interface, metaphors sneak up on you. That's because metaphors are *implicit* — that is, they aren't openly named and illustrated the way analogies are. Metaphors provide a context in which something else is understood. They're subtle and powerful because they do their work behind the scenes. Listen to some people who are speaking metaphorically:

Figure C-1: Microsoft Encarta uses muted colors and a simple, dignified graphical style to project the reliability and credibility of the reference work.

Figure C-2: The Save dialog box from the Incredible Toon Machine by Sierra shows how appropriate color and graphics can create a zany mood.

Figure C-3: The human eye is most sensitive to the hues in the middle of the visible spectrum: orange-yellow, yellow, and yellow-green.

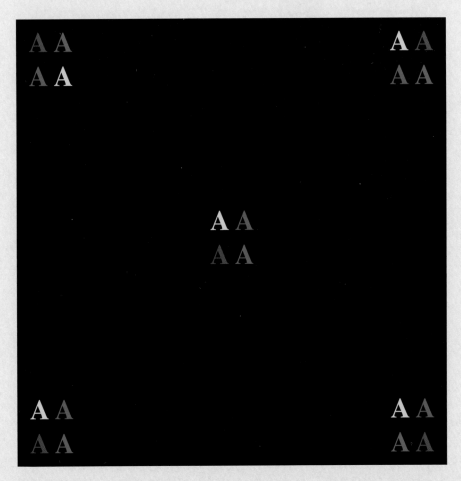

Figure C-4: Your eye is least sensitive to blue when a small blue area is in front of you. If you focus on the letters at the center of this figure, you may notice that the blue A's appear brighter at the corners, where they are in your peripheral vision.

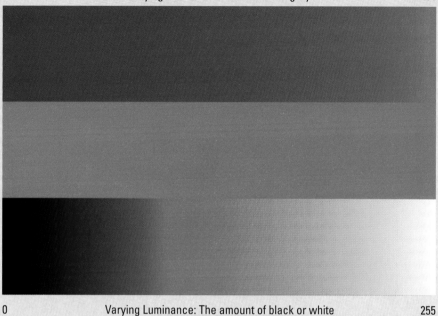

0
Varying Saturation: The amount of gray.
255
0
Varying Luminance: The amount of black or white mixed with the base color (Hue).
255

Figure C-5: The Hue, Luminance, and Saturation color-definition method is easy for non-artists to understand. Here the Hue setting is kept the same while Saturation and Luminance change.

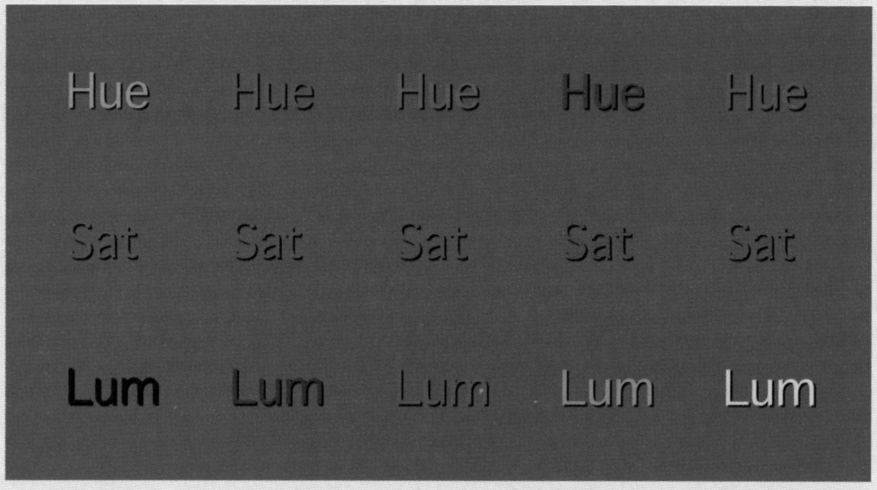
Hue Hue Hue Hue Hue
Sat Sat Sat Sat Sat
Lum Lum Lum Lum Lum

Figure C-6: For contrast that makes text readable, vary text luminance in relation to the background by at least 25 percent. More is better! Note that, if you vary only the Hue, colorblind users may have problems.

Figure C-7: What's around a color can change how we see the color. Are you sure that both circles in each pair are the same color?

Figure C-8: A small area of color like the O on the right may appear to change because of its surroundings, while a larger area of the same color does not seem to change as much.

Figure C-9: Which one looks bigger? Warm, saturated colors may seem to take up more space than cool, grayed colors.

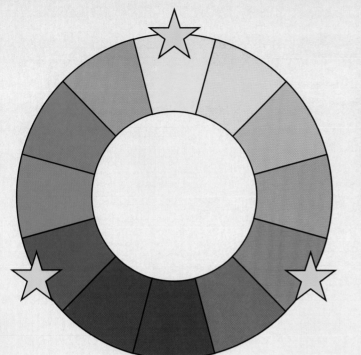

Yes!

Figure C-10: If you need a group of colors that are easy to distinguish from each other, choose colors that are evenly spaced on the color wheel.

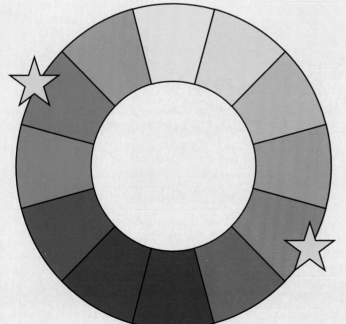

No!

Figure C-11: Don't use clear, saturated colors from opposite sides of the color wheel as foreground/background combinations, unless you want your users to see spots afterward.

Figure C-12: Here you see overuse of color coding in fields and text along with brightly colored graphics. Too much color is tiring instead of meaningful.

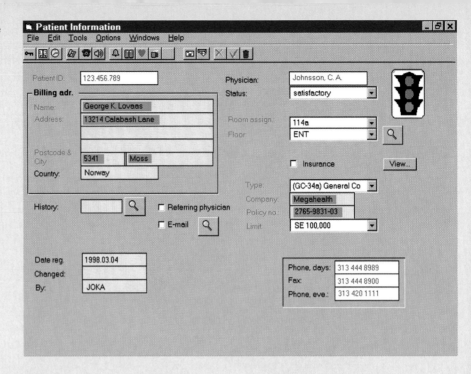

Figure C-13: Color is used to organize complex information and make difficult concepts more accessible at www.vashti.net/mceinc/phigraph.htm by Michael's Crazy Enterprises, Inc.

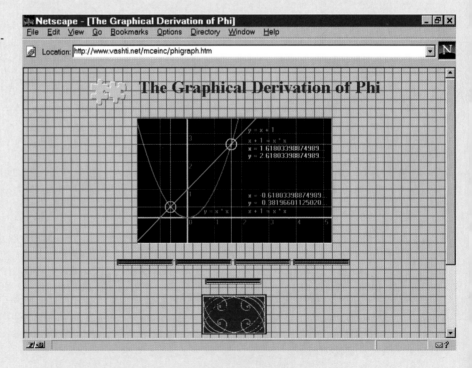

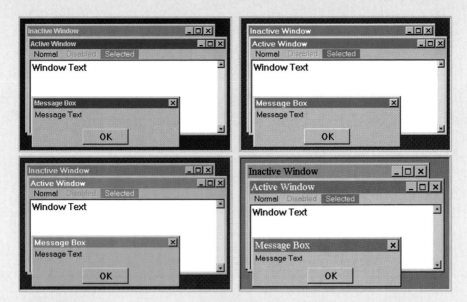

Figure C-14: The Display properties dialog box for Microsoft Windows 95 provides several examples of acceptable color schemes.

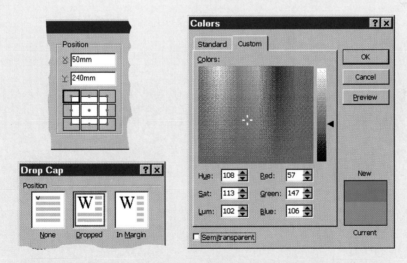

Figure C-15: Some ideas are easier to express in pictures than in text: Positioning from Visio 4.0 by Visio Corporation; Drop Cap dialog box from Microsoft Word 97; Colors dialog box from Microsoft PowerPoint 97.

Figure C-16: A typical amateur attempt at creating a toolbar mixes color, viewpoint, and graphical style. Don't do this.

Figure C-17: I like these icons from the Visio 4.0 "Lotus-style" toolbar, with a muted color palette and consistent approach to shadows and dimensions.

Figure C-18: Shown is a high-tech GUI reality check in a usability lab at SINTEF, Norway. You can record the user's expression, voice, and PC screen at the same time. Photo by Jan D. Martens.

✔ "I'm sure George is going to *go far*. He's just *made the jump* to vice president; never even *stopped off* at deputy."

✔ "Yes, he's *risen* very quickly, hasn't he? I wonder whether his *power-base* is really *secure*?"

✔ "Doesn't seem to matter with Carolyn as his *sponsor;* she's *firmly established* at the *top*."

The speakers share a concept of life, or at least working life, as a competitive, hierarchical pyramid. They understand each other perfectly. But if you hear this conversation without sharing the metaphor, you may wonder where George is going, why he jumped to the vice president instead of walking, and what that had to do with an uninterruptible power supply.

If you think I'm being silly here, you've just illustrated my point. Metaphors are so deeply ingrained that we rarely question them. We think that's the way things *are*.

Using metaphors involves several big hairy problems. First, the metaphors may be overlooked because they're not explicit. Second, a metaphor definitely confuses any user who doesn't share the underlying concept. Finally, designers often use metaphors without realizing it. Be on guard. Ask yourself, "Am I using a metaphor in this GUI design element? How can I be certain that my users share the underlying concept with me?"

The desktop metaphor

Although we talk about it openly all the time, the *desktop metaphor* is a true metaphor, not an analogy. You find no picture of a desktop on your computer, and you can't actually figure out what to do with the icons on your computer desktop based on what you do with the stuff on your physical desktop. Does your desktop have a wastebasket on it? Or a network?

The desktop metaphor is about the concept of a surface supporting two-dimensional objects. Maybe we should actually call it "the paper metaphor." Because of our experience with paper on flat surfaces, we can perceive which of several open windows is on top and use direct manipulation to arrange windows on our "desktop."

Safe metaphors

The following paragraphs list some other metaphors that I can detect in modern GUIs. These metaphors don't seem to give users much trouble, so I've put them on the safe list. You can count on people sharing these concepts with you:

The invisible desktop

I once helped a gentleman who had been using Windows for six weeks, with nothing but maximized windows. The user had previous experience with a character-based terminal environment. He was quite astonished after I showed him how he could look at his spreadsheet and his text document at the same time while copying numbers between them. Seeing the two windows overlapping slightly, he said, "Oh, so *this* is what they mean by the desktop. Now I know what they were talking about.

This situation could only happen with a metaphor, which is implicit, unseen, and taken for granted.

- ✔ **Time and order:** These shared concepts enable you to use commands such as Next, Previous, Go On, and Go Back. In all cases, you're speaking metaphorically. The next window isn't actually waiting in line — you cause the program to assemble it out of a jumble of bits and bytes after the user clicks Next.

- ✔ **Space:** You can use commands such as Up, Down, and Exit. You're assuming that the user applies spatial concepts to the program in the same way you do — for example, "exit" means to *go out of* the program.

- ✔ **Matter:** All people have a shared experience that things they can see and touch exist. In the metaphorical world of computers, you can see and manipulate "things," too. This shared basis of understanding applies to such commands as Delete, Create, Move, and Copy.

Don't read this sidebar if you believe in files

As computer people, you and I tend to agree that what goes on in a computer is real. The file system must be real; we're intimately acquainted with how it works. We can manipulate it.

As an exercise in mental flexibility, consider the following: The file system is not real; it's merely a way of organizing binary bits that computer folks have temporarily agreed on. You *could* actually organize things some other way, and then *that* way would be "real."

For novice computer users, the file system is just as strange and unreal as not having files would be to you.

I *told* you not to read this sidebar.

Dubious metaphors

On the doubtful list are a lot of things you and I take for granted as real. These things are *not real* to a novice computer user. In fact, they're not real to a lot of experienced users who use their computers by rote.

That statement, however, doesn't mean that you can't use these concepts.

It does mean that you should support your users' understanding explicitly with analogies, idioms, words, and pictures instead of taking for granted that the user understands them. Don't use these concepts *metaphorically* if you can help it.

Following are the most important concepts we techies take for granted, but that aren't shared by all humans:

- ✔ **Endless hierarchies with identical sublevels:** In the physical world, people don't store objects in endless hierarchies. They make stacks or groups of similar things in distinguishably different places. Even filing systems have cabinets, drawers, and folders rather than endless systems of folders in folders in folders. The file folder is a rotten analogy for a directory. The file folder doesn't support many of the essential properties of directories that users have trouble grasping. Directories go on spawning other directories; you can see the contents of only one at a time, and you must go back the way you came to get out of them.

- ✔ **The file concept:** A file is not a document. A file is there in the computer whether it's visible on-screen or not, but if you haven't got a document on paper, you haven't got it. A paper document is one *thing*, and a copy of the paper document is another *thing*. Changing the copy doesn't change the document. But if you work on a file, you're always working on a copy. And the copy of the file can change the original. Can you really wonder why new users have trouble understanding files if we keep saying that they're documents?

- ✔ **The data model and database concepts:** To us techies the following concepts are so real that we often use them metaphorically: one-to-many, many-to-many, record, field, selection criteria, selection list, transaction, table, key. Unless you're developing for other developers, don't assume that the internal structure of your database is as real to your users as it is to you.

Slow word processor or unconscious metaphor?

"We liked our word processor at first, but it seems to work more slowly every day," said the novice PC users at a certain office.

Sure it did. They'd started the first day with a blank file that looked like a blank sheet of paper. They typed the first document. When they needed to type a new document, they looked for help on "new page" and found the Insert Page Break command. For two weeks, the users went on adding a new page to the "stack of paper" in the word processor every time they created a new document. All their documents were in one long file, and the program did indeed run more and more slowly.

How does the program lead the users to believe that theirs is a right action? The program makes the assumption that all users share the "file" concept. The program "speaks" of files metaphorically, naming them documents in the title bar and using a paper analogy in the work area, assuming that all users will relate both document and paper to File, and so look in the File menu for commands to deal with the document and the paper. *Commonly accepted* is not the same thing as intuitive. I repeat: Watch out for the metaphors you take for granted!

Chapter 12

Making Your GUI Effective to Use

In This Chapter

▶ Considering the four sources of slowness
▶ Cutting response times — no easy answers
▶ Conserving human working memory
▶ Making the GUI easy to look at
▶ Cutting keystrokes and mouse clicks
▶ Asking if it just *feels* slow

*E*ffective is a dangerous word to use, because it means different things to different people. I know someone who thinks he's done a really effective job of cleaning up his room if he's shoved all the mess into the bulging cupboards or under the bed.

I propose that a user interface is effective if experienced users can work smoothly while using it, with the subjective feeling that the program is helping them and not slowing them down.

This chapter covers some of the things that you can do in your windows to make them fast to use. If effectiveness is an important goal for your project, remember that you also need to pay special attention to Chapters 9 and 10, which tell you how to make your application fit the task like the grapeskin fits the grape.

Sources of Slowness

Whenever you're using a computer, the following four things take time:

✔ Waiting for a response from the system
✔ Doing something: making a keystroke or performing a mouse operation
✔ Thinking
✔ Looking

Noticeable response times are never popular.

In the other three categories — doing, thinking, and looking — you must make a judgment call. You must decide what's necessary work and what's wasted work for the user's hand, mind, or eyes.

I cover the four "sources of slowness" in the following sections, one by one.

Getting Rid of Waiting

The only way for you as a designer to have a positive effect on response times is to understand the technical architecture backward, forward, and upside down. Develop a good relationship with the technical architect as early as possible. Sniff around the issues in the following areas:

- ✔ How does your development tool use and release system resources in Windows? What kinds of windows and controls are "costly" in terms of resources and which aren't?

- ✔ What causes heavy processing to go on locally? Centrally? Where is the dividing line between normal and "heavy" processing?

- ✔ Under what circumstances does the user experience a noticeable wait for data transfer?

Your challenge is to design the GUI so that the weak spots and bottlenecks in the technical architecture are rarely, if ever, visible to the user.

Suppose, for example, that your project uses a development tool that's not really especially clever at loading menus into Windows. You should choose an MDI (*multi*document *i*nterface) with a single main menu instead of a multiwindow interface with menus on every window. The user may notice that the application is slow to start up, but that happens only once per working session. If you insist on a multiwindow structure, your users find themselves driving in the slow lane every time they open a new window.

Don't Cram the Human RAM

Actually I'm not talking about the computer's Random Access Memory here; I'm talking about *human working memory,* or *short-term memory* as it used to be called. Memory is a bit of a misnomer, because you don't primarily use working memory to remember things; that's where you do your active thinking — or your processing, if you prefer.

Cognitive psychology states that, just as is true of computers, humans have a smaller, more limited working memory (your RAM) and a much larger long-term storage capability (your hard drive). Unfortunately, you can't mail-order additional megabytes for human working memory, and its capacity isn't measured in megabytes at all, but in information chunks. Chunks are quite elastic, since the essence of a chunk is that it is a meaningful piece of information. The letter *A* might be one chunk in some situations, *Alphabet* might be one chunk in another case.

The experts disagree as to whether working memory can handle 7 +/- 2 chunks of information or 4 +/- 1 chunks. While they're thinking about it, here are a few things that you can count on:

- ✔ Humans have a limited working memory. People work more slowly if they need to swap a lot of different information in and out of working memory.

- ✔ Working memory holds bigger chunks if chunks are meaningful to the user.

- ✔ Working memory may be able to hold more chunks if all chunks are related in a way that's meaningful to the user.

To demonstrate, here are three lists. For each list, read the list once. Then close the book and try to repeat the list out loud.

George Washington	Arthur	KLS
Abraham Lincoln	Piano	YUT
Franklin D. Roosevelt	Leann	BXS
John F. Kennedy	Grimace	MNI
Richard M. Nixon	Yellow	PGT

Although the third list contains the least information, it's the most difficult one for you to hold in working memory because the information is not meaningful. If you've had training in memory techniques, however, you can outwit me in the preceding experiment by assigning meaning and visual images to the arbitrary letters in the third list, making them easier to remember: Kevin's Little Sister; Yahoo, Uncle Ted!; Bananas eXit Slowly; Mother Never Itches; Pandas Growl Together.

Working memory in GUI design

Don't get overly focused on the magic number of chunks in working memory. For years, interface designers had a guideline stating that menus should have no more than nine items, because users could only think about that many items.

This guideline may possibly be correct if the user is completely new to the menu. At that time, the user *may* need to bring all the choices into working memory at the same time to compare them to each other and decide what they probably mean. Most of the time, however, the user is simply looking for a certain familiar word in the menu, and she compares one menu item at a time with the desired word.

What can you do to conserve your user's working memory? Try the following tricks:

✔ Use meaningful, distinct words instead of arbitrary codes.

✔ Put related information together; don't spread it around the window or put it in separate places.

✔ Put information in the right order to support the user's understanding of the relationship.

A simple example of this last principle is demonstrated in data-entry jobs. If your user types in data from software product registration cards, make sure that your GUI displays the same fields in the same arrangement as what appears on the card.

Look at the two windows shown in Figure 12-1. A junior high school offers a limited number of electives each year. Students submit their priority choices, and as far as possible, classes are made up based on student desires. Both windows shown in the figure enable the advisor to record a student's desires. Both require the same number of keystrokes. Research on similar windows, however, has shown an experienced user takes twice as long to complete the left-hand window as the right-hand window.

Research does not provide a guaranteed answer for *why* the left-hand window takes longer; but I can give you my theory:

The left-hand window requires more thinking steps — more swapping in and out of working memory. If I try to use each window and follow my own thought processes, I notice that, for the left-hand window, I need to keep reassembling the student's desired list in my head to count down to the correct priority. Alternatively, I can navigate back and forth between the fields and enter the numbers in the right order, but then I use more keystrokes.

Figure 12-1:
These two
windows
require the
same
number of
keystrokes
to
complete;
the left
window
takes twice
as long to
use.

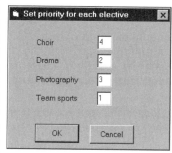 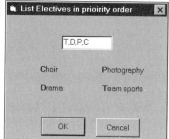

The right-hand window requires some practice. After I notice that the "codes" are just abbreviations and that I must type commas between values, I can work quickly. With the right-hand window, I seem to assemble the list in my head once and then "read off" the first letters of each elective title as I enter them.

Preventing inefficient windows

How can you prevent inefficiencies such as the left-hand window in Figure 12-1 from finding their way into your own interfaces? Consider the following:

- ✔ Try working with a window until you're proficient with it and then try to describe your own mental process as you perform the work.

- ✔ Consider designing a couple of alternatives for important windows that you expect to be used repetitively. Let people practice with each window until they're proficient and then hold a stop watch on them. If their use of one window is consistently faster, look for the reason in terms of mental work. Then apply what you learn to other windows.

If effectiveness is an important goal for your project, you need to plan for realistic testing with users. (See Chapter 17.)

Cutting Back on Visual Work

If your user must scan the window for the piece of information that he wants, he's performing *visual work*. Chapter 13 goes into detail about visual communication. For now, here are a couple of the most important ways to save eye mileage while designing a window:

- ✔ Clean up your act. Get rid of unnecessary visual information.
- ✔ Put things in order in the window. People in Western cultures work from left to right and from top to bottom.

The remainder of this section illustrates these principles for you.

Figure 12-2 shows two versions of a window from a personal-finance advice package. The window is supposed to emphasize how much of your recommended retirement income you're going to lack if you don't get off your financial duff and start investing your money wisely. The window uses both a diagram and a little table to make the point.

First, look at both windows. Which do you prefer to look at?

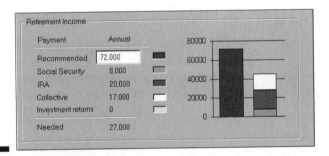

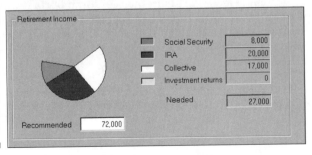

Figure 12-2: Which of these two retirement planning windows do you find easier to look at?

If you prefer the second window, the reason may be that it's simply *less work* to look at your choice. Here's what I did to make the second window more effective:

- ✔ Removed a redundant data axis.

- ✔ Switched from two columns that you needed to compare to one pie chart that needs to be completed.

- ✔ Changed the order so that your eye needn't jump so far to use the color key.

- ✔ Gave you clear signals about which texts are data values by having all the data values in fields.

- ✔ Right-aligned the amounts to make them easier to interpret.

Visual work tends to overlap with thinking; I can't say that the improvement in this window is solely due to less visual work. Some of the changes also cut down on thinking — the mental work that you perform to interpret what you see.

Whether something's more effective for one reason or the other, it's still more effective. So clean up your visual act! Chapter 13 tells you how.

Saving Keystrokes and Mouse Clicks

If you're aiming for effectiveness, get out your tally sheet. Keystrokes add up alarmingly if they're performed over and over again by large numbers of users.

The worst place to litter your interface with unnecessary keystrokes is in data-entry fields for the types of values that turn up again and again: dates, amounts, and ID numbers.

Good ways to cut keystrokes and mouse clicks are described in the following list:

- ✔ For those elements in which you know the possible values, save the user typing time by providing a list for the user to choose from. For example, don't make your receptionist type in an employee name to register a phone message; supply a list of names for the receptionist to choose from.

- ✔ Save scrolling by letting the user select items from the list by typing the first few characters of the selection: In a list including Dan, Danielle, David, and Davis, the user can select Danielle by typing "Dani".

- ✔ Put some extra effort into working out sensible default values.

- ✔ Give your program a memory. In many fields, the most likely value may be whichever one the user entered last time — either the last time she used this dialog box, or, in a data-entry window, the value that was entered in this field for the previous record.

Every keystroke counts

Suppose that you create a room-reservation window in a GUI application for a large hotel chain. On one part of the reservation window, your users enter the arrival date, the number of nights the guest is to stay, and the departure date.

The hotel chain has 100 reservation clerks who take an average of 20 calls an hour, with 7½ working hours on a shift.

You *could* have them type the following:

07-04-1998[tab]**3**[tab]**07-07-1998**

That's 23 keystrokes.

Or you could say, "They don't need to type the year at all, because reservations are normally made for the nearest future occurrence of the date. If they type the arrival date and the number of nights, I can calculate the departure date. And if I put in an editing mask to handle the single hyphen that's left, the users don't need to type that either. Because I require the users to enter exactly 4 characters for the

date, after they type 4 characters I can automatically move the focus to the field for the number of nights. And maybe I should add a text telling the name of the day so that they can confirm the day with the caller."

Operators are seeing more information, and you *leave the information editable in case of unusual needs* — for example, in case someone does want to make a reservation for the year after next.

But reservation clerks are now typing the following:

0704[autojump]**3**

That's only five keystrokes.

The difference that this change in design makes is 18 fewer keystrokes x 20 calls an hour x 7.5 hours a day x 100 reservation clerks, or 270,000 keystrokes in a single day. That number of keystrokes translates to 15 operator hours per day — the equivalent of a day's work for two clerks. Need I say more?

- Reuse data. Never require the user to retype data that he's already entered.

- Remember to provide keyboard shortcuts and mnemonics for keyboard users.

- Provide a pop-up menu, accessed from the right mouse button, for experienced mousers.

- Use editing masks to format data values instead of having the user type formatting characters such as spaces, hyphens, or slashes. When inputting a telephone number, for example, your user should *type* 1234567899 and *see* (123) 456-7899.

- In a well-designed dialog box, the box opens with the cursor (or, from the designer's point of view, the *focus*) in the first field that the user most likely wants to change. After the user presses the Tab key, the focus should move to the next field or widget that the user is likely to want to change. The *tab sequence* in a dialog box determines the order in which a keyboard user visits each widget.

Take special care to provide a suitable tab sequence and a default command button in dialog boxes so that keyboard users can work effectively.

The User Says "It Feels Slow"

"Well, it just feels slow to me."

This user gives an opinion, a subjective judgment. Does that mean that I can forget about it? Not for a moment. The user's subjective experience is the designer's objective input data. If the interface feels slow to the user, then the interface *is* too slow. End of discussion.

Getting this kind of nonspecific criticism can be frustrating. The following questions can help you pinpoint some of the places where you may be able to speed up the user's experience, even if you can't speed up the interface.

- Are you giving immediate feedback on user actions? Give people something to look at, and they judge time differently. Give them something to look at that moves — like a tumbling hourglass, a strolling dinosaur, or a growing progress bar — and they perceive that the computer is doing something.

- Can the user complete important tasks in a single window or at least with a minimum of navigation (overhead)?

- Have you got things — widgets, windows, or steps — in the right order according to the task the user is trying to perform?

- Have you provided keyboard shortcuts and mnemonics for everything so that the user doesn't have to move her hand between the keyboard and the mouse or trackball?

- Are you providing information where it's needed, as it's needed, or does the user need to figure things out or go look for data herself?

A Word to the Wise

Effectiveness is the most difficult design goal for your GUI design to meet.

If effectiveness is an important goal for your project, get people to define what they mean by *effective*. Is a design effective if it works fast, or does the quality of the user's work come into the picture? (Needing to do things over again is never very effective.) What *is* good quality work for this task, anyway?

If effectiveness is an important goal for your project, get to know the users and their tasks as well as you can. (See the other chapters in this part for more information on how to go about that task.)

And finally, plan for extensive and realistic "reality checks" all along the way (see Chapter 17).

Part IV
Designing Windows

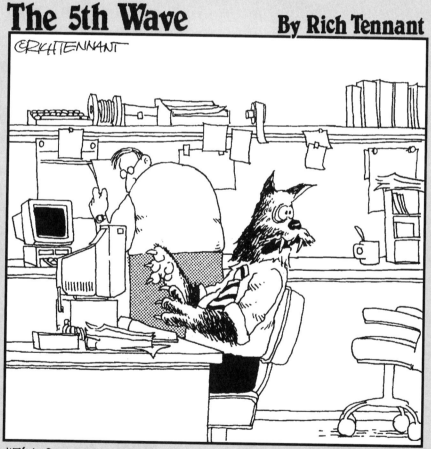

The 5th Wave
By Rich Tennant

"I'M GONNA HAVE A LITTLE TROUBLE WITH THIS 'FULL MOON' ICON ON OUR GRAPHICAL USER INTERFACE."

In this part . . .

The screen real-estate shortage, the pixel famine, the shoehorn syndrome — I don't know what you call it but I do know that everyone who designs a GUI struggles with the same problem. That's probably why the GUI designer's definition of *window* is "A rectangle, the area of which is given by the expression: Not big enough."

Tidy window packing skills are a plus, but that's the least of it. Good windows need to communicate clearly with the user. This part is bulging with illustrations that allow you to see how to choose and arrange your widgets, colors, graphics, and window space for more effective visual communication.

Chapter 13

The ABCs of Visual Design

*I*f you look at your own window designs, you can easily see how they're organized. You understand them because you've seen them progress from crumpled pencil sketches to sturdy, lively, colorful windows with real components and texts over which you've agonized. They look *right* to you. Yesss!

Then some uncouth stranger comes along for a look. Maybe he appreciates the exquisite logic of your window, and maybe he doesn't. Maybe he even thinks that the entire application looks like a college dorm full of unmade beds.

If you apply the basic principles of visual design to your windows, I can guarantee that they're at least going to look neat and tidy. Ideally, good visual design can also make your windows easier to understand.

This Looks Like a Job for . . . A Graphic Designer

Please turn to the color pages in this book and check out Color Figures C-1 and C-2. How do these two windows make you feel?

Sierra's Incredible Toon Machine uses neon color, crooked text, and cartoon graphics (and music) to create a slapstick mood. Even the save dialog box isn't a boring old rectangle — no way — but is shaped like a piggy bank.

On the other hand, Microsoft's multimedia encyclopedia Encarta uses sober colors and elegant lines to emphasize the dependability and authority of the product.

Toon Machine and Encarta illustrate that the concept of the program itself — what it does, whether work or fun — *must* be reflected in the visual elements of the graphic interface. Choice of lines, colors, shapes, and even text make the difference between a good GUI and a bad GUI just as much as user-interaction considerations do.

Sometimes, unfortunately, the project may fail if you don't get a professional graphic designer. You already know that games and multimedia presentations must look exciting or they don't sell. You should also get professional help for any walk-up-and-use, self-service application in which the owner benefits only when the customer chooses to use the system — self-ticketing programs at airports, for example, or commercial Web sites on the Internet. And what about a program that a sales rep carries around to the customers on a laptop? Just as a brochure does, this program needs to look exciting and express the company's graphical profile. Any time that "attracting the users" or "user satisfaction" is one of your high-priority goals for the user interface, professional graphics are a must.

What? You say you're *not* a graphic designer? Not by a long shot? You have trouble remembering what color shirt you have on? Don't worry. I'm not a graphic designer either — at least, not by any formal standards. The fact is that my fervent pleas to the boss to rent, beg, borrow, or steal a graphic designer for each project are rarely granted. I picked up the basics from books, from workshops, by interrogating every designer I met, and after a lot of trial and error. If you're lucky enough to secure the services of a professional graphic designer for your project, you can skip the rest of this chapter. Otherwise, take heart and read on. I clue you in on all the best stuff I've learned.

Aim to be a competent amateur of graphic design. Be proud when you achieve the following three qualities in the visual design of your GUIs:

- ✔ Clarity
- ✔ Simplicity
- ✔ Neatness

Professional graphic designers also aim for clarity, simplicity, and neatness in their designs, so nothing about these goals is second-best. The remaining sections of this chapter deal with each goal in turn.

Clear Communication

The human brain looks like a giant, gray, rubbery prune. Give someone a window to look at, and the prune, with a touching faith in the underlying logic of the universe, automatically tries to make sense out of what the eye sees. "What *is* this? What's important? What's related? How is this thing organized?"

What you see, maybe without noticing in your conscious mind, is position, size, color, value (how light or dark an area appears), direction, and texture. When you look at a window, your brain uses these qualities to decide which part of the window is important to look at first, and to determine what you're looking at — a button, for example. This decision process for most people is unconscious, involuntary, and nearly instantaneous.

Identifying visual cues

Play this little game to sharpen your awareness of visual cues: Look at Figure 13-1. Glance quickly at each grouping and then decide whether the group is arranged in rows or in columns.

Some of the groupings use a single visual clue to indicate the arrangement. You can tell what's happening at a glance. Others use two or more cues inconsistently: You find no clearly right answer to those. One grouping uses many cues to reinforce the same message; can you see which one? (It's the one in the lower left-hand corner, which uses shapes, spacing, and degree of darkness to denote rows.)

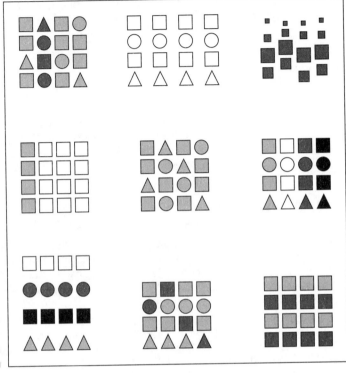

Figure 13-1:
Rows or
columns?
Conflicting
visual cues
can be
frustrating.

In clear visual communication, all the visual cues say the same thing. If visual cues contradict each other, users get confused and irritated.

As a GUI designer, you have a visual communication task that can be defined as follows:

- Decide what's the most important part of your window. Use big differences (or *contrasts*) in one or more visual qualities to emphasize the important part. Play down other contrasts.

- Decide which parts of the window should be interpreted together. Use several visual cues to support the grouping.

- Don't send mixed signals.

I show you a few examples of mixed-up visual signals in GUIs in the following sections.

Oh, Christmas Tree

The contents of the Patient Information window in Figure 13-2 are straight out of my imagination, but the visual design is true-to-life. I've seen this style of design in many applications created for internal use. Take a look at it in Color Figure C-12, and you see why I call it the Christmas Tree window. It just about sparkles with attention-grabbing colors and graphics.

Notice how your eyes play hopscotch as you look at the window. You shift from one high contrast point to another, looking for a place to start. What's important? What does the traffic light mean? I can count five different combinations of leading-text color, background color, and text color — what could the difference be? Why do some things appear sunken and others raised? Some groups are framed, and some are not. Do the frames mean anything special? The horizontal divisions between grouped fields are thin lines, but why does a thick vertical line divide Postcode from Country? Are these two fields *less* related than the others?

You can't ignore visual chaos. The brain is hardwired to go through the sorting and classifying process whenever you perceive differences, whether or not the differences are meaningful. Visual chaos increases your *cognitive load;* in other words, when you look at something visually complex, you think more slowly.

Don't load your user down with unnecessary or conflicting visual cues.

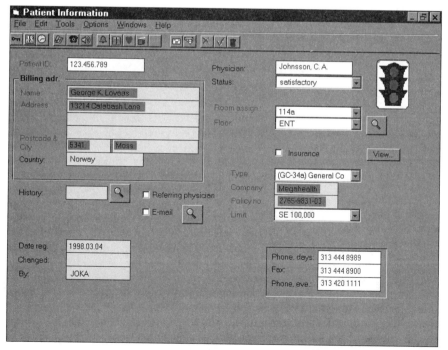

Figure 13-2: An example of visual chaos.

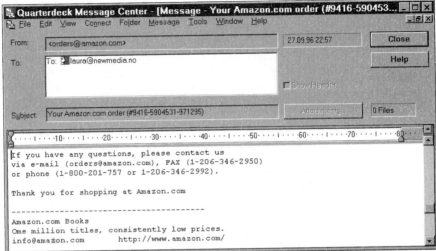

Figure 13-3:
A typical
e-mail
message
displayed in
Quarterdeck
Message
Center.

Figure 13-4:
When I saw
an e-mail
letter that
looked like
this, I
thought the
sender
made a
mistake.

Users miss small contrasts

If you use big differences in one or more of the visual cues, you create strong *contrast*. Strong contrasts gets noticed, but small ones are easily ignored.

Consider an example of one small problem that I had while using the wonderful e-mail program Quarterdeck Message Center. One time, I got tricked by a lack of contrast while reading my e-mail. Most of my letters looked similar to the one shown in Figure 13-3. Then I came to a letter that looked like the one shown in Figure 13-4 and I said, "Whoa — this one's empty; somebody goofed!"

What difference did you notice between the two letters? The strongest contrast is between the filled message area and the empty message area. I actually exchanged a couple of letters and calls with the person who sent the second letter before we figured out that nothing was wrong with our e-mail. The message was there, in the attachment.

Now I can see in Figure 13-4 that the Attachments button is active instead of grayed out, and the number of files listed has changed from 0 to 1. At the time I first tried to read this message, I didn't notice those small differences. My attention was caught by the big difference: the empty message space glaring at me in major contrast to the letter I'd just read.

I've never made this mistake with a different e-mail program that I some-times use. That program displays attachments as icons in the beginning of the message area. So, in a way, the design of the first e-mail program created a user error. Of course, the Quarterdeck program is an excellent one, and I'd never say otherwise. And the programmers of Message Center did a great job.

No one can think of *everything* while creating a window; the other half of the design process is doing a reality check on your creation. You can detect design features that lead your users into error in several ways: Try review-ing each window as you display several different sets of real data.

At any point in the design process, you can study your design in action with users to get new and useful insights. Chapter 17 tells how to try out your design with users.

How many buttons are there?

Tabs and command buttons provide a good example of the need to be careful what you say to people's eyes. And if *say* seems like the wrong word here, remember that program elements such as tabs and buttons are actually a form of communication — of *saying* something.

If the command buttons are placed on the tab surface, as shown in Figure 13-5, I have problems if I want to modify values on several tab cards.

If I click OK now to confirm my changes to the General tab, the window closes and goes away. But if I make a change here and go to another tab without clicking OK first, I no longer see these changes. Do they still count or not?

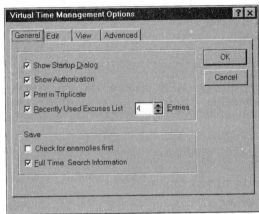

Figure 13-5:
The OK and
Cancel
buttons look
like part of
the General
tab here.

I'm unsure because of what I see: I see four tabs, and the front tab card has buttons on it. If the button was on a tab card in the real world, the same button couldn't be on another tab card. So the position of the buttons on the card implies that buttons are on *each* card: four cards, four sets of buttons. So I'm led to believe that I must click OK here and now if I want my OK to apply to this tab. Zip — away goes the window, but I wasn't finished yet. Grr!

A better solution is to place the buttons outside the tab set, as shown in Figure 13-6. Now I see four cards and one set of buttons controlling them all. I make all the changes and then click the OK button. I still can't see all my changes as I click OK, but at least I feel sure that I know what I am doing!

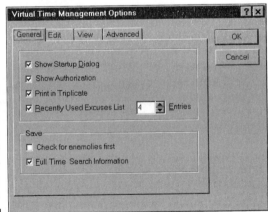

Figure 13-6:
Now OK
and Cancel
look as if
they apply
to the entire
tab set.

Two Quick Tests

To me, the examples in the previous sections don't prove that their developers are hopeless at visual design. They just prove that seeing other people's mistakes is loads easier than seeing your own. If you'd rather not go public with your mistakes, find a colleague with a critical eye for visual design.

The following sections describe a couple quick checks you can make with your own windows that may help you identify problems with your visual design before somebody else does.

The X-test

Imagine that a supernatural power has exchanged all the text in your newly designed window with *xxx*. Deprived of text cues, you can more easily see what visual cues you're sending. Do they reinforce the text cues or contradict them?

In Figure 13-7, what are the visual cues about the relationship between the two lists. What do you think the buttons do?

Figure 13-7:
The visual design of this dialog box implies that the lists are similar; what the buttons do is anybody's guess.

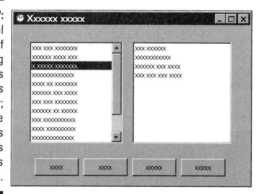

The two lists are the same height and width in Figure 13-7. The lists are positioned next to each other, and both figure prominently in the dialog box. Though the first list obviously has more in it, all other information says that these two lists are the same. The buttons are likely to include an OK and a Cancel; that leaves two buttons unaccounted for. Logic says they must be related to the lists, but no clues are available as to which buttons are list-related or as to what those buttons do.

Now look at Figure 13-8. What's the relationship between the two lists in this dialog box? What do these buttons do?

In Figure 13-8, the two lists are clearly different sizes; the first one is the "big list" and the second one is the "little list." The lists are positioned next to each other and are aligned at the top, so they appear to be equally important. Two buttons are placed close to the lists, implying that the buttons do something to the lists. The buttons are placed *between* the lists, indicating that the lists "share" the buttons in an equal way. The two buttons at the bottom must be the OK and Cancel buttons.

Figure 13-8:
Visual cues
say one list
is a short
version of
the other;
two buttons
are placed
with the
lists and
obviously
operate on
the lists.

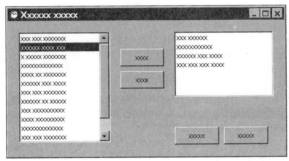

This two-list layout is a more intuitive alternative to multiple-selection list boxes. For example, in a GUI for the Los Angeles Dodgers legendary former manager Tommy Lasorda, the left-hand list is the Dodgers' roster (a big list), and the right hand list is the starting lineup for the next game (a shorter list of similar type). Two buttons move a player's names back and forth between the lists. (Two buttons are "shared" by the lists.) If you're designing Lasorda's dialog box, the X-test tells you that the layout in Figure 13-8 is best because that layout gives visual cues that match the way the dialog box works.

The squint test

Here's a standard trick that graphic designers use to check how the contrasts in a window work. I find it handy, and I'm sure you will, too. Just follow these steps:

1. Put realistic data in the window that you want to check.

2. **Close your eyes almost all the way and look at the window.**

   What you see now is what's most noticeable for the user at first glance.

3. **Decide whether this item is what you want the user to notice first.**

   If so, the window is okay. If not, you need to go back to the drawing board with this window. Make the elements that shouldn't stand out so much look more like the rest of the window. Collect your strongest contrasts — size, color, value, position in window, and amount of space framing the element — around the elements that need to stand out more.

Figure 13-9 shows a window that you can practice squinting at.

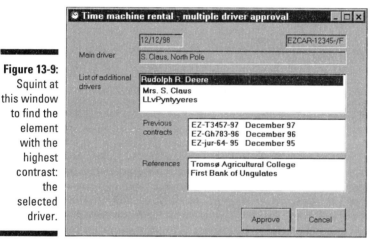

Figure 13-9:
Squint at this window to find the element with the highest contrast: the selected driver.

As I squinted at the original version of this window, the list of additional time-machine drivers didn't stand out enough. To make it stand out better, I made the list of drivers wider. Now that list is much wider than it needs to be in order for the data to fit, but the list stands out correctly, supporting the user's understanding that contracts and references are subordinate to drivers.

Simplicity — the KISS Principle

KISS is a well-known acronym for *Keep It Simple S<your choice of expletive>.* I prefer Keep It Simple (if you don't want to look) Stupid. The fewer things you put in each window, the easier they are for you to arrange neatly, and the easier they are for the user to figure out. To apply the KISS principle, check your window on the following points:

✔ Fill the window with typical data and then point to each element in the window, one at a time, and ask yourself, "Does the window still make sense if I take this element out entirely?"

✔ Are all items in this window essential to the task most likely to be performed with it? Can any of the nice-to-haves be placed on a tab or in an additional window?

✔ Are you using unnecessary *frames* — the box-shaped lines around groups of widgets? (I think that GUI frames may actually be virtual wire coathangers, because frames have the same tendency to multiply if you're not watching them carefully.) A frame's purpose in life (at least in a GUI) is to show that a group of things belong together, so putting a frame around just one thing is like putting two slices of bread around one olive.

✔ Can you replace a set of option buttons with a drop-down list?

✔ Do you have leading texts that are too long or so obvious that they can be omitted? (A lot of unnecessary leading texts are inserted because they help developers keep track of which fields they're working with while building the windows.)

✔ Use empty space, instead of frames or lines, to organize. That way, you reduce the amount of clutter in the window, as well as the risk of distracting the user.

Visual richness and complexity can be beautiful. Intricate graphics may be the best way to say a lot in a small space, like in a map or diagram. If you need to go beyond neat, simple and clear, check out the reading list in the Part of Tens. To see the KISS principle in action, read on!

Talkboard (fictitious product) is a simple application that helps patients who can't talk. The patient has a touch-sensitive panel with large buttons, and each button has a distinctive symbol; the patient touches a button, and the PC produces the corresponding word through a speaker.

Figure 13-10 shows the setup dialog box for Talkboard. Can you tell at a glance how to use it? My personal opinion is that it's a good candidate for a KISS makeover. To keep this exercise focused on visual design, I am not going to improve the functionality or suggest different widgets; I'll just work with the visual elements.

By using a tab, the Talk board window says, "Speech is one alternative thing that you can set up in this window." The fact that *no other alternatives are present,* however, says something else entirely. This function is not an alternative; this one's all there is. So I say just drop the tab and remove one layer of visual noise from the window.

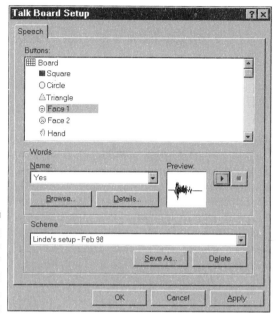

Figure 13-10: This window has a lot of visual complexity.

That takes care of the tab. What's left? The dialog box still has Buttons (unframed) and Words (framed) and Schemes (framed), in that order. Buttons come first, so they must be the most important of the three, right? Wrong. The matching frames around Words and Schemes tend to say, "These two things are alike." But that's wrong, too.

You get one Word per Button, but not one Scheme per Word. Buttons and Words are thus similar and related to each other, and each relates to Scheme in the same way.

A disrespectful word about standards

Should a setup dialog box that doesn't need tabs have a single tab merely because "All setup dialog boxes have tabs"?

I say no. Because the user must choose the Setup command to open the dialog box, he's unlikely to need the cue of tabs (which aren't exclusive to Setups anyway) to understand that this is a Setup dialog box. A more pressing question is whether he understands how to use this window to create, edit, and store a speech scheme, and the tab is not helping with that at all.

In general, users don't care a shake of salt about what categories of windows developers have created to make life easier for themselves. Users care about how to do what *they* want to do. Developers are supposed to help users do what they want without requiring them to think like developers.

One Scheme actually contains a whole set of Buttons, with a Word linked to each button. So I put Scheme at the top of the window and indicate its exclusive status with a single horizontal line. If one line is sufficient, why use a frame that is really four lines?

Perhaps I can help the user see what's going on by placing the leading texts in their own column, out to the left. That way, the texts emerge from the clutter and help to organize the other elements in the window.

Now the Words frame. Why both Words and Name? Name seems to be a filename, but as I scroll through the list of filenames I see that each file is (sensibly) named the same as the word it produces. No difference — no information. I'd drop the leading test "Name." What about the preview? When I try it out, it is actually pre-*hear*. The small tape-recorder buttons play the word, but the widget showing the sound waves is a waste — I can't tell which word it displays from looking at the sound waves. I toss out the sound waves widget.

The window still has a lot of buttons. The original window makes a good start by grouping some of the interior buttons with the widgets they control. I'd regularize the button positions, however. I'd also make the main buttons at the bottom of the window clearly larger than the interior buttons.

Figure 13-11 shows the resulting window. It's actually somewhat smaller than the original, but it looks more spacious. Remember to use space — the invaluable, invisible widget — as a way to separate and group logical elements of your windows.

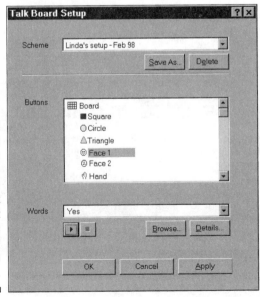

Figure 13-11:
This version
of the
window is
actually a bit
smaller but
looks
roomier and
easier to
work with.

Keeping Windows Neat

Graphic designers aren't born with their hair parted and the ability to toss their alphabet blocks up in the air and have them land in straight lines. Neatness is not genetically encoded in them. Instead, graphic designers have a secret weapon that anybody can use: They call it a *modular layout grid* or a *page template*. In print media, a page template helps layout artists line everything up neatly, and imparts a unifying "look and feel" to different pages and different issues of the same publication. Figure 13-12 shows how a page template governs and unites different page layouts from various issues of the same newsletter.

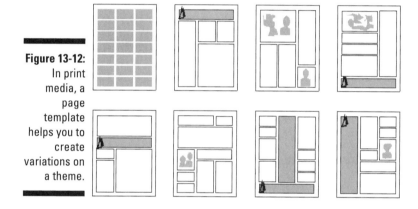

Figure 13-12: In print media, a page template helps you to create variations on a theme.

Messy, unrelated windows

Print media use page templates to organize layout in pages; how do you organize layout in windows? Most development tools have a built-in coordinate system to help you line things up neatly. The coordinate system allows you to precisely place widgets anywhere on the window. The coordinate system alone is not enough to ensure a good-looking layout throughout your application, however, because different developers use it differently and because the system is *too* flexible.

Figure 13-13 shows a couple of windows that were clearly made by different people in a project without a visual standard, let alone a modular layout.

In the two windows shown in Figure 13-13, the command buttons are in different places, the spacing between fields varies randomly, and field lengths vary, too. The developer of the upper window adjusted field length to field contents; the developer of the lower window seems to have taken a one-size-fits-all approach. Neither developer has aligned buttons with fields, and only one leading text has a colon after it.

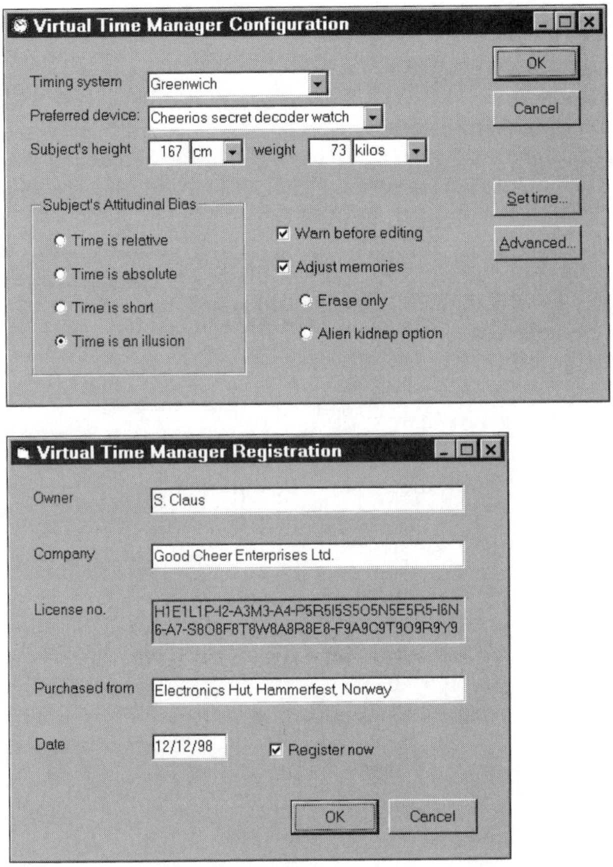

Virtual Time Manager Configuration

Timing system	Greenwich ▼
Preferred device:	Cheerios secret decoder watch ▼
Subject's height	167 cm ▼ weight 73 kilos ▼

Subject's Attitudinal Bias

○ Time is relative
○ Time is absolute
○ Time is short
◉ Time is an illusion

☑ Warn before editing
☑ Adjust memories
   ○ Erase only
   ○ Alien kidnap option

OK
Cancel
Set time...
Advanced...

Virtual Time Manager Registration

Owner	S. Claus
Company	Good Cheer Enterprises Ltd.
License no.	H1E1L1P-I2-A3M3-A4-P5R5I5S5O5N5E5R5-I6N6-A7-S8O8F8T8W8A8R8E8-F9A9C9T9O9R9Y9
Purchased from	Electronics Hut, Hammerfest, Norway
Date	12/12/98 ☑ Register now

OK   Cancel

Figure 13-13:
Different spacing and different plans for sizing widgets as well as different button placement make these two windows look unrelated.

Why use a modular window layout?

In GUI design you have the same layout challenges with your windows that every print publication has with its pages. You want your windows to look neat and tidy with a minimum of effort on your part, and you want all of the windows in your application to look like they belong together — even if the windows are actually created by different developers.

The coordinate system in your development tool is usually too flexible to be much help. In principle, a coordinate system enables you to put any widget anywhere. To make it easy to get things looking neat and tidy, you need to impose some extra rules: Make some coordinates out of bounds, and make all of your widgets start — and end — at predictable points.

You find that some of the same layout questions are repeated again for each window: Where should the first widget start? How much space between two related fields? How much space between command buttons? A modular window layout enables you and your colleagues to answer these questions consistently and automatically so that you can concentrate on more important things such as the order and the grouping of the text and widgets, choosing the leading texts, and selecting the right widget in which to collect or present data.

Applying a modular layout to different windows

Although printed pages are always a fixed size, windows may be different sizes. So instead of using a fixed number of columns and rows, base your window layout on a single rectangular layout module. Then size your widgets — and as many columns as you need in each window — in multiples of this rectangle.

Figure 13-14 shows the layout process for two different windows using the same layout module.

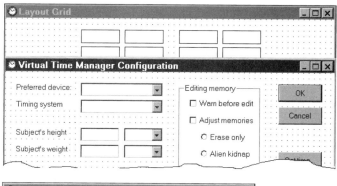

Figure 13-14: Two windows get tidied up with the help of a modular grid.

Just for illustration I drew a modular layout grid above each of the windows so you can see how I use the same rectangular module *differently* in the two windows. In practice, developers need this much flexibility to lay out very different windows in the same application: One window may have exceptionally long leading texts but few widgets; another may be crowded with widgets. In one window, you may have a group of 11 fields that need to stay together, while another window may contain several smaller groups.

The wide window on top in Figure 13-14 has long leading texts, so I've started the grid on the data fields. Three natural "groups" of widgets were in this window: the text fields, a frame full of radio buttons (which is visible in Figure 13-15), and the options. All three groups are about the same size and are squarish — about two modules wide (barring leading texts). I chose two double-module columns for this window. I needed to take one of the groups and make a rectangle out of it; the radio buttons were the only group that could handle that kind of treatment, so I spread their frame across the whole width of the modular layout grid.

The smaller window was simpler. Several of the text fields needed to be quite long, so I chose a single "column" four modules wide. Here, the leading texts (Owner, Company) were shorter, so I made them one module wide.

As you see, modular layout does not remove all your judgment and decision-making responsibilities from windows layout; you just get more regular, predictable results, as shown in Figure 13-15. Compare these versions to the original windows in Figure 13-13. The modular layout gives both of the new windows a subtle visual regularity that is especially noticeable in the lengths and spacing of the text fields.

Organize each window in a few clearly marked columns. As the user looks for the widget or the data she wants, the columns suggest a scanning pattern; the user "knows" she won't miss anything. To make sure that your column looks like a column to the user, remember to use plenty of space between columns.

Defining a modular layout grid

Base your module on the coordinate system in your development tool. Most tools offer a visible coordinate grid you can turn on or off; some others allow you to set up guiding lines. As a last resort, draw a text field to use as your rectangular layout module, copy it repeatedly at regular intervals in a window, and then use that window as a guide the way I have in Figure 13-14.

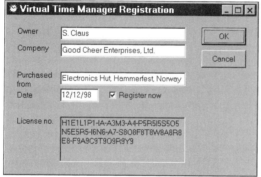

Figure 13-15:
These
windows
have a
subtle visual
similarity.
Widget sizes
are
multiples of
the same
module;
spacing is
predictable.

The height of the layout module should equal the minimum height of the biggest widget that *has* a minimum height — when that widget is filled with text at your default font size and enough space is above and below the text so that the widget looks attractive and readable. You need to test this with your own tool, but the definitive widget is often a combo box, which refuses to be compressed below the height of the button symbol on the end.

The length of the layout module is entirely your choice. Ideally, the module should be some multiple of the grid squares in your development tool — if you can see all those little specks to count them. Tying the module to a visible coordinate grid makes it easier to define standard spacing between modules, for example.

In addition to defining and using the rectangular layout module, you need to define the following standard spaces:

✔ **First text column or module:** Starting at the top left corner of the window, count the number of grid dots (or coordinate points) to move over and down before starting the first text column or module. Be generous here and all around the edges of the window — otherwise your widgets will seem to "fall off."

A generous margin is especially important for a clear visual definition of the dialog box's edges. Because a dialog box is almost always on top of some other window, you should make the edges of the box easy for your user to spot.

✔ **Between modules in a column:** Count and standardize the number of grid dots between two modules in the same column.

✔ **Between columns:** To create a standard space between columns, count the number of grid dots between two columns. (Use more grid dots between two columns than you do between two modules, please.)

✔ **Between related rows:** Getting this figure is simple: Count the number of grid dots between two related rows.

✔ **Between unrelated rows:** Another simple one. Set a standard for the number of grid dots between two unrelated rows.

✔ **Around main command buttons:** You need to set standard positioning of main command buttons *and* the number of grid dots showing on each side of these.

Whether you put the command buttons on the side or at the bottom of the window doesn't matter. (Just pick one and stick to it.) Do let the command buttons break out of the modular lockstep so that they stand out better. The command buttons shown in Figure 13-14 are both wider and higher than a module.

More Aspects of Visual Design

Now you've got the basic principles of visual design, but a few important questions are still hanging, such as "What are 'good' colors?" and "Does a GUI need to have icons?" and "Where do I ever find self-explanatory symbols for 117 different commands anyway?" The short answers: "Good colors are the ones the user likes; almost always; and they don't need to be self-explanatory, just different." If you want some longer answers, see Chapters 14 and 15.

Chapter 14

Color Is Communication

· ·

· ·

Color is the aspect of GUI design in which we most often forget about communication and sink back in pure aesthetic appreciation — or dislike. The human preference for color over monochrome is universal, but when people discuss specific colors, the fur begins to fly. Response to specific color schemes is personal and subjective, and in some cases cultural.

The ideal solution is to accept that color is a personal choice and let users set the colors that they want, as Windows allows through the Display Properties dialog box.

If your development tool prevents you from choosing the ideal solution, you need to make choices about color in your GUI design. You can base color choices primarily on an aesthetic appreciation of color, in which case one person imposes his or her taste on the interface. Or you can base color decisions on an understanding of color as a communication tool, in which case this chapter can give you a hand.

How (And How Not) to Use Color

First, decide what you want to achieve by using color in your design:

  ✔ You can use color to communicate a mood or a feeling, in which case one person must impose his or her perception of color on the interface.

✔ You can tie related information together with color, so that noticing and understanding the relationships is easier for the user.

✔ You can use color contrasts to make important information stand out to the user.

If you want color to do all these things at once, the design must continually balance the demands of clear visual communication with those of good aesthetics: Get a professional graphic designer. In the following examples, observe the important contribution that graphic design makes to the user's overall experience of the interface:

Check the special color section for Color Figure C-1 (you see a thumbnail-sized version of Figure C-1 on the left). The figure shows the Microsoft multimedia encyclopedia, Encarta. The Encarta interface uses subdued colors that create a mood of sober reliability around the information in the articles. Opportunities for user interaction stand out through the contrast of somewhat brighter, but still harmonious, colors.

Take a look at Color Figure C-2, which shows the interface from The Incredible Toon Machine (by Sierra On-Line). Here colors and graphics work together to say that this program is just for fun. Zany, hyper, and cheerful are words that spring to mind to describe this interface. So much goes on with color that the designer has added deep shadows and other 3-D effects to the selection list, the scrolling buttons, and the command buttons to help users see what they can click.

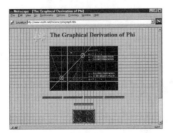

Color Figure C-13 shows how you can use color to group information. The main graphic, with its coordinate system, parabola, and line, looks like a cobweb in black and white, but color helps your eye to separate the elements. Color also links the coordinates and equations to the corresponding elements in the diagram. Finally, colored bars mark the links to the explanation of each element. Michael L. Wright's

"Derivation of Phi" Web page is designed within the relatively stringent 16-color palette, so that it looks equally good to Net surfers with limited displays.

You've seen several examples of color used purposefully; now look at Color Figure C-12. The patient information window in Figure C-12 is one that I made up, but the visual design (if you can call it that) and the use of color and graphics are typical in many in-house projects. This window is a truly unfortunate abuse of color.

Compare Figures C-12, the patient-information window, and C-13, the Phi-graph window. Both use bright colors. In the Phi-graph window, the colors draw your eye to the center of the window, while colors in the patient information window cause your eye to play hopscotch. Bright colors in the toolbar draw your eye to the edge of the window, and large yellow and intense green areas pull your focus down again. The Phi-graph window uses red on black, which provides acceptable contrast. The patient information window uses small red text on gray background, which is nearly unreadable. The Phi-graph window uses color to group information; you can see how all the yellow elements are related. In the patient information window, it's anybody's guess what the color combinations mean; what, for example, might be the difference between yellow fields with black text, and yellow fields with black text on green background?

If you want to use color to communicate in a business interface, the safest approach is to restrict yourself to just a little high-contrast color. Use that color for drawing the users' attention to the most important information *or* relationships in the interface. A plain Microsoft Windows-standard window like the one shown in Figure 14-1 illustrates these principles.

In Figure 14-1, the high contrast areas are the title bar, the selection bar, and the three white lists. These screen elements jump out at you when you do the *squint test* (see Chapter 13). The elements jump out even more at the user who sees this window in color. The selection bar stands out most because it is a slash of color surrounded by gray and white. Color contrast very clearly says "This is the central piece of information."

Follow these guidelines for using color in your GUIs:

- ✔ Enable the user to control color, if possible.
- ✔ If you want to get fancy, get a graphic designer.
- ✔ If you choose interface colors yourself, remember that color communicates best through contrast.
- ✔ A little bit of color communicates; a lot of color confuses.

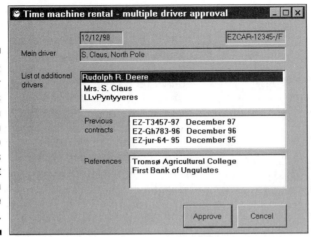

Figure 14-1:
Color
attracts
attention
through
contrast so
strong, it is
apparent
even in a
monochrome
rendition.

Color adds so much interest to a GUI that it's hard to resist playing around with it. Go right ahead and have fun. It can help to know more about how we see color, and how to define and choose colors. In order to take control of color *contrast,* you must first understand what makes colors seem alike or different to your user.

How We See Color

In project discussions about what colors to use in a GUI, I have heard various fractured versions of the physiological reasons why "You cannot, absolutely *cannot,* use blue in a GUI." Of course, you *can* use blue in most interfaces and in most parts of the interface. Just avoid bright blue next to bright red or bright yellow; and maybe you should be careful not to use little tiny blue letters on a black background right in the middle of the window.

In case you'd like to understand the basis for the rumors about blue being bad to use in GUI — and incidentally why you shouldn't use green text on a red background — I put the physiological explanations in this section. If you'd rather *not* take a journey to the center of the eye, do feel free to skip on!

We see *in color* to the extent that our eyes can tell the difference between different wavelengths of light. This differentiation is the job of receptors called *cones* on the retina at the back of the eyeball. Cones play favorites with colors: Some cones are most sensitive to reds and yellows, some to green, and some to blue. Very few of the cones pick up blue most effectively — the blue-loving cones mostly choose to live in the suburbs, out on the edges of your retina (as shown in Figure 14-2).

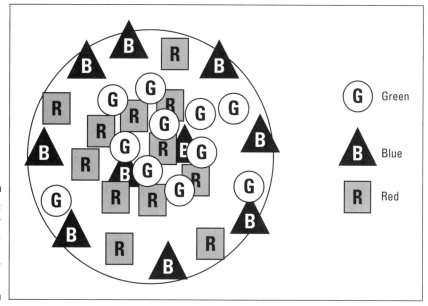

G Green

B Blue

R Red

Figure 14-2:
Color
receptors
are
unevenly
distributed.

Because of the uneven distribution of color receptors, the common wisdom is that GUI designers should avoid putting small blue areas (tiny blue letters, for example) in the middle of whatever the user is looking at. If you look at Color Figure C-4, you can try for yourself. Do you notice much difference in the brightness and clarity of the blue letters at the center of the diagram, compared to the red, yellow, and green letters? If you focus on the center of the illustration, do the blue letters out at the corners seem a little more distinct than the blue ones in the center?

To reach the color receptors on the retina at all, light has to pass through the *lens* — a thick, clear disk at the front of the eyeball, shown in Figure 14-3. The little muscles around your eye stretch the lens or relax it to focus an image so that it falls right on your retina — kind of like twisting the lens on the slide projector to sharpen the image falling on the screen.

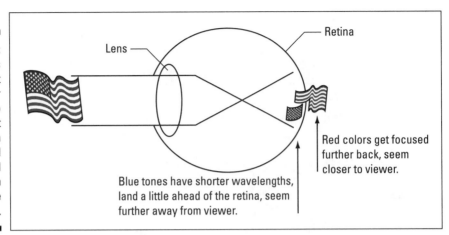

Figure 14-3:
The lens
doesn't
adjust for
color, so
you can't
keep both
blue and
red
perfectly in
focus at the
same time.

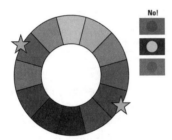

Your lens can't focus different parts of the image in different places, so when you are looking at adjacent colors with very different wavelengths, like blue (short wavelengths) and red (long wavelengths) things get a little blurry around the edges. You can observe this effect yourself in Color Figure C-11, which shows color combinations that make it difficult to focus on the edge between the two colors.

How to Define Color

If you want to choose a palette of related colors, predict what colors will be perceived as strong contrasts, or select foreground/background combinations, you'll find it helpful to understand how colors are defined.

A bunch of color definition systems are in common use. CYMK (an acronym for cyan, yellow, magenta, and black) is the most convenient one for people working with the four-color printing process, for example. For GUI design, I prefer the HLS system: *Hue, Luminance, and Saturation.* With HLS, you can check whether two colors have enough contrast to make a legible text color/ background color combination by looking at the *HLS numbers.* You can use the HLS numbers to define a group of colors that will look nice together. In effect, HLS is color-by-the-numbers insurance for people who don't trust their own artistic vision — like me.

Development tools (the ones which allow you to define colors at all, rather than offering a fixed palette) that don't offer HLS are likely to rely on the RGB (Red Green Blue) system. Follow these steps to use the Windows 95 Display Properties dialog box to get the HLS and RGB values for a color:

1. **Right-click on the Windows Desktop to pop up the menu.**

2. **Choose Properties from the menu.**

3. **In the Display Properties dialog box, choose the Appearance tab.**

4. **On the Appearance tab, click the drop-down menu for Color.**

5. **Click the Other command button.**

Hue, luminance, and saturation

Hue is what you're usually talking about when you ask, "What color is it?" Color Figure C-3 shows the rainbow — the colors in the spectrum of wavelengths that humans can see.

When you define colors with HLS, Hue starts with true red at 0. Clear yellow lives at about H=42 and neon green at H=89, and so on around to the bluish red at 255.

Color Figure C-5 shows how a color changes when you change its saturation and luminance.

Saturation refers to how much color is mixed with gray. When S=0, the color appears completely gray — no matter which hue you assign. As you move the S value up towards S=255, the gray gets an increasing tinge of color. When the S value reaches 255, the result is a pure or *saturated* color in whatever hue you pick. Hues that have a lower S value appear more subtle — less *colored,* in fact. If most of the colors in your interface have low S values and you use one color with a high S value, you get *contrast* between the colors. The saturated color stands out most distinctly.

Changing the *Luminance* (or L value) is a bit like taking translucent colored film and shining an increasingly bright light through it. When L=0, no light appears at all, and all you see is black. As the light goes from dim to bright (that is, the L value rises), you see first a dark color and then a bright color. Finally the light gets so strong that it overpowers the color in the film, and when L=255 all you see is white. Look at the Luminance values when you want to make sure you have a readable text and background combination.

Choosing text color and background color

Consider text color and background color together in order to ensure a legible result. To make colored text legible, you need to look for a big difference in Luminance, but take care using big differences in Hue.

Color Figure C-6 shows what happens with text each time you vary Hue, Saturation, and Luminance values by about 20 percent.

If you vary only the hue, the edge between the two areas is defined by the color difference alone. Because the human eye focuses without regard to color, if you chang_öonly the hue, the edges may look fuzzy and be hard to focus on.

Luminance makes a big difference in legibility. If you set at least a 20 percent difference in the L values of the text and background colors in your interface, the text will be visible. But why not be nice? Go for at least a 40 percent difference and make it easy for the old duffers like me. Most people see their best around age 20; but by the age of 80, many people lose more than half of their visual acuity . . . and glasses can't replace it completely.

As you see in Color Figure C-6, changing Saturation alone makes less difference than changing Luminance.

Individual users perceive color differently; color vision may be impaired in different ways and to different degrees. To check whether everything in your GUI will be visible to users with different color perception, use a graphics program that has grayscale mode to view your interface. Look at a screen dump in grayscale mode; if the colors in your window don't have enough contrast between them, you see something like the left side of Figure 14-4 (in which I changed the color of the leading text to robin's egg blue without checking luminance). The window on the right shows the text in black, for comparison purposes.

Figure 14-4:
View the window in grayscale to check whether you've got enough contrast.

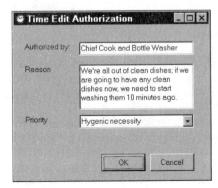

Choosing Colors

Competent graphic amateurs need to be aware of the pitfalls of using color in an interface: Color plays tricks on the human eye.

Color Figure C-7 shows how the same color can take on a slightly different cast, depending on the color placed next to it. Choose a pinky-beige skin color for a Caucasian face in your online tutorial, place the character against an unlucky choice of colored background in one screen, and all of a sudden your tutorial person looks like he's got a hangover.

In Color Figure C-8, note how a small patch of color — the letter O — is more vulnerable to its background than a large one. (The O is the same color as the large rectangle to the left.) If you use color to show that two items are related, make sure that both items appear to *be* the same color to the user.

Color Figure C-9 demonstrates that warm colors may look closer (and thus bigger) than cool colors. Two objects in the interface that are meant to be the same size may look slightly different if they happen to have this contrast.

Not only colors are quirky; the individual user's experience of color is just as unpredictable. Personal taste plays a role, and so does each user's physical ability to perceive color. External factors such as monitor quality, lighting, and fatigue add to the complexity.

Color *alone* is an unreliable communication tool. An old GUI design truism says, "Never use color as the sole signal of anything." For example, some users will confuse two toolbar icons, one for In-tray and one for Out-tray, if the only difference between the two symbols is that the In-tray is yellow and the Out-tray is brown.

Rather than relying on color as the sole communication tool, use color to support other visual cues. (See Chapter 13.) To be on the safe side, use *a few* colors that are very different from each other in your GUI designs.

Choosing distinct colors

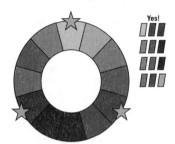

Yes!

Subtle differences in colors may be ignored. For color coding, or for grouping information, you need a set of distinct colors. To choose a set of distinct colors, look at a color wheel like the one shown in Color Figure C-10. Choose three or four colors that are evenly spaced around the wheel. If you're using HLS, vary the H value by 85 for three colors or 64 for four. Use distinct colors.

Choosing a palette of related colors

In most programs, toolbar icons should be distinct from each other, but should not be eye-catching or wildly colored. Define a palette of colors to use in your toolbar like this: Start with a group of distinct colors. To make them look related, mute the colors by adding the same amount of gray to each; lower the S value by the same amount for each color.

The colors in a palette constructed in this way may *not* appear different to a user with poor color perception, but color alone should never be the only difference between two icons. Besides the users who don't see color, some people simply don't notice color differences.

Avoid these combinations

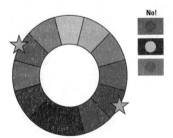

No!

Color Figure C-11 shows color combinations to watch out for. If you use a saturated color like bright red for text foreground or background, don't use it together with the saturated color directly opposite on the color wheel. Choosing opposite colors produces high-contrast pairs like red/green and yellow/violet that will quickly make your users see spots.

Suggested Color Standard

I'll say it again: The best thing you can do with color in your interface is to respect the user's choices. If your program can't pick up the user's choices from the Windows color settings (or the equivalent in your run-time environment), you need to set a color standard for your program. The following rules are suitable for an application that users will work with for hours every day (if you're making a utility for occasional use, you don't have to be quite so restrained):

- ✔ Use a pale, neutral color for the window background. Gray is fine.

- ✔ Use a white background for fields and lists with editable data.

- ✔ Repeat the window background color for the background of fields and lists displaying data that the user can't edit.

- ✔ Use black or a color with very low luminance for text.

- ✔ Define a small group of accent colors for your icons and graphics. The colors should be distinct but muted, with similar amounts of gray.

- ✔ Choose one highly saturated color for your high-contrast color. Use it for selection and anything you need to emphasize.

- ✔ If you need to group information or color-code information, consider using *one* additional color for one purpose. For example, use a light yellow background for obligatory fields or dark red text on a white background for data values outside expected ranges — but don't choose both. If you use an additional color, choose the aspect of the interface that it is most important for people to notice in order for them to work successfully.

 If you need inspiration, have a look at Windows 95. The Display Properties dialog box offers quite a few different color combinations, most of which comply with the standard suggested in the preceding list. Color Figure C-14 shows four examples. To see the dialog box, click Start on the taskbar. Choose Settings in the first menu and Control Panel in the second menu. In the Control Panel window, double-click Display.

Chapter 15
Icons and Graphics

. . . .

In This Chapter

▶ Remembering with graphics

▶ Using graphics and icons in your GUI

▶ Picking good icons

▶ Developing icons

▶ Working with a graphic designer

. . . .

*I*cons and graphics are all over the place in GUIs. They're a very visible sign of the difference between GUIs and older, character-based computer programs.

Because icons are a prominent feature of GUIs, and GUIs are more user-friendly than character-based programs, the idea that icons *make* GUIs user-friendly must logically follow. So to make a program more user-friendly, all we need to do is put in more icons — right?

Unfortunately, that logic is not just fuzzy; it's out-of-date. GUI designers now know that more icons do not automatically make a better product.

This chapter helps you make sure that you use the right icons for the right reasons. After you know what you want, the final sections of the chapter show you how to create your own icons or how to work with a graphic designer who creates icons for you.

Haven't I Seen You Somewhere Before?

Graphics and icons work to make GUIs more user-friendly by making parts of the GUI easier to understand or easier to remember — or both. Graphics aid memory because they provide rich opportunities for association, which helps us to assign meaning to what we want to remember.

If you like, you can use Figure 15-1 to experiment with the differences between remembering text codes, remembering symbols, and "assisted remembering" prompted by graphics. One column at a time, memorize the codes, the symbols, or the meanings. Give yourself about 45 seconds with each column, and then turn to the similar figure (Figure 15-10) at the end of the chapter to see how much you recall. Pay particular attention to how easy or difficult each task feels to you.

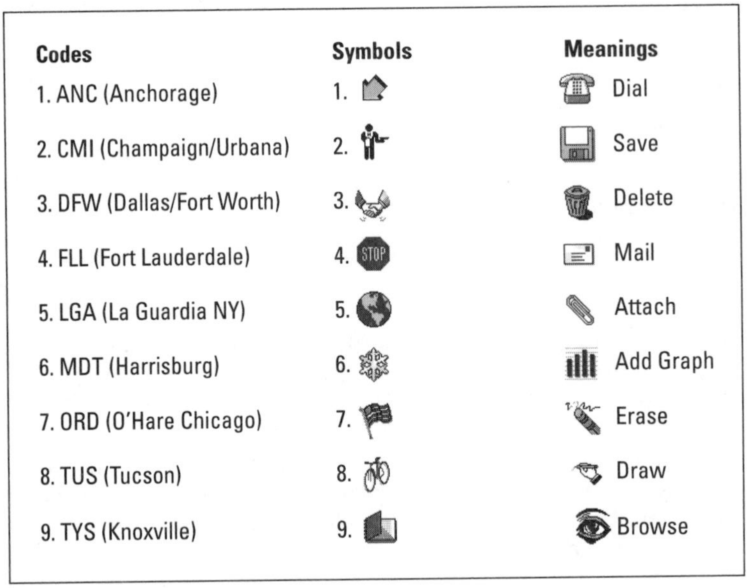

Figure 15-1:
Try memorizing and reproducing one column at a time. Notice which task you experience as being more difficult.

Codes	Symbols	Meanings
1. ANC (Anchorage)	1.	Dial
2. CMI (Champaign/Urbana)	2.	Save
3. DFW (Dallas/Fort Worth)	3.	Delete
4. FLL (Fort Lauderdale)	4.	Mail
5. LGA (La Guardia NY)	5.	Attach
6. MDT (Harrisburg)	6.	Add Graph
7. ORD (O'Hare Chicago)	7.	Erase
8. TUS (Tucson)	8.	Draw
9. TYS (Knoxville)	9.	Browse

Most people find the codes in the first column more difficult to memorize than those in the second column. The symbols in column two are easier, perhaps because they allow for individual differences. You could think of symbol five as "Mother Earth" or "globe" or "terra firma," but you still remember it. In column one, if you remember CMU instead of CMI for Champaign/Urbana, you have the wrong code.

In the third column, the meaning of each graphic is provided; all you have to do is associate the meaning with the appropriate symbol. Column three takes a lot of burden off your memory, just as the icons in a GUI enable associations for the user. Users needn't remember which symbols are there, just which commands the symbols stand for.

Icons work because they take advantage of how people are very good at remembering visually encoded information. Classic psychology experiments have shown that you can have people look at several *thousand* pictures and then ask them to pick out one image that they've seen before on another page full of otherwise new pictures. More than 90 percent of the time, people can correctly pick out the only picture that they've seen before. Pictures of concrete objects that people have seen before they recognize close to 100 percent of the time.

Using Icons and Graphics in Your GUI

GUIs seem to be more inherently satisfying to users than text-based interfaces with similar capability. Perhaps the reason is that our eyes and brains originally evolved in surroundings that were rich in visual cues.

Regardless of *why* they work, graphics and icons do more than just contribute to a satisfying visual environment: Graphic elements provide visual cues about how to use the interface; explanatory graphics support the user's understanding of some functions. Icons signal shortcuts to commands and contribute to brand identity.

Graphics to show what the GUI can do

Affordance is how an object *shows* what it can *do*. For example, the ridges on the edge of a jar lid help you to see that the lid is meant to be turned rather than pried off. Graphics provide similar affordances for your GUI. (You can read more about affordance in Chapter 11.)

Look at the two windows shown in Figure 15-2. Both windows have the same functions: Both can be minimized, maximized, scrolled, displayed in different views, or closed. Most people — even those who've mastered the keyboard shortcuts for all these operations — feel more comfortable with the window on the left, the one with visual reminders of what you can do with the program elements.

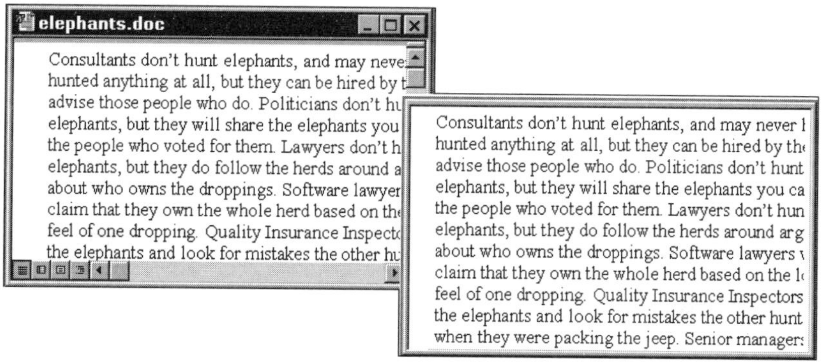

Figure 15-2: Do you prefer your window with or without affordances?

elephants.doc

Consultants don't hunt elephants, and may never hunted anything at all, but they can be hired by t advise those people who do. Politicians don't hu elephants, but they will share the elephants you the people who voted for them. Lawyers don't h elephants, but they do follow the herds around a about who owns the droppings. Software lawyer claim that they own the whole herd based on the feel of one dropping. Quality Insurance Inspect the elephants and look for mistakes the other hu

Consultants don't hunt elephants, and may never l hunted anything at all, but they can be hired by the advise those people who do. Politicians don't hunt elephants, but they will share the elephants you ca the people who voted for them. Lawyers don't hun elephants, but they do follow the herds around arg about who owns the droppings. Software lawyers v claim that they own the whole herd based on the l feel of one dropping. Quality Insurance Inspectors the elephants and look for mistakes the other hunt when they were packing the jeep. Senior managers

Graphics to explain

The old adage says "A picture is worth a thousand words." Take it with a grain of salt; sometimes you can explain more quickly and precisely with words. I'd rather explain the Thesaurus function to a user with words than with pictures, for example. On the other hand, sometimes you can communicate more effectively with a picture.

Color Figure C-15 (in the color insert) shows several examples in which illustrations help the user to understand a function better than words could. In the upper left corner of Color Figure C-15, Visio 4.0 by Visio Corporation uses a diagram to enable the user to show which of nine possible points she wants to define. This approach is more direct than simply describing the points "top left, top center, middle left," and so on, because many users need to visualize the diagram to make their decision. Those users who continually point left while they say, "Turn right," would definitely prefer the graphic!

In the lower left corner of Color Figure C-15, you see a bit of the Drop Cap dialog box from Micorsoft Word. Thanks to three thumbnail illustrations in the dialog box, any curious user who opens the dialog box immediately realizes that Word can create these fancy initial capitals. Here, graphics help make an "advanced" function easy to understand and use. This dialog box could get along without the illustrations, but fewer users would discover and use the Drop Cap feature.

To the right in Color Figure C-15, you see the Microsoft PowerPoint color definition dialog box, which has interactive illustrations. You can pick a color (hue and amount of gray) from the palette and use the slider on the right to adjust the amount of black or white mixed in with the color. Or you can type in values for Hue, Saturation, and Luminance and watch the indicators move on the palette and slider. In this case, the reality — color — is simply too complex to deal with in words. Oh, you could possibly set up a list of 256 evocative color names, but users would have difficulty deciding whether yellow-green or spring green is the green that they want to use without seeing it. And if the interface needed to deal with an infinite variety of colors, naming each color would be out of the question.

Consider using an explanatory graphic for functions that have concrete results — functions like formatting commands, for instance — not only are concrete results easiest to illustrate, but the user is also more likely to recognize an illustration of something that he has actually seen. Illustrations of processes or abstract actions such as *copy to clipboard* or *link to embedded object* or *index the database* are both more difficult to produce and more difficult for users to understand, though they may supplement text explanations.

Space-saving shortcuts

A window in a GUI is a workplace. You need the stuff you use all the time available on the surface of the window-workplace, not stowed away where you must open a menu and then a dialog box to get to it. Because you never have enough space on the display, GUI designers need to make the common tools available without taking up too much space. This requirement is the driving idea behind the toolbars, scrollbars, and all the other "fringe graphics" that flourish in GUIs today. Fringe graphics are shortcuts.

So, in creating a fringe graphic, you want something that's easy to remember and doesn't take up much space: a little bitty icon.

Figure 15-3 shows the Adaptec CD-Player by Adaptec, Inc. The real CD-Player is that modest little critter on the left. On the right, I manipulated the picture to produce a "text" version. The left-hand version is so small that I can leave it up on my desktop all the time; it rarely gets in the way. The text version is much larger, demonstrating one advantage of graphics: Often you can put more information in fewer valuable pixels by using graphics instead of text.

Figure 15-3:
The text version of the CD-Player is a real waste of space.

Graphics to reinforce brand identity

Program icons identify the program on the desktop, in the taskbar, or in lists of files. Program icons serve as shortcuts, but they must also contribute to brand recognition for their creators. This requirement isn't just marketing hype — it's also user-friendly: You like to know which programs are related and can be expected to work well together. In multiwindow systems with many main windows that can be iconized separately, users need to be able to see at a glance which windows belong to the application; icons fulfill that need.

Just as program icons should associate a program with its maker — and its sister programs, so to speak — file icons should help the user to associate files with the applications that created them. File icons appear primarily in file lists.

Repeated elements, either color or shape or both, are the most common way of showing that two things are related. Figure 15-4 shows icons from Lotus Development Corporation's SmartSuite 97 that reflect a strong, self-aware design program.

Product icons appear in column A. What is the common element among them? (The platform at the base of each icon is the most prominent repeated feature, but you may also notice the repetition of diamond shapes. The organizer notebook can be seen either as one incomplete diamond, or two irregular diamonds.)

I've put the file icons for each product in column B, but I mixed them up. Can you match up the file icons with the right product icons pretty easily, even in black and white? (The file icons are easy to match to the product icons because prominent elements are repeated: The letter A and diamond for Approach; the human figure and pencil for Word Pro, the numbers and graph for 1-2-3, and the notebook for Organizer.)

Figure 15-4:
Product icons from Lotus SmartSuite (column A) share a platform at the base and repeated diamond shapes; file icons in column B repeat important elements from the product that they belong to.

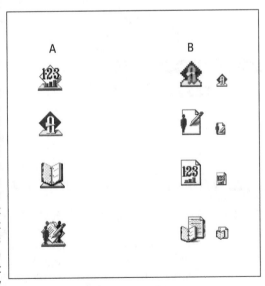

What's a Good Icon?

Okay, I've made the case for why you need icons and how to use them, but you're way ahead of me. You know you want icons, but how can you tell the difference between merely acceptable icons and really great ones?

Here are some clues:

- ✔ Great icon sets have a consistent visual style.
- ✔ Great icons are visually simple.
- ✔ Great icons are distinct from their neighbors.
- ✔ Great icons have an object or symbol that's easy to associate with their purpose.

Think of traffic signs: Curve ahead, school crossing, dangerous incline, slippery when wet — they have all the characteristics of good icons. The following sections help you to choose good icons for your program.

Avoid the art-gallery effect

Taken together, the icons in your program should exhibit consistent visual style. Watch out for the *art-gallery effect:* That's when the toolbar looks like a row of paintings by lots of different artists all hanging in a row.

 In Color Figure C-16 in the color section (shown in the thumbnail to the left), I've put together a mediocre row of icons. In the first place, too many of the icons in this row are too similar. Good idioms should be distinct, but all the little gray or red boxes look alike. This row also suffers from the art-gallery effect, mixing realistic icons with simple ones and muted colors with bright colors — choices that make this row show inconsistent visual style.

 Color Figure C-17 shows part of a toolbar from Visio 4.0 by Visio Corporation. These icons display a consistent visual style: Look at such elements as the degree of realism, the angle at which the objects are viewed, the degree of 3-D effects, and the color palette.

In Figure 15-5, I've jumbled together several icons created in two different visual styles. Can you find the clues to sort the icons back into two groups? In Figure 15-5, icons b, c, d, f, j, l, and m are drawn with some gray tones to make the objects look three-dimensional. Icons a, e, g, h, i, k, and n are drawn as flat outlines, using only black and white.

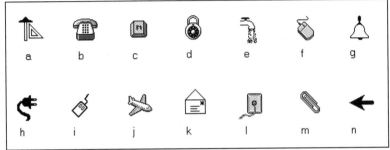

Keep icons simple and distinct

An icon is a shortcut for experienced users, so it needs to be distinct first and foremost. After you use a shortcut, you quickly become familiar with it; icons can serve their purpose as shortcuts as long as they are good idioms — once learned, never forgotten. Don't insist that your icons be self-explanatory if that means you end up making the icons too complicated or too similar to be distinct.

In Figure 15-6, the upper row is from WinFax Pro by Delrina Technology, Inc. This particular version was made back in 1992, when designers were just beginning to experiment with toolbars. The original icons are large and attractively drawn, and the stylistic aim seems to be to make the icons self-explanatory by combining one element that stands for an object with one that stands for an action. For example, the first icon gives information about faxes and the third lets you throw away files. The repeated pattern of two elements actually makes the icons visually similar to each other — and less distinct.

In the second row, I manipulated the picture to create a row that uses a single element in each icon; the icons in the second row appear to be simpler and are at the same time more different from each other. Though the second row is perhaps less self-explanatory, the simpler symbols are easier to remember and easier to distinguish at a glance.

Don't fall for the temptation to create a graphical language of your own by reusing the same symbol in different ways. This process makes your icons less distinct and harder for the user to differentiate from each other. In Figure 15-7, I use icons from the resource files supplied with Microsoft Visual Basic 4.0 to create two possible sets of toolbar icons for an e-mail program.

Figure 15-6:
Icons in the
upper row
are more
complex,
but also
more
similar to
each other;
icons in the
lower row
are both
simpler and
more
distinct.

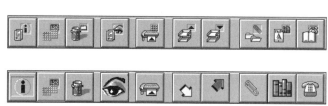

In the upper row of the figure, each individual icon is fine, but when you see them all together, they start to look alike because the letter symbol repeats in each one. You can't simply glance at the toolbar to find your destination and then click. You must look carefully to identify which picture of a letter you want this time. Sort of defeats the purpose of the shortcut, hmm?

For the second row of icons I've usually chosen a single object or a symbol that *can* be associated with the command (though not necessarily the best symbols for the job). Notice that the icons in this row look different from each other; you don't have to look closely to see which is which.

Figure 15-7:
Can you
find the
right icon
from the top
row if
you're in a
hurry?

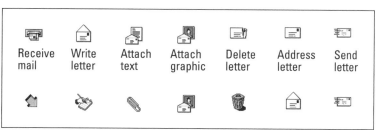

How to Get Good Icons

My brother-in-law the historian says, "History repeats itself; historians repeat each other." In GUI development projects, history repeats itself and developers repeat each other.

This conversation, or one very like it, takes place between two developers at the beginning of all too many projects: One developer says, "Let's have a toolbar here." And the other answers, "Okay, but where do we get the icons?" "Oh, we can just copy a few and sketch the ones we don't find for now."

Then, as the release date for the project gets close, the same two developers have this conversation: "What do we do about those icons on the toolbar? Do you have time to clean them up?" "Oh, they're fine — not stunning, but they make sense; we can just live with them."

Sound familiar? In my opinion, this strategy is the R&D equivalent of going to a job interview dressed in clothes you picked up off your brother's bedroom floor. Don't go to market with a haphazard set of icons; instead, start icon development early in the project and work on your icons in parallel with the rest of the design.

You're bound to need a few icons in addition to whichever copyright-free icons come with your development tool. Besides, you need to make them all fit into the same visual style, remember? You can draw your own; you can copy-and-modify existing public domain icons; or you can get a professional to do the job.

Icons in other people's products are part of their copyrighted property. You can look at them for ideas, but that's all.

Drawing your own icons

Drawing icons is not like any other kind of drawing, unless perhaps you're an expert at *pointillism* — painting with many tiny dots of color. Icons, too, are pictures composed of tiny dots of color.

Icon drawing is tough because the icon looks one way while you work on it and another way when you (or the user) see it at its regular display size. In other words, you don't get very good visual feedback while you're drawing. As Chapter 11 explains, immediate feedback is what helps you to master a new skill such as icon drawing or hedgehog training.

If you want to draw your own icons, look for an editing tool such as Microangelo by Leonard A. Gray, shown in Figure 15-8. You need the following features in such an editing tool:

✔ Your icon editor should have an automatic thumbnail display so that, while you're working, you can see what the user is going to see.

✔ If you're developing icons for Windows 95, Windows NT 4.0, or a later Windows platform, look for an editor that can handle several versions of an image in the same icon file. (Windows has the capability to select the best image for the user's display.)

One of the biggest problems in drawing icons is dealing with diagonal or curved lines — they tend to look jagged. To alleviate jaggies, you can use a technique called *antialiasing*. For an example of antialiasing, look at Figure 15-8, which is a screen shot of Microangelo by Leonard A. Gray. Notice along the edges of the three juggler's balls in the Microsoft Access icon displayed in the editor in Figure 15-8. The diagonal lines are drawn in two colors. The second color is halfway between the line color and the background color. When you use antialiasing, your drawing may lose a little sharpness, but it gains smoother lines and a welcome impression of depth.

If you're serious about creating icons yourself, I recommend *The Icon Book*, by William Horton, published by John Wiley & Sons Inc., 1994. I describe this book and other equally useful books for advanced reading in Chapter 23.

Figure 15-8: Magic the jaggies away from your icons by drawing thicker diagonal lines in two colors.

Capture and modify icons

The fastest path to good icons is undoubtedly to recycle them: Legal sources are your own products, icons provided with your development tool, and other icons in the public domain.

Remember that you can grab other folks' copyrighted icons to study, but you've got to make your own icons if you intend to use them in a product.

If you need some aid on your icon raid, try a little piece of freeware called *Icon Sucker*, by Copsey Strain, Inc. (A version of this program is on the CD-ROM that came with this book.) Icon Sucker, as shown in Figure 15-9, neatly displays the icons in any EXE or DLL file and enables you to save them to an icon file, a bitmap file, or to the clipboard.

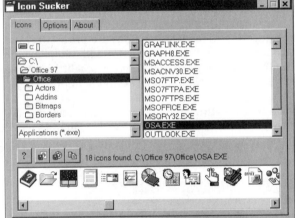

Figure 15-9:
The Icon
Sucker, by
Copsey
Strain, Inc.,
is a handy
piece of
freeware
for a GUI
designer.

Work with a graphic designer

Get a graphic designer to develop your icons if you want better results with less effort on your part. The main pitfall here is the same as with other parts of the program: You don't want uncontrolled iteration. And if you and the rest of the development team are going to be the customers for the graphic designer, remember that a customer who takes too long to make up his or her mind or changes it too often is always going to have higher development costs.

Here's a recipe for working with a graphic designer that makes the entire process run smoothly the first time. Remember to start early! Then just follow these steps:

1. **Specify what you need.**

   How many icons do you need? For what commands or products? What sizes, what number of colors, and what file format do you need?

2. Check out several designers and then choose one.

Ask for references, examples of previous work, and hourly rates. Ask each one to submit one icon in your preferred file format, and check it to make sure that it doesn't choke your compiler. Pick one designer to work with; don't start a contest — that wastes your time and theirs.

3. Get the right people to your first meeting.

You know how your company works. If you have marketing people or bosses who must have a finger in every pie, make sure that they're invited from the start. At the first meeting, give the designer your list of icons. Discuss possible shared elements, what graphical style or mood is appropriate, and what color palette marketing feels enthusiastic about. Have the designer come back with two or three examples to show alternative moods, common elements, and color palettes as soon as possible.

4. Make decisions at your second meeting.

Get the same people back and, on the basis of the designer's samples, have them agree on shared elements, mood, and color palette. Now get rid of the kibitzers, because all the choosing and opinions are finished.

5. Pick a small group of icons to do first.

Start with a small assignment to work out any kinks in the communication between you and the graphic designer. This step also enables you to establish an average price-per-icon and time-per-icon so that you can budget the rest of the work. Because you're starting early, you can start with a few icons that you know for sure you need, even if the full list isn't ready.

6. Test sketches of the icons.

Have the designer produce quick pencil sketches. Test the sketches to see whether people can easily associate the sketches with the right command and whether they can remember the associations a day or two later. Don't worry too much about whether people can instantly recognize what a sketch means. Let the designer observe the tests.

The tests show you which sketches need more work; the ones that need more work are the only ones you should send back for another iteration.

Don't, on any account, pass sketches around the project so that everybody can give suggestions. In contrast to user tests, which give you a chance to identify problems, asking for unqualified opinions at this stage merely adds an extra round of changes for no particular purpose.

7. Have the designer turn the sketches into finished icons.

8. **Check to make sure that the icons look right in their various sizes and on displays with different resolutions and numbers of colors, as well as on a monochrome display.**

Expect a few communication problems the first time around with a graphic designer in your project. Graphic design has its own professional culture, just like software development. While software developers primarily want to make programs that *work great,* graphic designers find their professional satisfaction in making things that *look great.* Even if working with someone who has different goals from yours takes a little extra effort, you'll find that the effort is worth it when you end up with a software program that looks as great as it works.

Experimenting with Memory

If you want to try the experiment at the beginning of this chapter (in the section "Haven't I Seen You Somewhere Before?"), you can use Figure 15-10 for jotting down the codes, symbols, and commands that you recall.

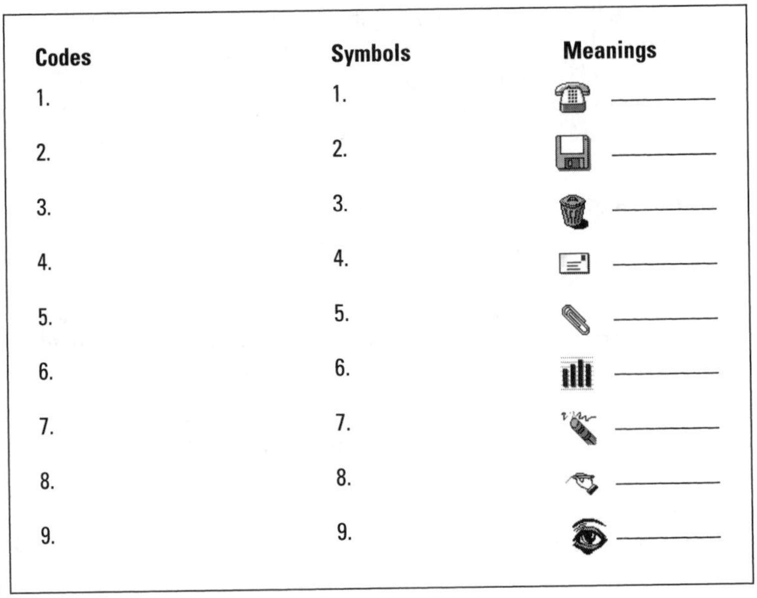

Codes	Symbols	Meanings
1.	1.	☎ _____
2.	2.	💾 _____
3.	3.	🗑 _____
4.	4.	✉ _____
5.	5.	📎 _____
6.	6.	📊 _____
7.	7.	✏ _____
8.	8.	✍ _____
9.	9.	👁 _____

Figure 15-10: Diagram to use for the memory experiment.

Chapter 16

The Right Widget for the Job

. . . .

. . . .

*T*he devil was conducting a newly arrived soul around his domain. A ragged looking fellow sat in one corner munching pretzels, pausing only to emit raspy moans. "This fellow is damned to eat pretzels perpetually?" the newcomer inquired incredulously. "No," replied his host, "We give him beer instead on alternate weeks." "And what has he done to deserve this fate?" "Oh, he's the one who invented the horizontal scrollbar," grinned the devil.

Other windows widgets have more going for them. Your development tool handbook doubtless tells you that edit fields are for presenting editable text or numerical values, check boxes are for binary fields, and so on. That's the implementation viewpoint.

Instead, this chapter takes you on a GUI designer's tour of Widgetville. You consider the role that each widget plays in communication and see what effect the main widget types have on user comprehension or user performance. I also cover some of the typical problems you may face with certain widgets and suggest possible solutions.

The Menu Is the Map

If your program is complicated enough to have a pull-down menu bar, you should think of the menu bar and its dependent menus as the *map* of your application.

Experienced users use the menu in different ways — some with the mouse and some with the keyboard, while others use shortcuts and rarely refer to the menu at all. Even so, think of the menu system as a map because of the special role the menu plays in orienting new users to your program. Look at what a good menu or a good map does for someone who is on unfamiliar territory:

- **A good map is complete:** Every function, feature, and window in your application should be accessible via the menu bar.

- **Different places have different names:** Don't put two commands called *Options...* in two different pull-down menus.

- **The map stays the same, even when you're not looking:** Keep the menus between windows the same. Gray out commands that don't work, but try to avoid having whole menus or groups of commands that appear and disappear.

- **A good map shows you where you need snow chains:** Collect the advanced and difficult commands into a single menu and give it a title that warns inexperienced users what they're getting into.

  For example, a groupware program should not place commands from various categories — such as those commands intended for e-mail users (end users) and other commands for database administrators and forms developers — in the File menu. I'd rather see a Database menu and a Designer menu toward the right of the menu bar, if these functions *must* share a main window with the e-mail users' interface.

- **A good map uses familiar symbols:** Users who have experience using programs with GUIs also have expectations about the menu bar. Don't disappoint them. Put Save, Print, and Exit commands on the first menu called File. If Cut, Copy, Paste, Undo, and Find are appropriate, these commands belong in a second menu called Edit. Place a Help menu at the right end of the menu bar. In MDI (multiple document interface) applications, users also expect to find a Windows menu.

Figure 16-1 shows more of the standard equipment GUI users expect in Windows menus. Don't overlook the dividing lines: Groupings help users understand commands from their context and make a long menu look less overwhelming. In addition to the items mentioned here, remember to list shortcut keys in the menus, such as Ctrl+P for Print.

Because the menu is a learning tool and a tool for maintaining overview, and because it's not always open and taking up space, you can afford to use enough space to make commands clear and specific. Using two words in menus is okay if the two words are clearer in meaning than one.

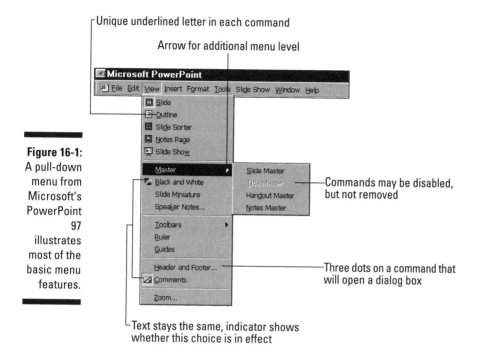

Figure 16-1:
A pull-down menu from Microsoft's PowerPoint 97 illustrates most of the basic menu features.

Toolbars are Shortcuts

Look at any recent version of an intensive-use application such as a word processor, spreadsheet, or financial package and you find it sprouting *fringe graphics* all around the edges — not only toolbars, but also rulers, scroll bars and other navigation tools, status bars, buttons to change mode or view, and so on, ad infinitum. Figure 16-2 shows examples of fringe graphics.

Toolbars are getting more and more sophisticated. Originally full of little square pushbuttons, today they've also got pushbuttons that toggle on or off, drop-down lists, and things I haven't got a name for yet.

Graphics on the fringe

Fringe graphics, headed by the toolbars, are the designer's answer to the chronic shortage of display real estate.

Fringe graphics use *idioms* and *affordances* to pack a lot of functional power into just a little bit of space. You can read more about idioms and affordances in Chapter 11.

Commands   Views or modes ⌐

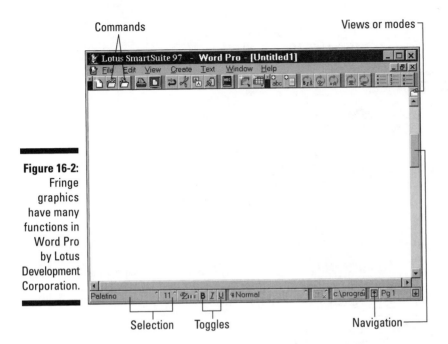

Figure 16-2:
Fringe
graphics
have many
functions in
Word Pro
by Lotus
Development
Corporation.

Selection   Toggles   Navigation ─┘

Applications intended for occasional use can't afford such a luxuriously thick fringe; the user doesn't hang around long enough to get familiar with all the idioms.

In most instances, a utility program is used only occasionally; it may be one of many such small programs the user sees, so the designer can't assume that the user will remember much about the interface from one visit to the next. Also, the user most likely will not spend much time learning a utility program. Figure 16-3 shows an appropriate toolbar for a utility program with the use pattern I've just described. The toolbar has just a few buttons; too many may seem overwhelming to the casual user. Buttons have text on them so the user doesn't need to interpret or remember the symbols. Finally, the toolbar shows all the main functions of the program right up front.

Large buttons with text on the toolbar would be a waste of space in a more complex, heavily used application such as a word processor. More functions compete for space on the toolbar. Also, because the application is more likely to be in daily use, few users remain completely inexperienced for long. Finally, the designer needs to reserve as much space as possible for the user's own work.

That's how fringe graphics work for designers. But how do they work for users?

Figure 16-3:
WinZip by
Nico Mak
Computing,
Inc.,
displays a
simple,
texted
toolbar
appropriate
for a utility
program.

Figure 16-3:
WinZip by
Nico Mak
Computing,
Inc.,
displays a
simple,
texted
toolbar
appropriate
for a utility
program.

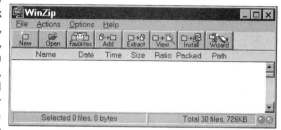

Usability studies performed by User Interface Engineering, Inc., and reported in their newsletter *Eye for Design* showed that users began using toolbars more quickly if the toolbar had an *automatic tip feature* like one of those shown in Figure 16-4. The tip feature pops up to explain an icon if the user points at the icon on the toolbar and leaves the pointer still for a moment. (Incidentally, you can get a complimentary copy of *Eye for Design;* see Chapter 23 for more details.)

Figure 16-4:
Top:
Microsoft
matches
tips to menu
commands
for
consistency;
Bottom:
Longer tips
from Lotus
offer clues
to a wider
variety of
users.

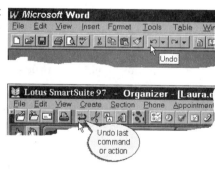

Wondering what to put on your toolbar?

The toolbar and other fringe graphics are shortcuts for people who like to use the mouse. Anything that you put on the fringe should also be available for keyboard users, and conversely, any menu command that seems to beg for a shortcut key should also have a toolbar icon for the mousers. The more frequently people use a command or function, the more likely you are to find that users want instant access to that command.

Often, a couple of site visits to different installations can give you enough impressions to set up a sensible toolbar for your users.

Exact data about how frequently people use different commands can be gathered via *logging software* — programs that record what happens on a user's PC. You can set up a logging program to record what happens at a user's site, or use one during usability tests. If you gather data during usability tests, remember that the task you set influences which commands the users give during the test.

Of course, you can make the toolbar configurable, but keep in mind that most users never change the default configuration of their applications. Those who do normally change the application soon after they begin using it to look like (surprise, surprise!) whatever they're already accustomed to.

For advice about good toolbar icons to choose for your design, see Chapter 15.

Open Season in Edit Fields

You have two reasons to use an edit field (also called a text field or data entry field) in your design:

- ✔ You need to give the user a place to type in data.
- ✔ You need a place to display data.

If you're going to display data that you don't want the user to touch, you don't want to put that data in a nice, white edit field that shouts, "Whee, lookit me, I'm editable!" at the top of its lungs and then have the computer make a disgusting beep after the user actually clicks in the field. That's called entrapment.

An empty, white edit field tells the user that it's open season — he can type anything into it that he thinks appropriate. For a designer to make that invitation and then come along afterward with a validation routine and reject what the user typed as "invalid data" is unfair to the user.

If you must be close-minded about what data you're willing to accept, then use a widget that clues the user to put in that kind of data, or one that constrains choice. For example, a spinbox (choose one of a set of numbers), or a drop-down list (choose one from a set of fixed choices).

If you insist that dates have a certain format, offer a visible editing mask. Or, better yet, craft your design to enable the user to type the date and then have the program convert it to the format you want. Have a dialog box pop up to ask the user to distinguish between July 4th (7/4) and April 7th (4/7), if you're in doubt.

Because edit fields have straightforward interaction, most of the design errors made with edit fields are layout errors. Figure 16-5 shows some layout errors to avoid.

Figure 16-5:
Watch out for these common layout mistakes as you're putting edit fields into your windows.

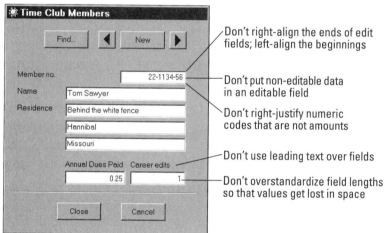

Radio Buttons Hail from Texas

Open and friendly, outgoing and expansive. That's a typical Texan for you, and radio buttons seem to come from Texas, too. Radio buttons put all of a user's choices up front. They present mutually exclusive alternatives in a completely intuitive way. Users who'd go goggle-eyed in horror if you asked them to define *mutually exclusive* watch that little black watermelon seed squirt from one circle to another and immediately realize that, here, they get to pick exactly one alternative.

Radio buttons are a good choice if the user may need to choose between some unfamiliar alternatives such as the ones shown on the left side of Figure 16-6.

Radio buttons must clearly appear in a group. You need not put a frame around related radio buttons if you can surround the group with sufficient empty space that it looks like a group. If not, use a frame around the group of radio buttons. Also, don't put two groups in one frame.

My personal preference is for vertical groups; I think that finding the start of each alternative is easier in vertical groups than in horizontal ones.

Figure 16-6:
Radio buttons take up a lot of space. Choose them if users need to compare options while deciding.

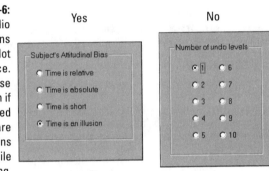

Like Texas, radio buttons take up a lot of space. Using radio buttons for more than a few choices wastes space, as the right-hand example in Figure 16-6 demonstrates. When the user can choose only one value from a large, predefined set, consider using a drop-down list.

Use lists instead of radio buttons within an application in which efficient data entry is an important goal. In the working situations that require this type of interface, users keep both hands on the keyboard. To choose a radio button with the keyboard, the user must either move one hand to the arrow keys to navigate between buttons or type an awkward Alt+ key sequence — if, of course, you remembered to underline a unique letter in each choice.

Check Boxes Can Fool You

Check boxes ought to be simple. You want the user to say yes or no to something — that's all — so you offer an option to check (for *yes*) or leave blank (for *no*).

Because a check box is just about the same size and shape as one radio button, and because several check boxes often appear together, you may find yourself tempted to group check boxes in a neat little frame, right next to the radio buttons, as shown in Figure 16-7. Don't fall for the temptation, however — some users are so influenced by the parallel layout that they treat the check boxes the same as radio buttons and assume that they can make only a single choice.

Figure 16-7:
The two frames look neat side-by-side, but some users may assume that, as with radio buttons, they can choose only one check box.

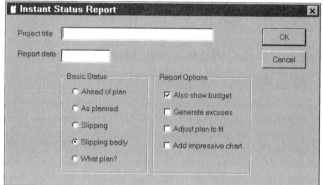

Binary boxes only

The older I get, the more I realize that the world is a lot less black and white than it looked when I was younger. Check boxes are like that, too. You just can't find enough purely binary relationships to use up all the check boxes in the world, so sometimes you find yourself trying to use check boxes to express relationships that aren't binary.

The left side of Figure 16-8 shows a pair of check boxes that really mystified me. They come from a window where I was supposed to enter data about an individual's terms of employment. Why does Expense account spit out its check mark and disappear if I click Hourly rate? Obviously, if you get paid an hourly rate, you can't have an expense account. But how are you getting paid then? And if you aren't getting paid by the hour and don't have an expense account — do you get paid at all?

Hidden alternative   Better

Figure 16-8:
If you find
yourself
designing
check
boxes that
depend on
other check
boxes, as in
the example
on the left,
you want to
think again.

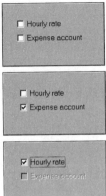

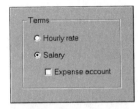

I went to the window's designer with these questions, and we took almost 20 minutes to puzzle out the problem. Finally the designer said, "Why is it so difficult to see that leaving the Hourly rate box unchecked is exactly the same thing as checking the box for On Salary?" "On Salary?" I asked, "Where do you see that?" "Nowhere," the designer replied. "The users just know it; they deal with hourly rates and salary all the time."

We showed the window to several other people who didn't "just know it" before we agreed to bring the hidden alternative out into the light and use the solution shown on the right side of Figure 16-8.

I've run into this type of problem often enough that I can give you a tip: If you find yourself designing check boxes with behavior that depends on other check boxes, think again. Are you sure you've got a purely binary relationship there?

Binary box exceptions

A design proverb says, "First learn to follow the rules; then learn when to break them." In that spirit, here's an example of some not-quite-binary check boxes that work pretty well. The search in Figure 16-9 can be in one, two, or all three of the categories, Private, Business, and Public, but it can't occur in no category at all. To prevent fruitless searches, the window designer programmed the check boxes so that, if only one box is checked, the check mark doesn't go away. If I want to switch from Private to Public, I must check Public first and uncheck Private afterward.

I've seen users test this window and fail to understand why they can't remove the check mark from the first check box. Even the ones who don't catch on, however, simply check the box they really want and search two categories instead of one.

Figure 16-9:
Sensible
use of
dependent
check
boxes: To
prevent
meaningless
searches,
this window
doesn't let
me remove
the check
mark from
Private
unless I
check one
of the other
choices
first.

So far, for this window I haven't figured out a solution that's equally efficient and more intuitive — and that uses standard widgets — so I must conclude that sometimes dependent check boxes are the best available answer to a design problem.

Lists Galore

Designers have several different list-based widgets among which to choose: list boxes, multiple-selection lists, drop-down lists, combo boxes (an edit field combined with a list), and drop-down combo boxes (an edit field combined with a drop-down list).

Lists tend to support safe data input: The user has confidence that she's chosen an acceptable value, and the database is happy that no garbage is coming in. You often choose drop-down lists and drop-down combo boxes to save space, but remember that you're trading away some efficiency, because interaction with these widgets is slightly more complex for the user.

With all the list widgets, you need to make certain that the user can easily navigate by typing the starting letter of his or her choice. If your list contains more than 100 to 150 values, a single starting letter may not bring the user close enough to the value he is pursuing. Consider using (or programming) a more advanced list widget that enables the user to type the whole beginning of a word and then navigate to matching values.

The code/decode problem

If you design a new GUI interface for an existing database system, you're likely to run across this problem: The system is full of values that already have codes, and some of the present users are familiar with the codes. How do you set up a list of values?

You may put the codes in the list as follows: LGA – New York. Then people must know the codes to navigate quickly. But GUIs are supposed to save us from memorizing codes, so perhaps you should put the values first, as in the following example: New York – LGA. This setup is great for new users and those who don't know the codes but penalizes the most experienced users. As long as you stick to a single list in such a situation, you're in a win/lose situation, as shown on the left side of Figure 16-10.

Figure 16-10:
If you put codes first in a list, as on the left, the user must memorize the codes to navigate quickly. On the right, an innovative solution has problems of its own.

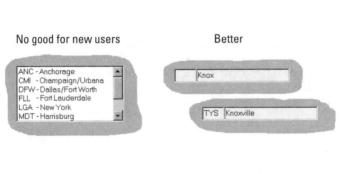

The right side of Figure 16-10 shows a more innovative approach. This solution comes from a database application in which the list of values is judged too long for a standard drop-down, or in which users want more-advanced search features within the value set.

In the figure are a pair of fields, one for the code and one for the decoded value. Users can work in either field. If a user fills one field with a valid value, the other field updates itself. Both fields are searchable: You can place the cursor in the field and hit Tab or a function key to pop up a dialog box with a complete list of values; or you can type one or more letters before you hit Tab to get a shorter list. If you type enough to locate a unique value, the rest of both fields are filled in for you, and no dialog box appears to complicate the interaction.

These widgets don't work like any of the standard widgets, so they don't look like standard widgets. To indicate that the fields are *constrained* (the fields will not accept values that are not somewhere in the database already), they have a pale yellow background instead of white. Using the color violates the general design guideline that "color should never be the sole signal"; however, this design does work in monochrome, as Figure 16-10 also illustrates.

Combo boxes

Combo boxes and drop-down combo boxes are really combinations of edit fields and lists. They enable the user to type a new value or select an existing one. Here again, you must be certain that the list scrolls automatically to the existing value closest to what the user types.

Preventing duplicate entries in a combo list box is the program's responsibility — not the user's.

One problem with combo boxes is that some users don't realize that they can type a new value in the field. You can help a little if you make sure that each combo box starts out with no value showing — unless, of course, a sensible default value *ought* to be showing. This situation is one of those times that you look back at your design priorities and ask, "Is effectiveness or intuitiveness more important in this project?" To make the combo box intuitive, leave the text field blank; if effectiveness is more important, fill in the default.

Multiple selection in lists

Here's a real weakness in the Windows GUI standard: a list widget that enables the user to make multiple selections looks exactly like a list widget that doesn't allow multiple selections. So how is the user even supposed to know that he can select item number two — telepathy perhaps? And what if the second selection is so far away from the first selection that the viewing area displays only one of the selections at a time? Then no visible difference is apparent even *after* the second item is selected.

A common solution is shown in Figure 16-11: The designer adds a longer leading text to encourage the user to select more than one item. The problem of getting a clear overview of what's already been selected remains. Because the user is accustomed to seeing the highlight bar "hop" to the current selection, she may be especially unsure whether items outside the current viewing area remain selected after she makes a new selection.

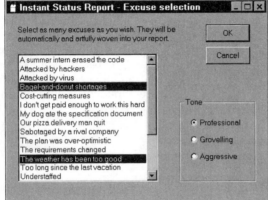

Figure 16-11:
Are other choices still marked in the part of this list that I can't see? I can't be sure.

Figure 16-12 shows two preferable versions of a multiple-selection list. On the left, I've added check boxes. These are analogies of paper checklists; the user has more confidence in the permanence of a check than that jumpy selection bar. A text field beneath the list reports the total number checked at any time.

The right-hand solution takes more space but is often easier to develop by using the standard widgets in a development tool. I've nicknamed this one the two-bags window. On the left, you have the big bag — the entire list. On the right, you have the little bag, showing only the selected items. In user tests, I've observed that users understand the window best if the items they choose from the big bag are "removed" from the big bag as they appear in the little bag of selected items.

Buttons Are Attention Grabbers

Before reading on, take a look at Figure 16-13, a window from Microsoft Visual Basic 4.0, and see whether you can figure out what you do in this window to create a new toolbar button.

Figure 16-12:
Two approaches to multiple-selection lists that make the user feel a little more secure.

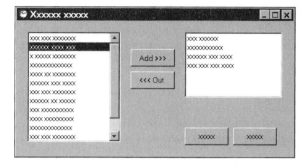

Figure 16-13:
How do you create a new toolbar button in this window?

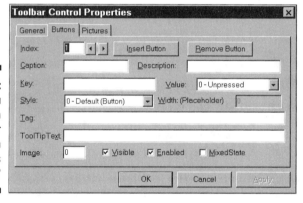

To create a new toolbar button in the window shown in Figure 16-13, click Insert Button. Can you recall where you focused your attention as you looked for the button-creation function? Most people check all the command buttons first. You probably decided on the Insert Button command, or at least lingered on it for a while, even though I deliberately avoided using the word *insert* when I set up this tiny user test.

Command buttons with text on them are the widgets that users notice and understand most easily.

Users' view of command buttons

Over and over again in user tests, I've observed that, whenever new users are in doubt about what to do in a dialog box or a window of any kind, they look for the command buttons with text and consider them first. In fact, some users don't seem to see anything else. Menus and toolbars may be lurking helpfully in the background of the window, but at the moment of truth, that's exactly where they are in the user's consciousness, too: the background.

Yes, a window can get cluttered with too many buttons. You needn't start out with buttons all over the place. But if your reality checks show that users have trouble figuring out what to do with a window or how to do it — if your window lacks affordance in the users' eyes — a nice, fat command button is often the quickest and cheapest answer.

I recommend that the main buttons — OK, Cancel, other buttons applying to the entire window, and buttons to navigate to other windows — be the same size and that you group them together.

Use smaller buttons if you need some within the window to regulate interaction between widgets — for example, to move data in and out of lists. Position the internal buttons in a way that communicates what widgets they work on. In Figure 16-13, the buttons Insert Button and Remove Button have their primary effect on the contents of the Index field, so they're well-placed right next to it.

Top or right side?

The battle rages as to whether command buttons belong stacked at the right side of a dialog box, or spread across the bottom. Choose one or the other and be consistent. I tend to recommend positioning your widgets on the right side for the following reasons:

- ✔ By positioning buttons at the top right of a window, you can more easily keep the OK and Cancel buttons in the same place all the time. If the buttons are at the bottom, any "extra" buttons get placed to the left — which means before — OK. And if I always put OK first in that location, it shifts around physically in relation to the lower right corner.

- ✔ By placing buttons vertically at the right side, I can usually add on more buttons if I need them without the button area getting crowded.

- ✔ I'm in favor of a few strong vertical lines in the window — columns — as starting points for the eye. The vertically placed buttons form a column of their own and contribute to the vertical organization of the entire window.

To be fair, here are the arguments in favor of buttons at the bottom of the window:

- ✔ Buttons at the bottom are far more common in UNIX, which also favors a horizontal organization (the way you read). Web pages, too, tend to have buttons at the bottom. Thus, this positioning is the new, cross-platform trend. Microsoft is using it, too.

✔ People finish reading and working at the bottom right, not at the top right. Why should they need to go up again to get finished?

✔ OK is always the first button. "Always first" is just as easy a position to find as upper right corner.

✔ Bottom placement limits the number of buttons, automatically imposing good design habits. You shouldn't have too many buttons on a window, anyway.

Before you make your top-or-sides call and write it into the project GUI standard, take a look at your key windows. Are you having more trouble fitting things in lengthwise or sideways?

If you've got a lot of multicolumn lists or tables in your windows, then you're usually short of space at the sides, and so standardizing buttons at the bottom of the window can be a good idea. If you've got more data entry fields, single-column lists, and plenty of check boxes and radio button sets, you may find that you typically need to arrange windows in several columns. In that case, fitting the buttons in at the side is usually easier than putting them at the bottom.

If you tend to need a lot of additional buttons for navigation to other windows, put the buttons at the side of your window. If you tend to have a lot of smaller buttons within the window to deal with operations on individual widgets, put the main buttons at the bottom.

Tabs Are Almost Perfect

Notebooks or tabs — call them what you want, but they're turning up everywhere in new GUI applications. Tabs are great. Designers love them because they relieve the space problem a little: You can recycle the same patch of window real estate over and over again. Users love them because they give a nice feeling of overview combined with a perfectly obvious navigation route. Usability tests show that they're intuitive if the designer uses them correctly.

Can such a wonderful widget be used incorrectly? You bet your sweet bippy it can!

Just say no

Tabs are an analogy for notebook dividers or file-drawer dividers. Besides offering an overview of the contents and a way to get there, the analogy sends a couple of additional messages that designers ignore at their peril:

   ✔ "You can choose whatever you want in whichever order you want."

   ✔ "Here are a bunch of roughly similar, related categories."

Don't use tabs if you want the user to complete a task in a given order. Create a wizard or a modal dialog box instead.

Don't use tabs to present grossly different, unrelated information or operations to the user. If you do, some users may misinterpret the application because they assume relationships or similarities that just aren't there. Use separate windows for unrelated information.

You can get too much of a good thing

You can't have unlimited tabs. And if your application is supposed to work in a long-winded language such as Norwegian or German, you can't even have as many tabs as you'd have with English titles on them. And if you fill up a whole row of tabs in this version, are you going to have anywhere to put the nice new features you invent for the next version? Must you redraw every sheet in the window if you add a new line of tabs, thus reducing the height of the space available for other widgets?

Of course, you could just create tabs in multiple rows. . . . Sorry to be a party pooper, but unless you're developing for other developers, the verdict is clear: One row of tabs is enough.

Again: One row is enough. And once more: One row is enough.

Tabs just don't work as well in multiple rows as they do in single rows. Figure 16-14, a pair of screen shots from Microsoft Word 97, shows that the complete context switch that occurs after a user clicks one of the back rows of tabs.

Not only does the card content change, which I expect, but the entire row of tabs under the pointer disappears for a moment. I tend to look where I'm pointing, so the shift is especially noticeable and disconcerting. Don't choose multiple tab rows for any application that you intend to be easy to learn or easy to use.

 If you have too many choices but all the information really belongs together in one window, use the "old-fashioned" solution of a list box at the left of the window. Let the various list choices control the contents of the right side of the window. You can see an example of this solution in Microsoft's new Outlook program.

Figure 16-14:
Having the
row of tabs
I clicked
jump out
from under
my pointer,
as happens
in Word 97,
is dis-
concerting.
Everything
in the
window
seems to
change at
once, and
I'm prone to
lose
context.

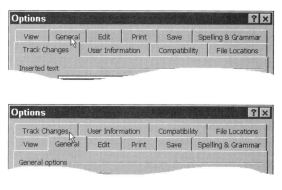

If you have too many choices, you can also consider going to some form of vertically stacked tabs instead of multiple horizontal rows. Lotus has chosen this solution for their SmartCenter application, which uses a hanging file folder analogy (see Figure 16-15).

Figure 16-15:
You have
more space
for vertical
tabs
than for
horizontal
tabs. Lotus
SmartCenter
uses the
analogy of
hanging file
folders.

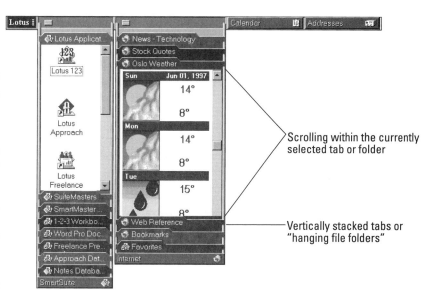

Scrolling within the currently selected tab or folder

Vertically stacked tabs or "hanging file folders"

The Invisible Widget

Widgets aren't just for displaying data or collecting data from the user. Widgets are also for communicating with the user about how to do parts of the task.

If you use widgets to communicate, remember the invisible widget: empty space. Keep in mind the following points about space:

✔ Space creates groups or separates widgets, expressing how data is related.

✔ Space leads the eye to a focal point.

✔ Space gives the user a rest and makes the application seem easier.

Space is what you never have enough of, I know. And that's a good reason to wind up the discussion of widgets with a little reminder about recycling space.

Because you never have enough of the invisible widget to go around, use it efficiently: Use the same space twice — or even more.

On the old character-based terminals, redrawing the screen was often an issue of response time. Changing anything on-screen involved a lengthy wait. Most systems were designed so that the user got one whole static screen, which she filled out and then submitted for processing. Too many GUI windows are designed as if this setup were still the case.

These days, you've got processing power. You can quickly change just one part of a window in response to a user action. Changing part of the window enables you to give feedback on user actions, which is usually good. Changing a part of the window enables you to use the same space again. Figure 16-16 shows a couple examples of dynamic use of window real estate.

Figure 16-16:
Reuse window space: Change the way a widget presents itself in response to a user action.

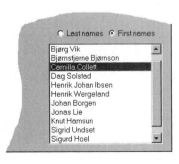

On the left side of Figure 16-16, one list box can present the same list in two different ways. A pair of radio buttons enables the user to switch between a list organized by first names and one organized by last names. The user doesn't need both lists at the same time; this solution adds flexibility to the window without using much additional space.

On the right of Figure 16-16, the Expense account option is grayed out — disabled — until Salary is selected. Dynamic presentation of the Expense account option helps the user to understand the complex logical relationships between the options.

Next Steps with Widgets

Would you like to get into more detail about each widget type? If so, I know just the book: Alan Cooper's *About Face: The Essentials of User Interface Design*, published by IDG Books Worldwide, Inc., 1995. (Read more about this useful book in Chapter 23.)

One widget doth not a window make. You need a team, all working together. If you'd like to know more about deciding how the window should work, check out Part III of this book, "Designing GUIs that Work."

Maybe you've got your widget team assembled and have given them their positions. If you're ready to try them out in a practice scrimmage, now's the time to read Part V, "Doing Reality Checks."

Part V
Doing Reality Checks

The 5th Wave   By Rich Tennant

COFFEE

GUI Design Team

"ALL I'M GOING TO SAY IS, THE USERS WEREN'T VERY HAPPY WITH OUR FIRST-DRAFT GUI DESIGN..."

In this part . . .

How fast do you think a baby would learn to talk if the baby said, "Oooh!" and its parents waited three months to respond with delighted smiles? Immediate feedback! That's the ticket to effective learning, whether it's a baby, a user, or a software developer who's doing the learning.

You want your users to say, "Wow, this is great!" Do you *really* want to wait for months after you have an idea to find out whether it works the way you planned? I'm heavily in favor of instant gratification rather than waiting. That's why I think testing with users is the best thing to come along since Chinese takeout.

The only thing that can stop you from testing with users is your own belief that it will be impossibly difficult, time-consuming, and unpleasant. It doesn't have to be. It can be cheap, fast, pragmatic, and under your own control, and this part shows you how.

Chapter 17

A Cookbook for Testing with Users

· ·

· ·

*T*ests can be very formal or very informal. You can test in a usability laboratory such as the one shown in Color Figure C-18. You can test at your users' workplace or where you sit and develop your application. You can take notes on paper or record the whole test on video and use an advanced logging program to link your sage observations to various points on the tape.

What all user tests have in common is that you first must get a user, a task, and some version of the system together, and then you button your lip, put on your best poker-playing face, and watch what happens.

In this chapter, I describe an informal way to test — methods that you can use without special equipment or special rooms. The focus is on testing with users as an integral part of your design work. The first section gives you the recipe for an informal test, and the rest of the chapter has the practical instructions for how to carry out each step.

If your company has a human factors specialist or a usability lab, you can skip this chapter and go straight to the experts for advice and training. Ask them, "How can usability testing make me a better designer?"

User Testing in a Nutshell

Creation is only half of the design process. The other half is evaluation — taking a close look at what you've created to see what's good and what can be improved. User testing helps you understand how your creation works. A user test has these steps:

1. **Decide which parts or aspects of the design you need information about.**

    You may be ready to test your conceptual model or your menu system. You can test a single window or an entire application. You can compare two alternative GUI standards to discover their comparative strengths and weaknesses. You can test something to see whether it's easily understood, or you can design a test of effectiveness.

2. **Choose or create a version of the system, window, or design aspect you want to test.**

    Sometimes all you need is a sketch, a printout of one window, or a stack of yellow stick-on notes. If you want to test how your program supports user effectiveness, you need at least one part of the system live and online with realistic data and response times.

3. **Define a task that the user must carry out with the test system.**

    Write down the task that you want the user to perform. Describe the task and the expected result, not necessarily the process you expect the user to follow. Written instructions ensure that different testers get the same input. Written instructions give users something to hold onto and refer to during the test.

4. **Get ahold of some test users who are similar to your future user group.**

    Use a sampling of your real users if possible. If you don't have direct access to your future users, test with hired temps, students, friends, neighbors, or relatives. Try to match your users' functional knowledge and level of computer experience. Or test with the most comparable people you can find inside your own company who are *outside* the development group.

5. **Practice the test on people within the development group.**

    Work the kinks out of your test instructions before you test with users.

6. **Get the task, the user, and the test system together; then stay quiet and watch what happens.**

    This step is the hardest part of the process. It's going to go wrong sometimes, and that's exactly when you need to keep quiet and let the user battle with your program without interference, without coffee and donuts and comforting words, and without explanations. *Especially* without explanations.

7. **Analyze what you learn and decide how you can use that information.**

   Whatever problems you observed the user having are not your defeats; they're your buried treasure. Perhaps you want to make a few quick changes before the next tester arrives and try out another idea?

   You don't always decide to make changes in the program. Theoretically, all problems should be solved by better design. In practice, you may end up making recommendations for training, documentation, or work routines instead.

User acceptance tests versus testing with users

User acceptance tests are the ones that happen right before somebody signs a check. User acceptance tests are not tests of the application; they're tests of your salesmanship. At a user acceptance test, you can talk and demonstrate all you want. The only information you want to collect is a "Yes," at best, or, at worst, a list of what you need to do to get the "Yes."

Testing with users is an entirely different process, because your goal is to collect the information that you need to make good design decisions.

What is a successful user test?

A successful user test is one where you learn something new — in other words, one where you get to observe problems.

If you run a user test where the user performs the task without any problems at all, that's the time to worry: Did you define your design question well enough? Did you define a task that would reveal the answer to your question? Was this a typical user?

Validity

A *test* with users gives completely different results than you get from *discussing* the design with one or more users, which is also useful but not the subject of this chapter.

Testing is valuable because what people say or what they predict that they'd do is different from what they actually do when push comes to shove. If you watch a test, you have a chance to detect some of the user's unconscious knowledge — things that he knows or expects about the task but takes for granted and thus couldn't explain.

Test results are facts, such as: I tested six users, and four succeeded in using the outline function to rearrange sections. Facts like these are a good basis for making sensible decisions about what to do with the design; for example, you can decide that you need to make it easier for the users to see that sections can be rearranged. Watch out, though, because you cannot safely *generalize* from test results, like this: "Two-thirds of all users will be able to use the outline function successfully."

Don't generalize, because you rarely carry out user testing according to rigorous scientific methods (nor is doing so sensible). In user testing, you don't calculate how many testers you need to obtain statistically significant results. You don't control all the factors influencing test results except the one you're observing. You're interested in observing some things that aren't quantifiable, such as which strategies users employed when they *failed* to rearrange sections using the outline function.

To make the right decisions based on what you observe during a user test, you must be completely honest with yourself about where you're taking shortcuts in relation to research-level standards:

- You don't usually have much choice about whom to test. Because you don't get a random group of representative users, you must consider how the test subjects differ from your user group and make allowances: If a manager suggests who you should test, consider whether you're getting the people he thinks are best at computers (a smooth test may not prove that the application will be usable for the others) or whether he is sending you his least productive employees because he can't spare the others (draw your own conclusion).

- Most of the time, you can't test in real surroundings on a live system with real data and real tasks. Look carefully at how your test conditions differ from real conditions and consider what the changes do to your results.

  Fudge least on the factors that are most important for your project: If ease of learning is the main design goal, don't help the user out during the test. If user efficiency is the main design goal, use a live system rather than a paper prototype to test with.

- The test user's actions can be influenced by the task instructions and by the person leading the test. Try to see how these factors influence your results. Strive to remain objective and neutral while you're testing. Try to lay your expectations aside and see what really happens.

How to invalidate your user test

In order to help test your own designs, you need to be as objective as possible. If you unconsciously lead the user through diffi-culties, problems you should catch in user testing will come back to haunt you after the product is released. Just look at some of the subtle ways you can skew a test, if you're not careful:

✔ Look back and forth between the test user's face and the part of the screen you think that he ought to look at now.

✔ Give "neutral" answers with embedded hints. Test user: "I don't know what to do next!" Test leader: "What do you think you ought to *click* now?"

✔ Hold a pencil and casually point it in the direction you want the test user to look.

✔ The user is on the right track. Lean slightly forward and smile.

✔ The user is on the wrong track. Sit back or look away with a slight frown.

The *test leader* is the person who talks to the user during the test. Usability labs traditionally ensconce the leader behind one-way glass to reduce these problems. In an informal test setting, I've found that having one observer concentrate on the test leader and give feed-back after the test on any nonneutral behavior helps test leaders to avoid this behavior in the future.

I don't mean to discourage you by mentioning all the ways that user testing differs from doing research. Researchers aim to uncover and prove new generalizable truths; designers are looking for information to use *today*: Did I forget anything? What did the user try first? Which functions did the user ignore? Which parts of the design worked? Which parts didn't?

Ethics

You just can't get around it — people aren't the same as bacteria, which are almost the only things you can run an experiment on these days without getting ethical qualms about your experimental subjects.

In any successful user test, users are going to run into problems, probably while two or more people are watching them and taking notes. Test users can experience this situation as being merely uncomfortable, as stressful, as embarrassing, or as completely awful. They can get upset. They can freeze totally. Some people cry. The need to test software doesn't give us the right to make other human beings feel this way. We haven't any right to use other people cynically or without their informed and free consent.

The Tester's Bill of Rights

Note: Use this as an example Bill of Rights for your test users.

Please read the entire list. As a test user, you should be aware of your rights:

1. *You* are not being tested. You're testing the product.

2. You are taking part in the test as a volunteer. You have the right to interrupt the test or withdraw from it at any time for any reason. You don't need to give a reason for interrupting or withdrawing.

3. If you're going to be observed or filmed during the test, you have the right to be informed of this fact and shown the arrangements beforehand.

4. Under no circumstances are you to be observed by a person who is your leader or manager at work.

5. Your anonymity is to be protected in any notes taken. If the test is taped or filmed, however, your face and voice are going to be recognizable in the records. You must give written consent for the test to be taped or filmed. You have the right to be informed what the records are to be used for. The records may not be used for other purposes than those you're apprised of unless your additional written consent is obtained.

6. You have the right to request that notes or tapes be deleted/destroyed even if you choose to complete the test.

7. You have the right to be treated politely and with respect during the test. Humor is allowed, but you're invited to set the tone with which you feel most comfortable. Other participants in the test are going to follow your lead.

Before a test, read "The Tester's Bill of Rights" (see accompanying sidebar) and take it to heart. After your test user arrives, give him or her the Bill of Rights to read and obtain a signed consent form similar to the one proposed in Chapter 8 for interview subjects.

Planning

If you want, you can test without doing any special planning.

In fact, after you've got the true designer attitude, you probably aren't going to let a chance for an informal test pass you by. Every time a fresh face turns up in your vicinity, you snatch up a sketch or pull up a chair. "Hi! Welcome to the project. Before you do anything else, why don't you take a look at this window and show me how you'd use it to order fifty basketballs?"

On the other hand, a well-planned test gives you more reliable results.

What do you want to know?

Some design decisions are trivial, and some make a lot more difference as to whether your project achieves its goals. The important design decisions are the ones that are worthwhile to support by testing with users.

The stage the project is in tends to influence both what you want to know and how you go about finding it out. Early in the project, you don't have a live system to test. Unless the budget is such that you can invest in a realistic (sometimes called *high fidelity*) prototype, you need to focus on questions that you can answer by using a *low fidelity prototype* — paper drawings or maybe a single window — at the beginning of the project. Later on, you can test with parts of the finished system, but at that point you're naturally reluctant to ask questions with answers that could turn the whole system inside out.

Figure out what you really, truly need to *know* as opposed to guessing. The questions you define determine what form of system you must have for the test and what tasks you give the test users.

Here are some examples of questions for which you may want to design tests:

- ✔ Can we identify any unnecessary steps in this dialog box for defining new products? You could test this anytime after designing the dialog box, with paper windows or live ones.

- ✔ Can the users start with the program icon and find their way to the right place to start each of the following tasks: add a new customer, correct an address, put in a new supplier address, or log an event? Test this one early, with the menu system simulated on a computer or on paper.

- ✔ As the users evaluate loan applications, do they take advantage of the decision support features the system offers? Test this in mid- to late project by using realistic windows. You need a realistic look and feel in order to find out what users actually do. Live data may not be necessary, but you'll need to hard-code realistic data. If you stick in just any old unrealistic values and customer information on a loan application, the test user will not exhibit the same behavior as she would for a real loan.

- ✔ Can a new user figure out what our program does? This one is an early test, with a paper sketch of the top window or windows.

- ✔ Have we chosen the right leading text for the fields in the patient chart? Check this one out early, on paper.

- ✔ How long does an experienced user take to log the results of the daily medical rounds? Can we do anything to make this test more effective? This one would be a late test, with live and realistic data.

A system to test on

Test the conceptual model with a paper sketch. (See the sidebar "Checking your models" in Chapter 5.)

Test your navigation model by using a paper prototype of the menu system and the top windows. You can also use a paper prototype to test the way you divide functions among windows. Paper prototypes aren't especially time-consuming to make. Figure 17-1 shows a setup for a user test of a paper prototype. As you can see, it's just a lot of pieces of paper!

If you're using Windows, just press the Print Screen key to copy to the Clipboard any window you have on-screen. You can edit the image in Windows Paint if you want to.

You can also sketch windows by using the simple drawing tools in a program such as PowerPoint or draw them with pencil and paper. On the CD-ROM, look for the PowerPoint file `Protkit1.ppt` with a prototype construction set of widget drawings.

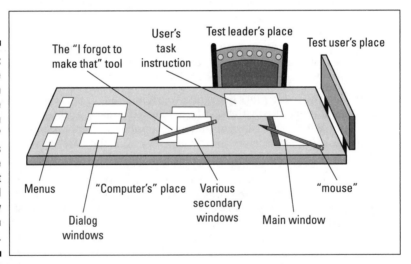

Figure 17-1:
See anything in the figure that you don't have? This stuff is all the equipment you need for an early test with users.

If you use pencil and paper, you may want to draw a bunch of components and window frames first and then photocopy them for use at this stage of user testing. Hand-drawn prototypes collect more active input from the users because the program doesn't look quite so finished. Hand-drawn prototypes also prevent unrealistic user expectations; most users can't tell that you haven't started programming yet from looking at the printout of a window because the window looks finished to them. You don't want questions such as, "You showed us that window three months ago, and *now* you say it's not ready?"

Test leading texts and button texts by using your paper windows.

Try out new widgets or dynamic relationships between widgets in a free-standing window made with your development tool or, if you prefer, a simple prototyping tool. Hard-code enough data to make the window look realistic.

Always test look-and-feel questions by using a prototype or a piece of the system created with the actual development tool. Different development tools create different windows: Standard widgets look a bit different when drawn with different tools; sizing and positioning capabilities vary and so does the color palette; and some widgets are unique to a development tool. In short, if you want to test look and feel, you need to show users what you actually intend to give them.

To test user effectiveness or system response times, you need a very high fidelity prototype or a piece of the system made with your actual development tool. If the entire system is not up and running, you may need to hard-code the estimated response times to produce realistic test conditions.

A task to test with

The task makes all the difference. The task is what separates a *test* with users from a *discussion* with users. Don't on any account try to run a test without a task.

Whether you're testing early or late in the project, on paper or live, you always need to do the following:

- ✔ Make a task, not a question. Tell the user: "Please sort these cards into groups and put each group in some order that seems natural to you," not "Tell me whether you're familiar with the words on these cards."

- ✔ Make the task specific, not general. Instruct the user: "Please register your own home as a new property for sale, using the actual address, description, number of rooms and other data," not "Register a new sale property."

- ✔ Give realistic input data. If the user must make up the data or you give typical programmer-test data (all numbers = 1, all texts = aaa, all names = Mary Smith), you miss some of the true problems with issues such as field lengths and error-handling routines.

- ✔ Make sure that the task has a well-defined result or outcome so that both you and the test user have a chance to see whether the task was successfully concluded.

- ✔ Provide a single task whenever you test a conceptual model or a single window. To test a menu system or a prototype with several windows, prepare a short list of tasks that will require the user to move around in the test system.

---

7 good reasons to test with users

You're already convinced that you need to test with users, right? These good reasons may help you convince your colleagues:

1. Everything gets tested by the users eventually. Do you want this testing to happen while you still control the program or after you've released it?

2. The earlier you discover a problem, the cheaper it is to fix.

3. You can test informally and with the people you can get hold of. Testing doesn't need to be expensive to get results — just objective. Objectivity is something *you* control.

4. Testing with users is the best, most cost-effective design education going. It compresses your learning curve amazingly!

5. Facts are a better basis for design decisions than experience; experience is a better basis than opinions. Testing with users produces something in the vicinity of facts.

6. Would Lotus and Microsoft and Sun spend millions of dollars on usability testing without seeing advantages in it?

7. What if you don't, and your competitors do?

If you did a task analysis (as described in Chapters 9 and 10), you already have some tasks that you can use for the test. Your prototype should work well with the tasks from the task analysis; after all, you designed it with those tasks in mind. Remember to add a couple of new, different tasks as well; you'll collect more new problems by trying out systems with new tasks.

For an informal test, figure that you can keep the user hard at work for anywhere from 15 minutes to an hour, but no more. You need time for introductions before the test and a closing interview after the test; even if the user is able to concentrate for longer periods, you and the other observers are going to start missing things. Based on my testing experience, to estimate how long a task is going to take during a user test, I perform the task myself and then multiply by about 3 for simple tasks and by about 5 for complex tasks.

Now, catch your users

At the planning stage, you need to set up appointments with your test users.

If you've never done testing with users before, this step may seem like the biggest problem to you. Starting out easy is okay: Try with a colleague close to your project but not directly involved in it. Administrative personnel, secretaries, and personal assistants are often willing to help out by acting as test users.

Another reason to start small and close to home is that you may be wondering, "Do I need permission to do this testing? How do I explain why I'm spending time this way?" You need some personal experience with testing — what it costs you to organize and what kind of information it produces — to take the step of saying to your colleagues or leaders, "This testing is valuable to our project, and I'd like to make a habit of working in this way."

If development leaders (or potential test users' leaders) are skeptical, offer them the chance to participate in a short test as test users themselves. (Need I encourage you to set up a task that they've *some* chance of completing successfully?)

As you gain practice and confidence in setting up and carrying out tests, go farther afield for your test users. You need people with a fresh perspective.

If you're doing custom development, your client usually feels reassured by the idea that you're actually tailoring the program to the users. Where the client leadership (or yours) prefers to isolate the development project, first establish user testing by using people on the periphery of the project and then suggest renting temps. A good temp agency can often provide people who have the right degree of computer experience and functional knowledge to represent your user group pretty well.

To find people to test a software package for the general public, try hanging posters in your own lunchroom or ask students, friends, neighbors, and relatives to participate. If you have a training department, see whether you can get access to customers who've come for courses.

How many test users do you need?

Dr. Jakob Nielsen, author of *Usability Engineering* (Academic Press, Inc.), has done both research and field work with this question. I summarize Nielsen's results here.

Nielsen's studies show that you find fewer new problems with each successive user you test. On the other hand, the first user is the most expensive user to test. To test one user, you have the costs of defining your question, choosing a task, and getting a system or a prototype ready to test. After the first test, each additional user you test costs only the time for the test and the analysis afterward.

Looking at the costs and benefits together, Nielsen shows that you get the best benefit to cost ratio if you test from three to five users.

I've been involved in tests with anywhere from 1 to 15 users, and I must say that my gut feelings based on these experiences match Nielsen's results: By the time you get to tests number six, seven, and eight, you very rarely see anything new. Could the observers be getting a bit jaded by then?

To test software that requires specific functional knowledge — for example, CAD/CAM — take your search for test users to the places where future users study — engineering schools, for example — or plan tests in connection with a local conference or a customer event such as a seminar planned by your own marketing department.

Whatever you're testing, try to find a variety of users to test. Individual differences account for a lot of usability problems: The program may make sense to everybody who thinks like you, but not everybody does. The more differences among the people who test your program, the more insight you gain into how it works for people who think differently from you.

Getting Ready

In the planning stage for a user test, you choose a question, a system, and some tasks and recruit your users. What's left are the practical preparations for the test. If you follow these step-by-step instructions, you won't forget anything even the first time through:

1. **Make appointments with the users.**

   Leave time for introductions before each test and discussions afterward with each test user. One to two hours total is about right. Leave time between appointments to collect findings.

2. **Make a test script.**

   The following section has a complete test script that can serve as an example. The same document is stored on the enclosed CD-ROM so that you can copy and edit it for your own test.

   The test script covers all the essential points of the introduction, opening interview, obtaining consent, and any training or system presentation. It contains the task. The test script also has any questions you want to make sure that you ask after the test.

   The test script helps you run the test in a predictable, professional manner. Giving the same information about the task and system to each user is especially important. If you're not certain what you told them and what they figured out for themselves, you don't know how to interpret the results of the test.

3. **Recruit the test team and assign jobs.**

   When I first learned to perform user tests, I thought that my trainer was going overboard. Why get at least three people — and maybe four or five — to perform one user test? I was certain that I was already getting the same information far more effectively from my conversations with the users. "Ivory tower theoretician," I mumbled to myself. Experience, however, changed my mind.

You must have one test leader. If you're using a paper prototype, use a second person to act the role of the computer. I recommend using at least one observer. Additional observers are fine. Also, note that the test leader is the only person who communicates with the user during the test. The test leader encourages the user to think out loud during the test.

If you have a person acting as the computer, then that person makes the paper windows respond to user actions: If the user "clicks" on a menu by tapping it with a pencil, for example, the computer finds the slip of paper representing the pulled-down menu and puts it in place.

The test leader and the observers all take notes on the problems and any particularly successful features that they notice during the test.

How many people from your project to involve is your choice. I now prefer to use three or more people in the test team for three reasons: First, the quality of the observations improves, because we correct each other. Second, project members who take part develop a shared understanding of the problems they have seen. The resulting discussions about how to solve the problems are more constructive. Finally, seeing is believing. Those who observe a test don't doubt its findings, and they tend to become more positive to using testing as one of their design tools.

4. Set up work space for the test.

Decide where the test user, the test leader, and the "computer" are to sit. Also, decide how to make sure the observers can see what's going on. I've solved this visibility problem in various ways: I've made a giant paper prototype on flip-over paper or, once, on a whole whiteboard. I've also used a document camera from a videoconferencing setup to transmit a picture of the paper prototype and the user's hands to a big-screen TV in front of the observers.

If you're working with a live system, consider letting the user work on a laptop; use an extra long cable to hook up a screen that the observers can stare at.

5. Rehearse the test.

You often find problems with the test script, usually somewhere in the description of the task or the instructions for it. A rehearsal is the best way to find and correct the problems.

If you're using a paper prototype, the person playing the computer needs a rehearsal or two to decide how best to arrange the multitude of paper bits.

Finally, the observers and test leader need to be quite certain how the task is supposed to proceed so that they can be alert if the test user departs from the expected: That's when the good stuff turns up.

To rehearse the test, team members can take turns being the test user. Be prepared to take notes, because you often notice usability problems yourselves during the rehearsals. Project leaders are also good rehearsal subjects. Rehearsing helps them understand how the test process works, and they may find a few problems, too, which makes them feel useful.

A Sample Test Script

This section contains a sample test script for testing the overall usability of a Directory Assistance CD-ROM, a substitute for having telephone books for the whole state. A copy of the test script is on the CD-ROM in the back of this book, and it is ready for you to use as a basis for the script for your own test.

Scenario

Here's the scenario for the test of the Directory Assistance CD-ROM: The project is nearly ready to release a beta version. The GUI designer's question for this test is as follows: Suppose that I have a user whose most advanced computer experience is to use a Windows word processor for correspondence. Can this user successfully install and use the product?

Earlier tests with prototypes covered the search features; at this test, the development team can confirm the effects of their improvements. They can also check how the test user reacts to the response times involved in different searches.

Each of the following sections covers one step in the test (such as welcoming the test user, obtaining consent, and so on) through the closing interview.

Welcome

In the welcome, you aim to help the test user feel comfortable with you. You begin to establish your role as the listener. Use dialogue similar to the following:

✔ **Good morning. Welcome to the Directory Assistance product test. I'm** *<your name>*.

The test user supplies her name.

✔ **I'm glad you could come today to help us test this product. How did you hear about the test?**

The test user explains, and you listen attentively.

✔ **Have you participated in a product test of a computer program before? How do you feel about it?**

The test user explains, and you listen attentively. If a response is called for, remind the test user that she is testing the product, not the other way around.

Bill of Rights

The Tester's Bill of Rights is in an earlier section of this chapter. Use dialogue similar to the following:

✔ **Because you have/haven't performed this test before, you may/may not be familiar with the Tester's Bill of Rights. Please read through these and see whether you have any questions or reservations.**

Give the user a sheet with the Tester's Bill of Rights. Wait quietly while the user reads.

✔ **Do you have any questions or reservations?**

Listen and respond to the test user's comments.

Consent

Always use a consent form if you plan to record audio or video. Chapter 9 suggests the points that should be included in an interview consent form. Have a qualified lawyer help you with the wording of the consent form. Ask the user, "Please read through and sign the consent form." Give the user the consent form and wait quietly for any questions.

Opening interview

You want to know how this test user compares to your projected user group in terms of computer experience and functional knowledge of the task. Try not to ask obvious questions such as "Male or female?" Invite the user to describe herself rather than treating her as an experimental subject.

Use dialogue such as the following: "Directory Assistance is intended for people who already use Windows, whether they have very little computer experience or quite a lot. Could you describe how you fit into that group?"

Note especially products or tasks that the test user mentions and length of PC experience. Ask concrete follow-up questions if necessary. Note answers in keyword form.

Introductions and "Tour"

Present the observers to the test user, not the other way around. Show the arrangements for monitoring and (if relevant) recording the test. Reassure the user if necessary. Prepare the user for your role during the test.

Throughout the introduction, encourage the test user to respond by pausing, waiting, and listening. Getting the test user loosened up and accustomed to talking in front of all three of you before the actual test begins is important. Use dialogue similar to the following:

- **Here is the work area we use for the test. <*test user's name*>, this is Javier and Sharon. Javier and Sharon are observing and taking notes; after we get started they kind of fade into the woodwork.**

    Observers and test user exchange a few friendly words.

- **You sit here and use this computer; Javier and Sharon can see what's happening on their monitor over there, and they've got a card they can flash at me if they need you to speak up or anything like that.**

    Stop and enable the user to respond to your comments or make her own comments on the room.

- **By the way, the computer's safe — we have copies of everything here, so nothing you do can possibly "hurt" the computer or destroy anything, okay?**

    Wait for a response.

- **I'm going to be here, too. My job is to remind you to talk out loud during the test, but I'm not allowed to help you, because we need to know what happens for our customers/users who don't have a test team right next to them as they use Directory Assistance!**

    Wait for a response.

Training or introduction to system

For some tests, you need to give an introduction to the system at this point. Do write down the points that you intend to cover.

Practice the test user's role

Practice helps the user over the threshold of touching the computer and gives you a chance to observe mouse technique and typing ability. Use dialogue such as the following:

- ✔ Okay, let's sit down and make sure that everything is in working order here.

- ✔ Would you start the Word program, just to try out the mouse and see that it's working? Thanks, that looks fine.

- ✔ Can you type a few lines there? How's this keyboard for you?

- ✔ Now I need you to practice thinking out loud, like this: "Oh, I see I need to sharpen my pencil. Do you have a sharpener here? Yes, I see one over there; okay, I can go use it. This handle is hard to grip; it's too small for my fingers. Okay, I'm ready to go. . . ."

- ✔ Now, can you turn the Word program off again and give me the same kind of play-by-play comments on what you're doing?

Again, practice at talking out loud may get the test user started. Individuals vary enormously in whether they can speak their thoughts out loud. If you get a true introvert as a test user, don't push her to talk and work simultaneously, but rather ask her to pause now and again, think back, and tell you what she thinks happened.

Start the test

Asking the user to read the instructions out loud ensures that she does read through the instructions before beginning and also gets the user speaking out loud as the test begins. Use dialogue similar to this.

- ✔ Okay, that takes care of all the preliminaries. Ready to go?

  Wait for an affirmative answer and hand over the test materials.

- ✔ Here are your instructions and the materials you need. From now until you're finished, I'm going to say as little as possible and just remind you to speak your thoughts.

  Perhaps you may begin by reading the instructions out loud and commenting on them.

Task instructions

Try to make the task instructions brief and concrete. Focus on goals and results; don't describe how to perform the task. Make sure that both you and the test user can see whether a task has been successfully completed.

Debug the task instructions in rehearsals; many tests fail because the instructions are misunderstood or create problems by themselves, and that's a waste!

Title the instructions something neutral, such as Directory Assistance Test Instructions. Explain the task using introductory and instructional language that's similar to the following:

- ✔ **Besides these instructions, you've received a packet with the Directory Assistance CD-ROM. Suppose that you'd just come home from the store with this packet, and this is your own computer.**

- ✔ **Please do whatever you need to do to make Directory Assistance work on this computer. After you see a window saying "Welcome to Directory Assistance," you've succeeded.**

- ✔ **Use Directory Assistance to find the following information and note down the answers on this paper.**

  1. **Find the telephone number for John Hubert Urban, who lives in San Diego on Littler Drive, and write it on the first line of the paper.**

  2. **Find the switchboard number and the street address for the Department of Public Health in Sacramento and write them on the next line of the paper.**

  3. **Find the telephone numbers of a restaurant in San Francisco that serves Italian food and write it on the third line.**

  4. **Find out who lives at 234 W. Main Street in Carlsbad and write the name on the fourth line.**

Closing interview

The closing interview provides closure for the test user, who may easily be frustrated if she's been unable to complete the task.

Observers get the chance to ask questions, but the test leader should prevent observers from getting into discussions with the test user about why the program is designed the way it is.

Finally, ask specific questions to ascertain the test user's familiarity with key tasks. Wait until the end to ask questions similar to the following so that you don't clue the user in as to what she's supposed to do or create too many expectations in your own mind about where the test user may fail:

✔ Do you have any questions for us, *<test user's name>*? Would you like to make any suggestions about the Directory Assistance program?

✔ How would you describe the experience of acting as a test user with our test team?

✔ Sharon and Javier, do you have any questions for *<test user's name>*?

✔ Does either the computer you use at work or one that you use at home have a place to insert a CD-ROM? A disk?

✔ Do you ever copy things to or from disks?

✔ Have you ever used a CD-ROM to put new things on your computer? What?

Good-bye

Especially if you're doing custom development, remember to use this opportunity to create realistic expectations. External test users are usually paid; I like to give internal test users a diploma or a coffee cup marked "I survived the <product name> usability test." Hand over a check for $40 (or whatever you have promised in order to lure users into the test) and get a receipt.

Escort the test user back to the reception area and say good-bye in a manner similar to this: "Thanks very much for testing Directory Assistance for us, <test user's name>. Seeing how the program performs with a real user is a big help for us. We're going to use what we've learned from you to improve the product, but you should know that we may not be able to solve all the problems you've pointed out to us in the first version that you see."

What to Watch Out For

After you're prepared, carrying out the test is just a case of following the script. Until things start going wrong, that is. As soon as the user departs from the task the way you've rehearsed it, sharpen your attention. Does the user say anything to show what she's thinking? How long does she take before she begins to realize she's hit a problem? What seems to make her aware that she has a problem? How does she try to solve the problem?

Sometimes the test leader needs to intervene. The following list of events (in bold) and responses gives you some ideas about what can happen and how you may respond:

- ✔ **The user clams up.** Ask her, "What are you thinking about now?" or use two testers at the same time and ask them to perform the task together. They should talk to each other.

- ✔ **The user gets stuck.** Ask: "What are you looking for now?" "What else would you like to try?"

- ✔ **The user indirectly asks for help or confirmation before doing something.** Ask: "What do *you* think that you should do?" "What do you think may happen?" "What do you think it means?"

- ✔ **The user asks directly for help.** Say, "Please show me what you'd do if I weren't here."

- ✔ **The user shows signs of frustration or other strong feelings.** Acknowledge the user's feelings neutrally: "I can see that you have some reactions to this situation."

- ✔ **The user gives up on the task or expresses strong negative feelings.** Suggest: "Let's take a break for a while. After you're ready to begin again, I can help you solve this problem and then you can go on." Use clear body language as well as words to mark the break. Move the user away from the test system for a little while. Take a coffee break if necessary. Reassure the user that problems give valuable information about the system and that you all appreciate the tester's efforts. After you return, hop over the difficulty. Set the user in a place where she can go on with as little fuss and explanation as possible. Say, "Now you can go on," and mark clearly that you're back in test mode.

- ✔ **The user is lost in space.** If the user repeats the same unsuccessful approach over and over again or is so far off track that you see no chance she can wander back, follow the same procedure described in the preceding paragraph for a user who has given up.

- ✔ **The user decides to withdraw from the test.** Break off the test immediately. Thank the user and ask whether she'd like to go through the closing interview.

- ✔ **Observers need to communicate with the test leader.** Write and unobtrusively pass notes.

- ✔ **Observers lose it.** Observers are not supposed to be talking, laughing, or waving their eyebrows around (or sobbing in despair). If anything such as these actions occur, the observer should make an excuse to leave the test room. The test leader must, if necessary, send the cracked-up observer out: "*Xxxx*, could you please go out and tell the reception clerk that the test is going fine and that we should be finished on time?" *Xxxx* can either return or not, depending on whether he or she regains composure.

Figuring Out What It All Means

Whenever I've held a test with other developers, I've enjoyed seeing their immediate reactions. Usually, they want to gallop back to their workstations and start fixing things right away: "That was great! I know just what I want to change; we can fix half of these problems in a couple of minutes apiece!" If you can keep the test team working together for a couple more hours, you can obtain more complete and systematic results.

After each test user leaves

Go through your notes as soon as the test user is out the door, while everything is still fresh in your minds.

All you need to do is collect all the observed problems in a single list. Have one person in the test team mention one problem and cross it off in his notes and then go on to the next person, who mentions the next different problem that she saw. This way, no individual view of the test dominates the analysis. Go around the table until all the problems are crossed off and then discard the observation notes.

A "problem" may be anything from a spelling error in the interface to a missing piece of the design. A problem may be something that the user did wrong or something that the user did not understand. Here's an excerpt from a test of a word processing function to merge a list of addresses with a standard letter:

- ✔ Couldn't find the Merge command. Looked in the Print dialog box.
- ✔ Did not associate Merge command with standard letters even after looking at the Merge command.
- ✔ Created letter first and had no merge fields to insert.
- ✔ Got list of standard merge fields. Tried to select from list when should have deleted unwanted fields.
- ✔ Did not recognize the standard Save As dialog box after it appeared on exit from the Field Definition dialog box.
- ✔ Saved without realizing had done so or where file was located.

This session sharpens attention. You usually think of something that you didn't see in the test. Then you think, "Well, I'll look and see whether that happens with the next user."

This stage is also the time to give feedback on the test leader's performance. Was the test leader both neutral and respectful toward the user? Did you get the impression that the test leader influenced the user? If so, what specific behavior or comments did you observe?

When you come back to the collected list after the next user leaves, the job goes a little faster. You can put an extra mark by problems that recurred and just write down the new ones.

After the last test user leaves

You already have a collection of raw data. Follow this procedure to organize your findings and feed them back into the creative process:

1. **Sort the problems according to which window or which order they occurred in.**

2. **Remove or consolidate duplicate findings.**

3. **Categorize the problems.**

   I use the following scheme:

   - **Class A: Problem must be solved.** Put it in the project plans.

   - **Class B: We can solve the problem if we have time.** Make sure that it doesn't get forgotten; if we don't solve it, treat it as class C.

   - **Class C: We can't solve this problem now, so define it as a training/documentation problem or a feature.** Inform the people who are going to need to deal with it.

   - **Class D: This problem is minor and easy to solve.** We can fix this glitch in a few minutes.

4. **Discuss how to solve the problems in Classes A and B.**

   The categorized list and a written summary of your proposed solutions in Step 4 make up the documentation from the user test.

Remember to distribute the test results within the project. They may also be a useful tool in making the case for testing with users.

Upgrading to a Usability Lab

If you're testing an electronic, live protoype (as opposed to a paper proto-type), you can use the testing technique described in this chapter in a more formal setting. A usability lab has some advantages over the informal setup described so far in this chapter, among them those described in the following list:

✔ You can let the user work alone in a room and communicate via microphone or telephone. This setup tends to cut down on problems with "leading the user," but the user tends to say a lot less, too.

✔ You can set up a more realistic working situation. People rarely work with a gang of observers peering at them.

✔ Labs have equipment to record what happens on the user's screen onto a videotape as well as recording what the user says and does. By using editing equipment, you can mix these two images together and record them onto a single tape, with a result similar to that shown in the diagram in Figure 17-2.

You don't have to build your own usability lab from scratch: You can contact a professional usability consulting firm that runs its own laboratory; expect to purchase both consulting services and lab time. Alternatively, you can rent recording and editing equipment for a short period, or you can buy a portable usability lab. A portable lab includes a PC card to enable direct video recording of a screen image and the other recording and editing equipment you need. A portable lab enables you to conduct even more realistic tests because you can visit the users where they normally work.

Before you get hooked on the idea of video, keep in mind that reviewing a video and collecting observations takes much longer than reviewing notes does. An edited tape with just the highlights of several tests is great for communicating test results to a larger audience, but such a tape is also time-consuming to produce.

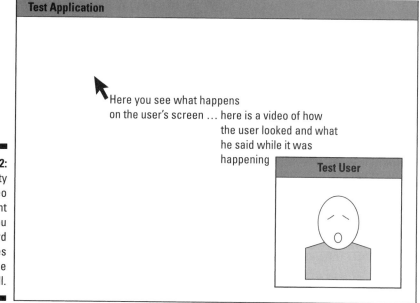

Figure 17-2:
Lab-quality video equipment enables you to record two images for one tape that tells all.

The same considerations apply whether you're recording user tests or interviews — you may want to check out the sidebar "To record or not to record" in Chapter 8.

If your company doesn't use systematic usability tests today, you're better off starting with inexpensive, informal tests. Establish testing with users as a Good Thing in the eyes of management before you go shopping for recording equipment. Testing with users requires the development project members to be objective and open to self-criticism. I've found that this process is easiest for people if they feel some control over the testing process and how the results are presented.

If you want to get away from theory and look at some more real examples, in Chapter 18, I discuss four actual projects. I show you excerpts of what we tested and what we learned in each project.

Chapter 18

Testing Stories from True Life

- -

- -

Storytelling is not just something to do with children or around campfires. What's after-dinner speaking, after all? At college, we called it a bull session; at Norsk Data, we spoke of the company legends; and in a consulting firm we relaxed after work and told "war stories." Stories and anecdotes are a way to share experiences.

I'd like to share some of my testing experiences with you. In this chapter, you find stories from simple, inexpensive tests done on four different projects. I hope they whet your own appetite for testing. If not, well, stir up the coals and get out the marshmallows!

Conceptual Model for Search

In Chapter 5, I recommend that you make and test one or more conceptual models for your system.

If you can draw a conceptual model of what the program is going to do and you find out that the users understand the drawing with no trouble, you can safely design the program to work like the drawing.

In this project, I'm designing a public-service interface for a library. The interface is to help visitors to the library search to determine whether the book, video, or music they want is available and to print out instructions for how to find it. I want to design a search function that people can understand whether they understand databases or not.

The design

I began by drawing a one-page conceptual model for the search process, and my first draft is as shown in Figure 18-1. The drawing attempts to communicate the following information:

✔ The drawing starts in the upper left-hand corner. The first step shows a person picking one of three categories, books, music, or video.

✔ In the second step, the person decides what he wants — a specific book, such as *Tom Sawyer,* or a category of books, such as Autobiography or Mystery.

✔ The system offers books that suit the user's criteria, and he picks one. The arrows indicate that maybe he doesn't see anything he likes or he wants another book or some other item in addition. After he's satisfied, he can choose to quit.

✔ The result of using the system is that the user gets printed directions for how to find what he wants.

Figure 18-1:
A conceptual model for searching for a book at the library.

The test

To test my model, I printed the drawing on a transparency and presented it to a group of 15 people on an overhead projector. They knew that it had something to do with a library system. I simply put the drawing on the overhead and asked, "What's going on in this picture?"

What I learned

One of the first problems was that determining where the process begins and ends was difficult in the picture. Although I thought I'd created a clear progression from top left to bottom right, most people found that the central position of the third picture, its "on-top" format, and the arrows leading away from it all made it the natural starting point. And if they started in the middle, they didn't understand the overall picture at all.

The discussion group came to the conclusion that a comic strip format would have solved their problem with the picture. I agreed, but what was most valuable for me was to realize that the *sequence* would be an important clue for my users in understanding the functions that the search system offers at each step. I understood that sequence was important because I listened to the discussion group's confused questions, incorrect statements, and disagreements about the order and meaning of the steps in the picture.

For example, those who found it natural to start with the third frame saw a lender choosing between three *books,* so they interpreted the whole picture as being about choosing between books, rather than about choosing among all of the library's resources. When they tried to make sense of frames one and two, members of the discussion group had trouble recognizing symbols for music and videos because they had already decided that this was a picture about choosing books.

The discussion group also pointed out that I'd failed to allow for a return between steps 1 and 2, and they wondered whether they'd lose the directions to item number 1 if they didn't finish the process and receive those directions before they went back and searched for a second item.

Finally, interesting questions to the functionality of the entire system arose: Does the user have any guarantee that the book is actually on the shelf after he gets there? What's the benefit to the user in using this system as opposed to just asking a librarian, which is what the understaffed library is trying to prevent?

The questions that you can clear up by drawing and testing a conceptual model — even within the project — may seem very basic. In many failed projects, the problem is precisely that these basic questions were never asked and never answered.

Analogy for a Training Program

Several years ago, I was paired with another designer to create computer-based training for user interface design. Because the training program would be used for a short time by each user, and the user's focus should be on the subject content rather than on how to use the training program, we set the following design goal: A student who looks at the initial screen should be able to say what she must do to complete the course.

Analogies were hot right then, so we did the brainstorming routine and decided that a gameboard analogy was just what we needed. It has a clear start and a clear finish and lots of positive associations to make learning fun. We thought.

The design

The original sketch is lost to me now, but I recall that it looked something like the one shown in Figure 18-2.

We believed that the user would point at Start and say, "I start here. First I must go there, to the supply store, and get some things, although I don't know what yet. Then I go on past the library, which I can visit any time, and I end up at this castle. A key's there, and I see some other keys and, oh, here at the end is a chest with three keyholes, so I guess I need to get all three of the keys by going to the three places where the keys are. Looks like I may have do battle with this knight or something to get the keys to the chest. And then I put the keys in the chest and open it and something good happens, and I'm done."

The test

We did a quick-and-dirty sketch of a gameboard on a single sheet of paper. The sketch took about two hours. Then we arranged to spend 20 minutes each with half a dozen new employees, because the course was aimed at people in their first year of employment. We simply gave them the paper and said, "This diagram is the first screen of a new on-line training program you must complete. What do you think you need to do to complete this training course?"

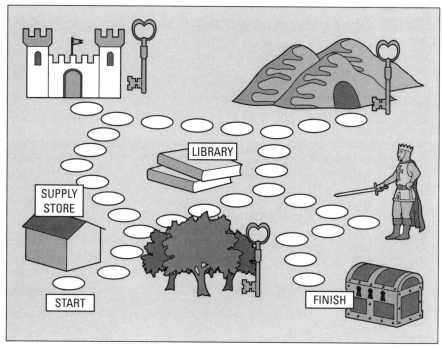

Figure 18-2:
Gameboard
analogy for
a training
program.

What we learned

By the time we'd finished listening to the first three testers, we realized that the analogy was hurting more than it was helping.

One woman said, "Well, the cave looks dangerous; I'd certainly try to avoid that." And that was the primary problem: The graphics, crude as they were, put the testers in a strategic frame of mind. They imagined dangers; they imagined competitors; they started plotting how to collect keys without doing anything risky.

The library and the supply depot were ignored as resources; in our drawing, users couldn't see how to get into them or what good it would do to visit the library and supply depot. But more important was that the tester's attention was focused by the analogy on "treasure" and "strategy."

We postponed our appointments with the last three testers and went back to the drawing board. Although it wasn't quite as satisfying to our creative souls (at first), we came up with what we called the flow-chart analogy, as shown in Figure 18-3.

Figure 18-3:
A flow-chart
analogy for
a training
program.

With the last three testers we'd arranged to meet, we performed the same test on our new design. The second design met the design goals: Each user could say immediately what steps the course would consist of.

Total elapsed time was about $1^1/_2$ days for two designers and a total of 2 hours for the six test users.

Later in the project, we made a working prototype of the course window with the flow chart buttons at the top. Testing with the prototype, we found that it was an advantage to hide the three alternatives under the View and Evaluate buttons until the user actually clicked View or Evaluate.

Which Window Layout is Best?

Recently, I worked on a GUI standards project for a client whose various applications contained many windows, each having a list box and a detail area. The list box may contain a list of products, for example. The user selects one product from the list, and the detail area of the window shows information for the selected product: the product number, product name, product description, wholesale price, retail price, packaging information and shipping weight, and so on.

In some applications, the developers chose to put the *details* first, at the top of the window, because that's what the user spends most time with. In other applications, developers argued that the *list* should always be at the top of the window, because the item that's selected controls which details are shown.

Each faction believed that their solution was the most logical and should be written into the new standard. "Who's right?" they wanted to know. The standards group could have gathered six or eight developers and spent four hours discussing the matter, but we wouldn't get any smarter from doing that, so we did a test instead.

First, we needed to decide what we really wanted to know. To ask "Which is better?" without knowing what you mean by "better" is a waste of time. Looking at the user groups and design goals for each of the applications, we saw that almost all the applications had broad user groups with many new and inexperienced users starting all the time. Furthermore, ease of use was the highest priority. Based on these goals, we decided to try to determine which alternative was easiest for the users to understand.

The test

In a word processor, we typed a list with one highlighted line and a set of details. Because we did not want people to answer on the basis of the company products that they were familiar with, we used data that would probably be easy to understand for any employed adult: descriptions of homes for sale. We printed the list and detail on two sheets of paper, as shown in Figure 18-4.

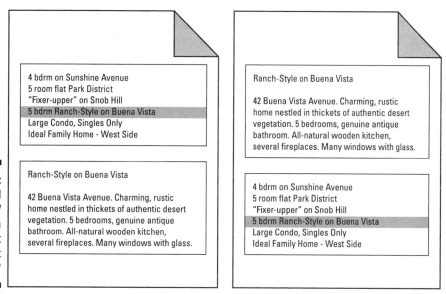

Figure 18-4:
List/detail or detail/list. Which arrangement is most intuitive?

Then we simply walked around the rest of the company, mostly outside the R&D department, handing one piece of paper or the other to random people and asking, "What is the relationship between the information in the two boxes on this piece of paper?"

We listened carefully to what they said. Some people found answering difficult because they didn't understand what we wanted to know or why. The question was a bit abstract.

After they'd answered about one of the pieces of paper, we'd give them the other one as well, give them time to realize that the two were the same, and ask them which of the two alternatives they preferred.

What we decided

Of 21 users, 14 preferred the alternative with the list on top. They gave a wide variety of reasons, from "It is more logical this way" to "I am familiar with this arrangement from working with our products." Different people gave the same reasons for preferring different alternatives.

What was more interesting was that those who received the list-on-top paper first had less difficulty in answering the question. They were more puzzled by why we were asking such an obvious question than by what they saw.

If the list was on top, most people looked at the high-contrast item in the list first. In fact, it was the only thing that they really looked at in the list. Then they glanced at the details and immediately related it to the list. If the details were on top, more people started at the top of the detail box and read the entire thing, puzzling about our question all the while — those were the ones who tended to get really stuck.

We concluded that list/detail was *more likely* (not proved) to be intuitive for the majority of new users than detail/list and wrote our conclusion into the standard.

Two members of the standards groups spent about two hours on this activity.

Testing a Menu System

This example is based on a custom development project for an administrative system with lots of functionality. The menu contents you see here are fictional, but the rest is taken from real life.

The system was supposed to be easy to administer and easy to add to in the future. Therefore, we were trying to design a flexible menu system that could hold lots of choices. One user group would be large, with many users who had limited computer experience. This group also had high turnover. Another group would be a smaller, stable group of expert users.

The design goals for the system were, in order, that it be easy to understand, effective for experienced users, and easy to modify or maintain.

The design

All the users would need to learn enough about Windows 3.11 to use the File Manager anyway, so why not have the menu system work like the left side of the File Manager? The menu system could grow to as many levels as necessary. Users would automatically know how to use the menus.

The top-level menu is shown in Figure 18-5. Users can click on one of these folders to open a submenu in which each choice is represented by another folder.

Figure 18-5:
The top
level of a
menu
system
based on
the
Windows
3.11 File
Manager.

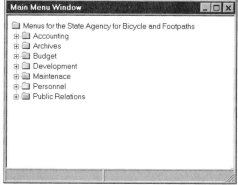

The test

Because we were using an interaction form that was a well-established part of Windows, we had no reason to test it. Our test was planned to show whether the menu *texts* were clear and easy to understand.

We made a live prototype of the entire menu system with the development tool; that was easy, because we were using a standard widget. At the lowest level of the menu, each command was intended to take the user to a different window in the system. Instead of making many windows, we used a single window with text that varied, reflecting the command that had opened the window: `This is the <course participation registration> window.`

We recruited a group of testers from among the client's employees and then we made a list of 11 tasks, such as "Use the menus to go to the window where you'd register the name and other data of someone who's signed up for an internal training course in asphalt maintenance." We asked users to start at the top level of the menu system and click around in it until they got to the window they'd use and then write down the text in the window next to the task. The 11 tasks took users all around the menu system.

We wanted to know how many users would go to the correct window on their first attempt at each task.

We got a surprise

Only about half of the tasks were solved correctly on the first attempt. This was disappointing, but it showed that we still needed to work on some of the menu texts. What users would find in Budget as opposed to what belonged in Accounting was not always clear.

The big surprise was that, after users made an incorrect choice at the first level, *they went on making incorrect choices.* If they opened Accounting when they should have opened Budget, they'd have trouble finding exactly what they were looking for at the second level of the menu. They'd choose the choice that seemed least wrong from the second level, however, and go on. They'd go on making choices until they got to a window that was obviously not the one they wanted. Then they'd try a couple other windows from the lowest level menu, and then many of them would give up in some way or another.

Watching closely, we concluded that something about the design of the menu system discouraged users from reconsidering their first wrong choice.

Figure 18-6 shows what happened. After the user opened the second level, the first level of the menu changed. It was still there, but choices were no longer in the same position. Furthermore, the user needed to scroll both up and down to see the entire first level.

I first noticed the problem as I watched a user wavering between Development and Personnel at the first level. He incorrectly chose Personnel. As he talked about the choices in the Personnel menu and dispiritedly compared them to the task, he absentmindedly and repeatedly moved the mouse pointer to the spot where Development used to be, now occupied by Employee Database. He never said explicitly that he wanted to go back and try Development, but at some level, he obviously did want to.

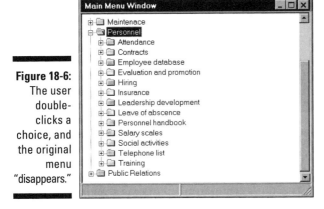

Figure 18-6:
The user double-clicks a choice, and the original menu "disappears."

Our testers were all like new users. They hadn't stored the menu system in their heads. After they made an incorrect choice, working memory was occupied with evaluating what they now saw. By having the first level menus jump out of sight, our design changed the working context and removed the visual cues that the users needed to reconsider their first decision.

Our test revealed a problem that we hadn't expected — a problem with something that we were certain was all right. That's one of the real benefits of testing with users.

If the project had expected low turnover in the user group, we could've defined this turnover as a mere problem of training and familiarity. Because turnover in the largest user group was high, we decided to make changes to the design. A design such as the one shown in Figure 18-7 would give the users an opportunity to go back and reconsider their first choice if they didn't like any of the options it opened to them.

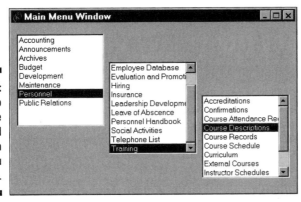

Figure 18-7:
One way to preserve context and flexibility in a menu system.

Other Good Reality Checks

Testing with users is a reality check. It clarifies your perceptions and gets your feet back on the ground. Here, in Chapter 18, I've shown you how simple and enlightening a user test can be. Chapter 19 offers some alternative ways to make sure that your GUI does what you hope: walkthroughs, evaluation with guidelines, and site visits.

Chapter 19

Other Paths to Enlightenment

● ●

● ●

A designer needs a nicely balanced blend of curiosity and backbone: curiosity about what other people think, and backbone to take responsibility for making the final design decision after gathering feedback from a variety of sources. So wait until your perfectly natural delight in your own creation has settled to a warm glow of appreciation, and then do a reality check. Make these reality checks part of each major step in the design; specifically, during the early design phase, during task design, and as part of the design process for each window.

Chapters 17 and 18 cover testing with users, which is the best way to collect feedback. But user testing is not the most practical or most cost-effective way to garner feedback in every project, every time. This chapter suggests alternate ways to collect the input you need to fuel the design process.

Walk-throughs

Perhaps you already do technical *walk-throughs* or technical reviews, where several people go through a design step-by-step. To review a graphic user interface design, just utilize the same old techniques — with a new twist.

If you haven't performed a walk-through before, here's a quick, ah, walk-through of the process.

1. Put walk-throughs on the project schedule.

Schedule a walk-through when you would schedule a usability test: As soon as you have a design document or prototype you can review, but before you get to the stage in which making any changes will give the project leader ulcers.

2. Decide what the walk-through is to find out.

You don't need an agenda for a walk-through if you know what you're trying to find out. If the walk-through is to ensure that a three-window module follows the project standard, for example, you can either go through the normal point-by-point process and check the windows, or you can take each window piece-by-piece and determine whether the window complies with the standard.

The most useful type of walk-through to me is more of a *work-through*. To do a work-through, choose a specific task (see Chapters 9 and 10) and work through the design, explaining in detail how a user would carry out each step in the task. Repeat for several different tasks.

3. Invite the gang.

Say that you're the designer for the object of this delightful little walk-through exercise. You need someone to run the meeting, and you need a couple of authorized reviewers — also called *critics*. Your job is to be as stoic as possible while taking copious notes. The meeting leader keeps everything on track and reminds everybody to stay as neutral and impersonal with their comments as possible. The critics get to have the time of their lives.

Try to invite at least one critic with a fresh viewpoint on the design. (That is, someone who has not been involved in the design process yet.)

Consider your goals when you decide who to invite as your reviewers: If you want to check whether the design conforms to company standards, invite critics who are familiar with the standard. If you want to find out whether the design will work with current task routines and forms, invite the people who are recognized as "old hands" at following the routines, and so on.

4. Go through the interface design bit-by-bit.

Encourage a reviewer-critic at a walk-through to look for trouble, problems, and possible difficulties with the interface as the leader goes through it, point-by-point. The reviewer should be admonished to mention potential problems in neutral, impersonal terms. Questions can be a good form.

Yes: "That list box has multiple selection, but it looks just like the other one."

No: "Quentin, you fool! They'll never understand that list box!"

The meeting leader uses diplomacy, direct orders and, if necessary, a referee's whistle to keep the discussion on track. The leader shouldn't let the participants argue about different ways to change the program or how to implement changes. Keep the discussion focused on listing potential problems for these reasons:

- If you stop to try to agree on solutions, you won't get finished.

- If you allow discussion of whether something is a problem, the meeting will often become a "critics attack/designer defends" situation where feelings and the desire to be right or to win obscure the more important design issues.

If you're one of the critical reviewers, do take the time to mention things that you think will work well, in the same fairly neutral terms. (In this way you demonstrate to the designer that at least some of your opinions are worth listening to.)

5. Remember that results belong to the designer or design team.

The comments belong to the designer, who is free to ignore them or use them. However, a good idea is for the designer to begin the *next* walk-through — which will normally be for a different part or stage of the design — by telling which design improvements resulted from the previous session. This custom means that the designer must seriously consider comments. If the designer has no changes to report, all concerned parties understand that walk-throughs are not a roaring success in this particular project. Try some other method instead.

Cognitive Walk-through

Do the Funky Chicken, do the Mashed Potato, do the Cognitive Walk-through. Almost fits in there with the '60s dances, doesn't it? *Cognitive* means having to do with thought processes. A cognitive walk-through means going through how designers *believe* the user will think about the application, step-by-step. Do a cognitive walk-through whenever testing is out of the question, yet you feel a need to check whether your application is easy to understand.

You need an interface design, a task to perform, a designer, and someone willing to take the role of the *skeptic*. (Funny; it's never a problem to find volunteers for this job!) With the skeptic, go through one task a small step at a time. For each step, the designer says what the user would do next. The skeptic then asks, "Why does the user understand that this is the next step?" The designer explains what signals in the GUI make the user realize that this is the next step. The skeptic gets to present an opposing view if the designer is being overly optimistic. Designers and skeptics don't fight the design issues to a gory standstill — they just register their opposing views and move on.

The only difference between a cognitive walk-through and any other walk-through is the special focus on what you expect the user to understand, and why. Follow the walk-through guidelines described in detail in the previous section: Focus on collecting potential problems, keep the discussion neutral and not personal, let the designer decide what to do with the results, and finally, report decisions back to the participants in the walk-through.

A simple cognitive walk-through

The following is an example of the dialog that takes place in a cognitive walk-through.

Jill: The user is an administrative employee in a real estate agency. He has used a Windows-based word processor for two years already. A potential home buyer calls and wants to know what properties that are in his price range will be showing during the upcoming weekend. The buyer wants a home on the west side of town for under $300,000.

The user starts our application.

Jack: Why does he do that?

Jill: Because he knows that our application is on his computer, so he looks for it, and because the desktop icon with a house and a question mark reminds him of the task he is trying to carry out, which is answering a query from a buyer.

The user sees our opening window. The list of listed properties is always showing in the opening window, but the user needs a filtered view, so he clicks on the View menu.

Jack: Why does he know he should go to the View menu?

Jill: Because it's a view he wants.

Jack: But perhaps he thinks that he wants to find something, so the user goes to the Edit menu and looks for Find, as he would in his word processor.

Jill: Well, that won't work. Find will only find a term in the list, not a combination of criteria. He needs a filtered view.

Jack: I don't see how the user is going to know all by himself that he needs a filtered view.

Jill: Okay, I'll note that as a potential problem and we'll go on.

Heuristic Evaluation

In a *heuristic* method of education, students are trained to find things out for themselves. In *heuristic evaluation* of a user interface, people discover the potential usability problems by looking for them directly in the design, rather than by observing users. Many developers find a heuristic evaluation useful because it's quite simple to perform, though you get the most accurate results when you use experienced reviewers.

Heuristic evaluation does have one thing in common with usability testing; just as you find more of the problems by testing with more users, you find more of the problems by using more evaluators.

Here's how to do a heuristic evaluation:

1. **Gather a group of three to five reviewers.**

    Try to get people who are experts in user interface design or *functional experts* — people who have experience in the work to be done with the interface. Preferably, you want a mix of both.

2. **Present your reviewers with a short list of the principles that are followed by all well-behaved user interfaces.**

   The list in Chapter 21 will do just fine. If your reviewers are inexperienced, go through the principles in detail. Encourage the reviewers to discuss the principles and to give examples of interfaces that comply or fail to comply.

3. **Introduce the design or prototype.**

   Explain the purpose of the product and the user group and use pattern it is designed for. If the application is complex, rather than self-explanatory, you may need to hold a demonstration. Don't allow discussion at this point.

4. **Ask the reviewers to go through the design, noting all the potential problems, both large and small, that they spot.**

   It's very important that reviewers don't talk with each other while they do this evaluation. You want to benefit from the independent thinking of different minds. Actually, this element of the evaluation is one of the beauties of heuristic evaluation, because the reviewers don't necessarily have to be gathered in one place or do the review at the same time. (You don't necessarily have to hang around while they're hard at work, either.)

   If you're evaluating a live system (or a design that's currently being developed), a good idea is to assign one note-taker and helper to each evaluator. Let the evaluator work with the system and dictate comments to the helper. The helper can also solve any technical problems that turn up.

5. **Gather the comments together, check with reviewers about any comments you don't understand, and remove any duplicates.**

   Foster a healthy sense of competition in your reviewers by making sure that each one gets credit for her finds in the final report (which you, of course, distribute to the evaluation team). This process keeps the reviewers keen on doing this for you — you may want to use them again, after all.

Review with Checklists

A *checklist* is a list of items or characteristics that should be present in an interface or a part of an interface. Typically, projects make a checklist for reviewing individual windows.

A checklist can include items like these:

- ✔ Correctly spelled window title in title bar.
- ✔ Standard-sized OK and Cancel buttons correctly placed in upper right-hand corner.
- ✔ All texts correctly spelled.
- ✔ Unique underlined letter in title or leading text of each control.

To do a checklist review, you look at the item on the checklist, look at the window to decide whether the item or characteristic is present, and then make a checkmark next to that item on the list. After all the items are checked, you conclude that the window is okay. Some projects require a completed and signed checklist for each window as part of the quality assurance documentation.

I'm no fan of checklists; this is a personal failing. Give me a checklist with more than a dozen items on it and my mind goes absolutely numb with boredom. I start off conscientiously reading each item and checking whether the item in question is fulfilled; within three minutes I have to stop myself from merely setting tick marks at random. If I must check a half-dozen windows with the help of a checklist, I start missing blatant mistakes on the second window, mainly because I watch the list instead of the window.

Are you any different from me? Do you know someone who does the same thing when presented with a checklist?

If you *must* use a checklist of review considerations, make sure that the checklist is short, well-formulated, and covers points that people are actually likely to forget. Here's a checklist for making your checklist:

- ✔ **Do stick to items that can be checked without involving opinions.** "Data listed in alphabetical order" is okay, but not "Data grouped logically."

- ✔ **Do state all items the same way, preferably as requirements.** "Texts spelled correctly," and "One frame around each group of radio buttons" are okay; but not "No misspellings," and "Radio buttons should usually be framed."

- ✔ **Do skip requirements for things that your development tool does automatically.** For example, skip items such as: "The window must have a title bar."

Instead of a checklist, I recommend using a *window proofreader*. When your project nears completion, have the most eagle-eyed project member look through printouts of all the windows and circle spelling mistakes, alignment errors, inconsistent terminology, or departures from the project standard. Documentation people are often great at this. By using one person to do the job, you get a single standard that's consistently applied, and the focus of the task is on finding errors rather than making checkmarks.

Site Observations

You perform a site observation by visiting present (or future) users of your product at the place where they work. You watch, listen, and take notes as users either do their work or use your product to do their work.

Site visits have a certain "I'm on a getaway" effect: You are more open to a fresh perspective on your design when you come to a new place and don't know what to expect. Site observations work best when you perform them in salubrious climates. If, for example, your development project takes place in Cincinnati, a site visit to Honolulu or Acapulco would probably give the — sorry, my evil twin got the better of me for a moment.

You may find it helpful to do site observations either very early in the development project or soon after a product release. When performed early in the project, site observations are a good way to learn about users and their working environment. You can gather information about the tasks users need to perform and also get an idea about whether your product really will solve a problem for the users.

Customarily, development projects conclude with a beta release or pilot release of the product to a limited number of users. The pilot is really a large-scale usability test. As long as this test is taking place, why not seize the opportunity to observe at least part of it? During pilot tests, users call attention to major barriers such as installation problems. If you're observing users at the site, though, you'll see things that the users never talk about, such as how they approach the new application and what features they find first. Though you can seldom make design changes in the coming release, a lot of what you learn will help in future releases:

- ✔ What design problems showed up here that I *didn't* catch with my earlier testing? Are they problems I could catch next time? How would I have to change my testing strategy?

- ✔ Which of the assumptions I made about users, working environment, and tasks at the beginning of the project were correct? Which were wrong?

If you're designing a commercial software package, a new version is always something to look forward to. Never pass up the chance to make a site observation. While you are in the middle of designing a new version, the users are just getting to be old hands with your previous version. Efficiency problems require the most advanced and expensive form of usability testing, because you need to set up realistic systems, realistic tasks, and realistic working conditions in order to evaluate efficiency. A site visit provides all the realism you need, so you can hunt for efficiency problems for a fraction of the cost of a usability test to find the same problems.

Site observations don't have to be complicated, but a few practical tips may be in order, such as:

- ✔ **Prepare your mind.** Consider the difference between observing and interviewing, which is the difference between watching without judgment and going out in the field to find proof of one or more of your favorite theories.

- ✔ **Prepare your welcome.** After you identify a site you'd like to visit and receive clearance from any necessary top brass, write to either the users you would like to observe or to their immediate supervisors. Request *their* permission to come, explain why you want to observe their work and emphasize that you will be evaluating system performance, not user performance. Suggest a couple of alternate dates. Some workplaces have weekly or seasonal hectic periods when they're not especially thrilled about an extra pair of feet to trip over.

- ✔ **Ensure your welcome.** I've never turned up for a site observation without some small, appropriate token of my appreciation, whether it's a box of donuts or a bunch of flowers. Explain that you'll be a fly on the wall, that you won't have time to talk or ask questions because you'll be busy taking notes. Also, offer to show your notes to the users and supervisors at the end of the observation period so that subjects can comment, correct, or censure any material they wish. Be innocuous!

- ✔ **Take thorough notes.** If you're writing notes as fast as you can, you won't be tempted to break out of the observer role. My favorite tool for note-taking is a laptop computer. I sit a few feet behind a user, perch the laptop on a credenza or an upended briefcase, and get down as many notes as I can.

- ✔ **Hold a short closing interview at the end of the observation.** Show your notes to the users and ask for their comments. Also ask for clarification of things you haven't understood. And remember to say thanks!

- ✔ **Be polite.** Take the time to write a thank you letter.

Site observations sometimes have an interesting side-effect: Users who have been observed feel honored. They may become more efficient or develop more positive feelings about the product. This reaction is called the *Hawthorne effect* because it was first noted in a 1939 study of Western Electric Company workers in Hawthorne, Illinois.

Changing over to a new computer system is very, very low on a user's list of Things I Just Love to Do. A little judicious publicity around carefully conducted site observations can help pave the way for the new computer system that your project is developing. Together with interviews and user tests, site observations show that you acknowledge users' competence and knowledge of their own work.

Just as we developers get frustrated by people who make demands or criticize our work while they display a total lack of technical understanding, our users get fed up when we give the impression of thinking that a computer system will solve all their problems.

What Next?

You've just read the final chapter on reality checking. Reality checks are a necessary complement to the creative part of design; one succeeds the other in a chicken-and-egg cycle. The user tests described in Chapters 17 and 18 are also reality checks.

If you're ready to start a project of your own anytime soon, look at the Part of Tens for a list of tips for project leaders, or for where to find more information about GUI design, whether on the Internet or at a professional gathering. Or you may want to take a look at the CD-ROM, which has example files and utilities for the GUI designer.

Part VI
The Part of Tens

In this part . . .

Welcome to The Part of Tens. This part is the place where all the good stuff that didn't fit elsewhere came to roost. This is where you can dip in just for fun and pick up a tip, an idea, a reference, or a funny story. You won't need to read the section just in front or the section just behind; each tidbit is self-contained.

As you may have noticed, I am not in favor of following standards for the sake of consistency. Standards are there to make things act like users expect them to. I figure that you expect me to give you all the good stuff I've got, so even though this is called The Part of Tens, don't too be shocked if you find more than ten good tips or interesting resources.

Enjoy!

Chapter 20
Murphy's Laws of GUI Design

● ●

In this Chapter

▶ Appreciating individual differences

▶ Identifying the users

▶ Designing with your customer's priorities in mind

▶ Taking responsibility for user errors

▶ Resolving design conflicts

▶ Assigning responsibility for usability

▶ Leading a project to user-friendly results

▶ Satisfying the users

● ●

1 know some people whose entire approach to life is based on Murphy's Law: the premise that if something can go wrong, it will — in the worst possible way.

"The sun is shining in a blue sky and we're going to walk only 500 yards to the mailbox, Uncle Sebastian, so why are you putting on galoshes and getting out your raincoat?" asks Kathy. "As long as I'm prepared for rain, it won't rain," Uncle Sebastian replies with supreme confidence. Kathy and Uncle Sebastian end up getting hailed on.

Murphy's Law and its relatives are wry wisdom based on experience in the real world. Because GUI design is a real-world activity and not a purely theoretical exercise, in this chapter I take a look at some of the things that can go wrong in the software development process and some ways to stay on old Murphy's good side.

The Law of Maximized Misunderstanding

The Law:

> If something can possibly be misunderstood, it will be.

The corollary:

> If it can't *possibly* be misunderstood, it will still be misunderstood.

The following stories illustrate ways that users can misunderstand computers and computer applications. Many of these stories may just be urban myths of the computer variety, but people who have worked on support lines don't find them unbelievable or even unusual:

- ✔ There is the story of the user who called and asked for a replacement cup holder for his PC. "Cup holder?" inquired the mystified support person. As it turned out, this user was using the CD tray to hold a coffee cup, at least until the disc tray broke.

- ✔ One user was asked to "copy a diskette," which she did — with her office copier. She sent the support team an $8^1/_2$-x-11-inch piece of paper with a nice photocopy of the diskette cover.

- ✔ A user was installing an application using $5^1/_4$-inch floppy disks. The installation instructions said, "Please insert diskette #2," and so on, resulting in a call to the support team: "I managed to get #2 in, but there's no way to get #3 to fit in there, as well."

"If it can be misunderstood, it will be" serves to remind you that understanding is based on shared experience and vocabulary. Just as no two people are exactly alike, neither are any two sets of experiences. As a user-interface designer, you need to allow for individual variation among your users by recognizing that they may think differently from you or differently from each other.

Guard against the assumption that your own background and experience with computers is universal. Accept that somebody is sure to misunderstand even the best design. Take the time to create Undo features and graceful exits from error situations in your interface.

User Identification Theorems

All those concerned with software development agree that GUIs should be designed to suit the users, but who *are* the users? Developers, clients, and user representatives all occasionally masquerade as users; the user identification theorems will help you expose the imposters.

The Theorems:

- ✔ If you think that *backup* is something you do to get your car out of the garage, you might be a user.

- ✔ If you design or develop software for a living, you are definitely not a user.

- ✔ If you're developing software for other software developers, you are allowed to consider yourself as one of your own users . . . just this once!

- ✔ If it bothers you that you have to click OK when the computer says, "Irrecoverable error, your file has just been destroyed," you might be a user.

- ✔ If you are a *user representative,* you might be a user, but you are probably not a typical user. Most user representatives get awarded the job because they are more than typically interested in the computer system and better than average at using it.

- ✔ If it bothers you to put file folders inside file folders inside file folders unto the *nth* generation, you might be a user.

- ✔ If you sign the check that pays to have software designed or developed, you are *not* a user; you are a customer.

- ✔ If you're never sure whether you should click once or click twice, you might be a user.

- ✔ If you can define any two of the following acronyms: TCP/IP, http, JPEG, TIFF, ROM, MDI, LPT, OSI — you are *not* a user.

- ✔ If you'd rather go to lunch than redefine the parameters governing the fish in your screen saver, you might be a user.

- ✔ If you don't know what a *parameter* is or what parameters have to do with electronic fish, you're definitely a user.

If you'd like to get to know your users better, try interviewing users (Chapter 8) or performing a site visit. (Chapter 19).

Arlov's Observation

The Observation:

Results are achieved not when systems work, but when users work.

Customers don't purchase or develop systems because they are afraid their hard drives might perish of undernourishment. Customers invest in new software to achieve some goal such as better customer service or more economical operations.

Arlov's Observation points out that the new software can sit there perfectly installed on the customer's computers until pigs fly, but nothing good will happen (no results!) until *the users* are able to work with the software as you and the customer have assumed that they will.

The interaction between user and computer forms a kind of bottleneck for the desired results. Functions, processes, or improvements in speed or quality designed into the system won't show up for the customer unless the interaction between the users and the user interface is successful.

As a system developer, you do not and cannot control the users. You can write handbooks and recommend courses and hope for the best. But even if you rely on training, different people will learn and remember differently. What you *do* control is the user interface. The quality that you design and build into the interface will always be there. It is in your best interests as a system developer to take responsibility for making the best quality user interfaces you can.

To make sure the software you supply translates into results for your customers, do the following:

1. Consider the project's or purchaser's overall goals when setting your design priorities, as described in Chapter 1.

2. Know your users, as described in Chapter 2.

3. Take a task-oriented approach to design, as described in Part III.

4. Perform user tests with realistic tasks and typical users, and make use of the results to improve your design as described in Part V.

A Faultless Admonishment

The Admonishment:

The user is always right — even when the user is wrong.

 The admonishment reminds you to look at problems from the user's point of view. Okay, so the user may have made a mistake. But blaming the user for what goes wrong doesn't improve your design. You don't learn anything useful by blaming the user. In any error situation, assume that the user did what he or she thought *was* the right thing. Ask what your program did that encouraged the user to take such an action. Now you have started a train of thought that can lead to improvements and new insights.

The Axiom of Inversely Accessible Information

The Law:

> The best basis for a design decision is the information that is the most expensive or difficult to obtain.

Base your design decisions on the following, in order:

1. **Relevant research,**

2. **Test results,**

3. **Relevant experience, and failing all else,**

4. **Opinions.**

If what you decide is important, don't waste time arguing about it; go do a test.

Reserve your testing efforts for questions that are critical to achieving your design goals and make certain that you are testing what you really want to know. To test the quality of your icons, for example, don't test whether users can guess which icon represents each command. Rather, ask a tester to look through the tool tips at the beginning of a test. Then do an interview and have the user perform some task unrelated to the icons. Just before concluding the test, ask the user to say what each icon does *without* looking at the tool tips. In this way, you can test whether your icons are memorable and easy to distinguish — icons need to exhibit these qualities in order to act as effective shortcuts for users who are familiar with the program.

The Law of Inversely Accessible Information is closely related to Spencer's Laws of Data, from Arthur Bloch's *Murphy's Law Book Two* (Price/Stern/Sloan Publisher, Inc.). Spencer's law states:

1. Anyone can make a decision given enough facts.

2. A good manager can make a decision without enough facts.

3. A perfect manager can operate in perfect ignorance.

The Buck Location Principle

The Principle:

> Those who have the knowledge to control the technology in a project are ultimately responsible for the usability of the product.

I can hear the graphic designers and human factors experts groaning loudly at this one — and even many GUI designers. "We specialize in making things user-friendly; how can you say that it's not our responsibility?"

I believe that the buck ultimately stops with the project's most knowledgeable technologist. If you are a technologist, I believe that your mastery of technology carries both power and responsibility. Look at the following:

- **Why I equate technical mastery with power:** No matter how much a design idea might improve the usability of an application, the people who are going to build the application have the veto power. If they say it can't be done (or it can't be done in the available time, or would cause too many other changes, or would create unacceptable response times), the only way to reverse that decision is to find someone who knows *more* about the technology and who is willing to prove that the designers are wrong. The CEO can march down into the project and demand a user-friendly solution, but that solution won't materialize until someone can be found who will say "I can build what you're asking for within the time and money constraints that you set."

- **Why I equate technical mastery with responsibility for user friendliness:** If you are the top technical authority in a project, your mastery gives you veto power. You can veto the design ideas that make the product more user-friendly, or you can use your technical mastery to discover creative ways to implement user-friendly design ideas. The end result is not going to be any more user-friendly than you will allow or any less user-friendly than you will settle for — in other words, you're responsible for user-friendliness.

Though I am rarely the top technical expert in a project myself (sigh), I am content with this situation. It seems fitting to me that, at least sometimes, knowledge is the key to power.

The Law of Just Desserts

The Law:

> R&D managers get the software quality they deserve, and user-friendliness is no exception.

The managers who complain that their R&D departments produce more bugs than an open landfill are usually the same ones who delete training time, vacation time, review periods, and testing from the project plans. In other words, they have earned all the bugs that they get.

An R&D manager who *wants* user-friendly software can *earn* user friendly-software by encouraging developers to:

- ✔ Make field observations.
- ✔ Talk to customers.
- ✔ Design before building.
- ✔ Employ graphic designers.
- ✔ Meet with user representatives.
- ✔ Take part in customer training.
- ✔ Participate in user focus groups.
- ✔ Request, perform and observe tests with users.

Grudin's Law

The Law:

> If those who do the work required by a new or changed system do not perceive any benefits, the system is likely to fail.

Grudin's law is attributed to Jonathan Grudin, HCI researcher at the University of California at Irvine. This law goes like this: people are human. You may think "What's in it for me?" is a cynical reflection of an egotistical age, but if it isn't clear to your users how they will benefit from using the system, don't be surprised if Grudin's Law scurries out of the woodwork and nibbles your program to death.

Beating Grudin's Law is not merely a case of explaining things well when the new system is installed. To beat Grudin's Law, you have to start thinking about it at the beginning of the design phase. In prioritizing and designing functions, take care to find a few things that are important to the user and that are difficult, irritating, or time-consuming to do today. Let your system make *those* tasks markedly easier, more pleasant, or more efficient in the future.

Watch out for customers who want you to solve their leadership problems by designing a system that forces users to work in a certain way. As one of my favorite techies says, "There's only so much of management's job a computer can do."

The Copenhagen Conclusion

During a delicious Danish lunch at a software development conference in Copenhagen, a developer gestured at the buffet table overflowing with pickled herring, smoked salmon, sliced meat, salads, fruit, cheeses, bread, and pastry as if to illustrate the question she asked her companions: "There is too much to choose from. *What do the users really want?*"

After some hearty discussion, and some equally enthusiastic munching, a small party of diners concluded that the easiest way to answer the question was to say what the users *don't* want. I think their conclusion is a fine watchword for GUI designers:

The Conclusion:

New users don't want to feel stupid. Old users don't want to feel slowed down.

Chapter 21

Ten Ways to Tell Whether Your GUI Is Good

1 was once handed a checklist for good GUI that included the questions, "Does the program have drag-and-drop capability?" and "Does the program have icons?" Use a checklist like that one if you need help picking out the GUI from a police lineup of interfaces.

Use a list of criteria such as the one in this chapter if you need to *evaluate* a user interface — your own or someone else's. The list reminds you of what to consider. You can't give an objective yes or no to each point; you must make judgments.

To judge a GUI correctly, you need to know the answers to the following questions, described in detail in Chapter 2:

✔ Who are the users?

✔ What is the technical platform?

✔ What are the tasks?

✔ What is the environment?

Solve a Problem for the Users

Even the best-designed program in the world doesn't see much use if it doesn't do something the users really want done — or at least that they *believe* they want done. Consider these assertions:

- ✔ WordPerfect sailed to popularity in the late '80s partially because it supported nearly every printer on the market. Who needed a word processor that couldn't guarantee print capability?

- ✔ The IBM concept for home computing — to get the non-techies to invest in home PCs — got off to a rocky start because application offerings such as *keep track of your LP records/your recipes/what you have in the freezer* were met with "Why would I need a computer to do that? I can keep track just fine the way it is now." After home computing was presented as *a way to help your kids succeed in school,* its success became another story entirely.

Be particularly careful with this point in custom development projects where the people who specify requirements are rarely the ones who are going to be using the program. If the first release requires users to register mountains of data but doesn't include the functions to create the reports they themselves need, watch out!

Support Project Goals

A good GUI, or any user interface for that matter, should be designed to support the project's overall goals. If you look through the interface, you should be able to see which design goals have received top priority. Is this interface designed for speed? To be attractive to the users? To be self-explanatory?

Then ask yourself the following question: Does this type of design serve the project's overall goals?

Consider, for example, a virus-control utility. To continue to sell well and to sell upgrades — the overall goal — this program must protect its users from pesky virus infections. The user interface is designed to be as automatic as possible, a design priority that clearly supports the overall goal. Would you choose an antivirus program that works only if you remember to use it or one that protects you all the time? (Actually, I would choose the one that could tell the difference between installing new software and a virus attack. . . . Sigh.)

For the rare occasions that the user interacts directly with the antivirus program, windows must be designed to be clear and self-explanatory. This feature is a more appropriate choice than, for example, speed. A user with a virus problem wants to know exactly what's happening and what to do; meeting these needs is more important than saving seconds.

Give the antivirus program an A for supporting project goals.

Suited to the Users

Two important questions lurk behind this criterion of whether a design is suited to the users.

First, has the project identified the users or user groups correctly? No one's been forgotten? You're most likely to forget a group of users if they're underrepresented in your particular project environment: Women, disabled users, elderly users, children, foreign-language speakers, non-academics, users from the branch offices, and even end-users occasionally get forgotten.

Second, does the design show that the characteristics of important user groups have been taken into consideration? You need to decide which characteristics and which groups are important on a case-by-case basis — that's where judgment comes in. Don't reduce your users to statistics such as age and computer experience. You need to consider users' motivation, preferences, and use patterns — intense or occasional. You must also consider attributes of the group as a whole. A user group with a high turnover rate, for example, always has a high proportion of new users to experienced users.

Suited to the Task

First, get to know the task without looking at the GUI. What are the steps in the task? What's the result? How do you know whether the task's been successfully completed?

Now examine the GUI, considering the following questions:

- Can the user easily find where to start the task?
- Can the task be completed without undue navigation?
- Do the steps come in natural order?

> ✔ Do you see all the information you need to complete the task without needing to search through unnecessary information? Is information presented in the most helpful way?
>
> ✔ Can you tell when the task is done and whether it was successful?

Easy to Get Started

A good GUI has *clarity of purpose* — the program tells the user what she can do with it, eliminating any guessing. Where and how to begin working also should be obvious.

How can you tell just from looking at a GUI whether the intended users are going to understand the program?

Try to think of how the users view their work. What are the main activities and objects from the users' point of view? Now look at the first or main window of the GUI and the texts in the menu. Do you see text and graphics that reflect the users' view of the work? If not, the most common problem is that the GUI simply displays the structure of its own modules and its own database, leaving the user to puzzle out the relationship between database tables and tasks.

Consistent with Users' Expectations

Nowhere does this list of criteria say that a good GUI is "consistent with the standard." Users don't read the standard. If their new Windows program does what they expect it to, they're happy and they tell you, "Yes, this program is a standard Windows program."

If the program doesn't do what the users expect it to, it's not a standard program in their eyes. Users' expectations are based on the program or programs that they use most, not on the printed standard. To know what your users expect, look at the programs they spend most of their time with.

Attractive

A GUI that follows the principles of good visual design is rarely judged completely ugly. Some people may like the interface a lot, while others may give it a ho-hum. You can probably determine whether you find a GUI attractive just by casting a quick glance at it. Table 21-1 shows some things to look for if you want to give *reasons* for your conclusion.

Table 21-1	Why Do You Like the Way the GUI Looks?
Category	*What to look for*
Mood	A well-designed graphical user interface has a mood you can put your finger on. Relaxed, sober, or re-served. Informal. Humorous. Peppy. The mood is appropriate to the GUI's purpose and user group.
Graphical style	Dimensional effects are consistent. Fonts, icons, layout, and choice of colors contribute to the same mood. Icon symbols and other graphics are drawn in a consistent style, with similar degree of realism and consistent light source.
Space and harmony	Windows and frames have pleasing proportions. Windows appear clear and restful or organized. Windows don't look crowded, confusing, or busy.
Neatness	Texts and widgets are consistently positioned and correctly aligned. Consistent spacing and widget sizes give an impression of rhythm and predictability.
Color	Colors are related, yet distinct. Strong colors aren't overused. Color-on-color combinations give a comfort-able degree of contrast: You can see edges clearly, but colors used together do not vibrate. You see agreeable proportion of color to gray, black, and white.

Intuitive

A GUI is intuitive if the users feel that they know what to do without thinking too much. Ask three people whether a program that they use is intuitive, however, and you get three different answers.

If you must make an educated guess on the basis of a short acquaintance with the program, look for clues such as the following, which are described in detail in Chapter 11:

✔ Can you spot the *affordances*: Do windows and widgets show what they can do?

✔ Does the program give immediate *feedback* when the user does some-thing? Is the feedback in a useful form?

✔ Are *metaphor, analogy,* and *idiom* used appropriately?

✔ Does the program have good *mapping?* Do you find a natural, one-to-one relationship between the GUI and the user's task or mental model?

Effective

An effective GUI is speedy. The program doesn't drag its feet and produce noticeable response lags; it requires no unnecessary keystrokes or mouse clicks, and the user has little need to jump from window to window to get a job done.

Look at data entry for a quick check of basic effciency, as the following list describes:

✔ Do fields appear in the correct order? Can the user press the tab key to move through the task in natural order?

✔ Does the program provide sensible defaults and reuse previously entered data?

✔ Do editing masks enter the spaces and hyphens for dates, product numbers, and the like?

✔ If the user types a few characters of a known value, does the program fill in the rest?

If the end result isn't good enough, fast is just fast, not effective. To truly evaluate effectiveness of a GUI you need to consider not only what the user is trying to produce, but also how good the result needs to be.

A truly effective GUI is one that helps the user do a good job without working harder than he needs to.

Ergonomically Correct

I certainly don't want to offend the Ergons, now do I? *Ergonomics* is the study of human efficiency in the workplace. A tool, a workplace, or a GUI is ergonomically correct if it's correctly designed to fit the physical characteristics of the person working with it.

Check whether the GUI is well-suited to the user's eyesight.

Ideally, the user should be able to control font, font size, and foreground/background color combinations. If these features are hard-coded into the program, you should leave a good margin of error for visibility. You can't know whether the user is blessed with good lighting conditions and a nice monitor or sitting in glare city with a flickering 13-incher. An ergonomically correct GUI should have enough spare visibility to be acceptable even under poor working conditions or to a user with mildly impaired vision or impaired color vision.

Check how the GUI enables the user to input data. A good GUI doesn't play favorites. Both mousers and keyboarders should feel welcome. Frequently used keyboard commands should be brief and centrally located. For heavily numeric data, the user should be able to use the numeric keypad and enter data one-handed. Mouse users should not need to wave the mouse back and forth. Dragging and double-clicking are both more difficult than a single point-and-click interaction, so think twice before creating an interface with heavy emphasis on dragging or double-clicking.

An ergonomically correct GUI is accessible for disabled users and is prepared for interaction with adaptive devices. (See the sidebar, "Users with special needs," in Chapter 2.)

Secure

A good GUI protects the user from inadvertent or malicious loss of data. This level of protection includes providing a good Undo feature and graceful ways to exit an operation if the user changes his mind.

 A good GUI also has enough self-confidence — and enough confidence in the user — that it doesn't beg for continual reassurance on routine operations: "Are you *sure* you want to delete this paragraph? Are you really *sure* you're sure?"

Tested with Users

At last, here's one checkpoint that needs only a yes or a no. If a GUI is tested with users during the design process, some of the problems that are *not* obvious to the designer's judgment get discovered and corrected. You can safely say that a GUI that's been tested is better than a comparable untested GUI.

Chapter 22

Ten Things a Project Leader Can Do

*A*ll the best project leaders I've worked with have been alike in certain ways. For one thing, they all *guide* their projects rather than controlling details.

So how do you guide a project toward a great user interface? This chapter lists ten useful actions you can take if you're the project leader. Some of them help project members understand what they're aiming for. Others help create the working conditions that foster good user interfaces. Finally, you find some things that you can do to make sure that project members receive clear, early feedback on their design efforts so that they're not working in the dark.

This chapter collects the advice found throughout *GUI Design For Dummies* that's most important for project leaders. After all, another way my favorite project leaders are alike is that that they never have enough free time to read a whole book!

Get Agreement on the Facts

Working on a GUI design attracts sidewalk supervisors like pouring fresh concrete at an elementary school playground.

In custom development, you have client leaders, potential users and their managers and trainers, and probably client technical personnel who all have opinions.

If you're doing package development, you usually find that sales, marketing, training, service, and documentation representatives all have legitimate concerns about the user interface.

I call the people with legitimate concerns about your interface your *stakeholders* (or your kibitzers). If you want your project to create a coherent design, you'd better get the kibitzers organized. Invite them to a meeting to define the important conditions governing the design. These conditions fall into the four categories: technology, users, tasks, and environment. For each category, I've listed the questions you need to answer in cooperation with your stakeholders.

Following are the technology questions:

- ✔ What is the technical platform for the project?
- ✔ What are the development tools?
- ✔ What are the known strengths and weaknesses of the technical platform and the development tools? Do you have sufficient knowledge on this point?
- ✔ What is the minimum run-time configuration your users are required to have?
- ✔ What are the security issues? What about system performance?

Naturally, a GUI must be suited to its users. The following questions ensure that you and your stakeholders agree who the users are:

- ✔ Which different groups with different demands can you identify among your users?
- ✔ What range or level of computer competence do you find in each group?
- ✔ What's the approximate size of and turnover in each group?
- ✔ What's the use pattern in each group? Regular or irregular use? Hours or minutes per day? Repetitive tasks or unpredictable tasks?
- ✔ What do the users lack today that your system is supposed to give them?
- ✔ How can the project stay in touch with the users?

Although you need far more information about tasks as the project proceeds, what you need from your stakeholders is agreement on which tasks have top priority. Ask them the following questions:

- ✔ What are the critical tasks?
- ✔ Which tasks are frequently repeated?
- ✔ Which current tasks do users most dislike?
- ✔ How will the project get access to more-detailed functional information?

Neither your project nor the program you create exists in a vacuum. If you and your stakeholders consider the project's environment and the environment in which the program will be used, you get wind of other important design considerations, as noted in the following list:

- ✔ What demands does the users' physical environment make on your program?
- ✔ Does the users' cultural environment (national, professional, or organizational) make any particular demands on the program?
- ✔ Does the market in which the program or the users must compete impose any constraints on your project? Time to completion? Available resources? Critical success factors?

Get those who have a stake in the design to agree on the answers to these questions. Write the answers down. In a long project, review these design considerations every three months to make sure that you catch the inevitable changes.

Set a Few Goals for the User Interface

In an ideal world, every user interface is both easy to learn and efficient to use; completely flexible but always suited to the task; user-driven and error-preventive at the same time; and runs like greased lightning on even the oldest PCs and monitors, even though the program's full of features, options, and fancy graphics.

If your goals for the design read like a spoiled seven-year-old's letter to Santa Claus — Dear developers, please give us everything that's popular this year, for free — you're setting yourself up for a disappointment.

The answer is to get your stakeholders and key project members together, just as you did to establish the important design considerations. Consider your project carefully. Consider the overall project goals, what type of users you have, and what the users' working situation is. Pick three goals — just three — and put them in order of priority. Say that you want to go for flexibility first and then ease of use, and your third goal is that the interface should be attractive to the users. That decision means that you need to ask the project members to design the entire interface with those qualities in mind. If they come to a design tradeoff where the most flexible solution puts a dent in the window layout, they know to consistently sacrifice a little beauty to maintain flexibility.

As project leader, you need to make certain that everyone who joins the project understands the design goals. (I like to print out the goals, frame them, and hang them on the soda machine.) If design disputes land on your desk, ask "Which solution is in keeping with the priority of the design goals?"

By the way, prioritizing design goals with stakeholders is a great way to help them develop realistic expectations for the project.

Don't Treat GUI as a Side Effect

To produce a good GUI, you must either define the GUI design as a separate project or give a single person or team leader responsibility for it and authority over it.

I admit that this approach doesn't seem necessary or sensible at first glance. With modern development tools, each developer designs one piece of the user interface while creating each window. In this way, the design work is divided between many people and proceeds according to many different visions of the end result. No wonder the results are patchy.

In a project large enough to need a project leader, any of the following strategies can help:

- ✔ In a small project, put one or more GUI design deadlines in the project plan. Define which design documentation must be completed and reviewed by each deadline. Do the reviews together.

- ✔ Assign responsibility for the GUI design to the person who's most qualified for the job in a medium-sized project. The GUI designer guides the rest of the team in this aspect of the design work.

- ✔ In a big development effort, define GUI design as a project in itself. You may need to assign an entire team to the job, or you may assign several people to spend part of their time on the GUI design job. As is true of any project, the GUI design project should have a defined goal or result, a plan for reaching the goal, and a leader who has the authority and resources to carry out the plan.

Think Twice about Standards

A GUI standard *can* help your project make a GUI that looks and behaves predictably, but the standard *can't* make all the design decisions for you. A well-written standard covers only a fraction of the design decisions your project needs to make, and even a well-written standard is useless unless you're willing to require unwilling developers to follow it.

Here's what a project leader needs to know about standards:

✔ Don't waste time producing a standard if you're going to duck the difficult questions of actually using it in the project: Does everyone need to follow the standard? Who ensures that they do so? What happens if they don't? Who decides whether the standard can be changed, interpreted, or bent a little? What's the procedure for communicating changes?

✔ "We can follow the Microsoft/Apple/IBM standard." Sorry, but if you look closely, you find that these folks don't always follow their own standards, and, in fact, the standard changes for each new version of the operating system. Understand that what you're really trying to do is to meet user expectations. If the users spend most of their PC time working with Microsoft Excel, they're going to have one set of expectations; if they mostly work with QuarkXPress from Quark Inc., they expect something entirely different.

✔ Users are never going to read your standards; make your document usable for the developers. Keep standards short and specific. Write the standard to conform to the development tool: If the tool measures distance in millifoos, the standard should give distances in millifoos, too.

✔ For consistent product appearance, do include a layout grid and include widget sizes and spacing in the standard. Don't put in sermons and principles. Think of the standard as the building code rather than inspirational literature. If you can provide an online repository of windows and widgets in standard formats along with the standard attributes, so much the better.

✔ Don't copy the standard used on a previous project unless both projects have the same design goals, users, and technical platform and the same types of tasks and environmental considerations.

✔ Don't decide too early or you may end up with the wrong standard. The project shouldn't be starting mass production until after key windows are designed and tested. Do your best creative work and then write the standard on that basis.

Get Professional Graphics

Good amateur graphics look like what they are: good and amateur.

If your project can't afford to have some users cast a glance at the interface and snort, make sure that you get professional help with the graphic design. You face a real increased risk of snorts these days, as user expectations are inflated by gorgeous computer games, exciting Web sites, and innovative business software.

If you're worried that adding a visual designer to the team may have unpredictable effects on the look and feel of your product — or on your schedule and budget — here are some things that you can do to guide the design process:

- ✔ Pick a visual designer who has previous experience working with your technical platform.

- ✔ Define the parameters that govern the visual design. Make sure that the development tools, file formats, font sizes, and number of colors to be supported are specified in writing.

- ✔ Provide a technical expert to help your designer explore the visual possibilities and limitations offered by your development tools. Emphasize to the designer that the development tool is a "given" — rather like the dimensions or printing process for a publication.

- ✔ Make sure that you know which stakeholders feel that they have a constitutional right to opinions about the visual design and invite them to an initial meeting. At this meeting, agree on a couple theme words for the mood you want or the effect you want to produce. Select a color palette. Then impose severe limits on the number of kibitzers and further meetings.

- ✔ If possible, make your visual designer a full-time member of the development team. In any case, create a design plan that matches the steps of controlled iteration in your project plan.

- ✔ Document design decisions and resist the impulse to change your mind or ask for multiple alternatives.

Don't get professional graphics by stealing them from other people's products. Icons, for example, are part of the copyrighted product. Make sure that your graphics are legally yours!

Go Multidisciplinary

"Two heads are better than one," says the old proverb. But two heads of the same age and the same sex, with the same educational and occupational background, are a lot closer to one head than two. Unless all your users are clones, you find a lot of individual differences among them. The best way to create a product that appeals to more than one kind of user is to have more than one kind of person participate in the design.

- ✔ If you have a small project, pick someone with broader-than-average experience as your GUI designer. Look for the one who took a double major in computer science and drama or the programmer who gets around in a wheelchair. Look for a people-oriented person who draws pictures while talking.

- ✔ An ideal design team has a few multidisciplinary members. Together, the team should have functional competence, technical expertise, visual design ability, teaching skills, and good "people" skills.

- ✔ Help an incomplete team or a single designer by approving time and funds for design reviews with functional experts, a graphic designer, or a trainer.

Because you're the project leader, your attitudes are contagious. If you're seen to respect and appreciate diversity, the chances are good that your project members are going to follow suit.

Keep in Touch with the Users

I know that you're under pressure to make sure that the project gets done on time.

Don't try to save time by isolating the project from all outside influences. Developers who spend months on end discussing their work with other developers tend to turn out products that are very developer-friendly. If you want the result of your project to be user-friendly as well, make sure that the developers meet your users.

To keep your project in touch with users without triggering uncontrolled iteration, encourage activities such as site visits or meetings with groups of users at specific points, early on in the project.

If your designers don't have enough functional knowledge to start with — if they don't really understand what the users are going to *do* with the program — you're going to have a lot of unplanned redesign work whenever the lightbulbs finally blink on. Prevent this problem by securing good functional competence for your design team as early as possible. Why not let designers start the project by spending a week or two as trainees where users do their work?

Testing with users can be a great help, but that's so important that I give it a heading all its own.

User Testing — the Silver Bullet

Suppose that you waited until the very end of a client/server development project to test the communication between the server and the PCs? What if, when you did test, you discovered that half the packets were getting lost in space? Would you then decide that the PCs were useless and send them out to be repaired? You'd have a short career as project leader if you did.

Now consider whether you're treating the communication between the GUI and the users in the way I've just described.

Testing with users is not so very different from prototyping the technical architecture and module tests and string tests. You start testing early and test small pieces at a time to make sure that you don't get any big, expensive surprises after you're too far into the project to do anything about them.

If anything is close to a magic formula or a silver bullet in this whole book, it's testing with users. Encourage your project to view testing as a way to get important information, not as a sterile quality-assurance exercise that leads to somebody getting yelled at. To this end, encourage your project members to take part in defining and observing the tests themselves.

Testing doesn't need to be expensive and time-consuming. Your designers can discover how to conduct simple tests with the help of Chapter 17 in this very book.

Plan to Test

The unplanned activities and the unanticipated problems are what threaten to sink your project.

Plan from the very beginning of the project to have the following test cycles. (A *test cycle* includes testing with at least three to five users and usually a quick set of design changes and a retest with three to five new users.)

- ✔ Test your project's conceptual model.
- ✔ Test a paper prototype of your main windows and navigation system.
- ✔ Test live prototypes of the menu system and several key windows.

Plan time for project members to take part in testing with users and plan time to make modest changes in the design as a result of these tests.

Chapter 23

Ten Resources for GUI Designers

*W*ould you like to dig further and deeper into the field of GUI design? If so, you can find something here for every personality and every pocketbook.

If you're the people-loving type or you'd just like an excuse to travel, try a conference. Perhaps you've got a generous employer to pick up the bill? Or you're self-employed and can justify it as a business expense? If you're a poverty-stricken student, several conferences have good deals for student volunteers.

If you're in a hurry and you're online, investigate the World Wide Web. I've listed a couple of major link sites that can help you home in on the information you want.

Perhaps you prefer to curl up in peace and savor a good book? You can choose between technical books, philosophical books, and artistic books. Given the multidisciplinary nature of GUI design, you have a huge variety of useful reading matter from which to choose. Doing so was a tough call, but I've picked my favorites for you.

Resources on the Internet

Because you're interested in software design, I'm going to assume that you are "Net-enabled" or know someone who can help you check out these interesting resources on the Net. If not — if you *wish* you were on the

Internet but it just seems so impossibly difficult — why not get yourself a friendly boost from *The Internet For Dummies*, 4th Edition? This book, by John R. Levine, Margaret Levine Young, and Carol Baroudi, is published by IDG Books Worldwide, Inc. — the same people who published the book you're reading!

Jump in here

Mikael Ericsson, at the Department of Computer and Information Science at Linköping University, in Sweden, maintains a comprehensive Web page with links to events, publications, people, and companies in the field of Human-Computer Interaction (HCI).

You find Mikael's page at `http://www.ida.liu.se/~miker/hci/`.

A California firm called Usernomics has an especially user-friendly HCI links page. Usernomics provides a concise description of each link; most of the links are to sites with HCI content, as opposed to sites that offer only more links.

Visit Usernomics at `http://www.usernomics.com/hci.html`.

Halls of fame and shame

Kudos to Isys Information Architects, Inc., of Greensboro, North Carolina, for their outstanding pages *The Interface Hall of Fame* and *The Interface Hall of Shame*.

Here you can see real excerpts from real products and read short, sensible explanations of what's so good or bad about the examples. Even if you don't always agree with the comments, you should find these pages both fun and thought-provoking.

The good examples are at `http://www.mindspring.com/~bchayes/mfame.htm`.

The bad ones live at `http://www.mindspring.com/~bchayes/mshame.htm`.

Comp.human-factors

`Comp.human-factors` is the cyberspace hangout for folks who're interested in improving human-computer relationships. You find postings from all kinds of people here — from cognitive psychologists, to techies, to usability testing specialists. Interface designers turn up with practical design questions and the resulting discussions can get pretty interesting — and occasionally a little heated. `Comp.human-factors` also has job and conference announcements, mentions of new books and papers, and directions to new Web sites that may be interesting. I'll see you there!

If you're new to the Net, you may want to note that `comp.human-factors` is a *newsgroup,* not a Web site. Look for commands such as News and Subscribe to Newsgroup in your Web browser to access these groups.

Interaction design

Delft University of Technology, in the Netherlands, sponsors an extensive and well-designed site with up-to-date links. The site is called *User Interaction Design Web*. The site has useful lists of books and publications and a good list of multimedia tools. This site also has links and references to industrial design resources.

Visit *User Interaction Design Web* at `http://www.io.tudelft.nl/uidesign/#`.

Windows 95 standard

If I need to know specifically how a user interface element is supposed to work in Windows 95, I visit Microsoft's site. It's an easy place to get lost.

The following address takes you straight to the user interface department:

`http://www.microsoft.com/win32dev/uiguide`

Downloading software and icons

Lots of places let you download software, but ZDnet's software library is my favorite because the creators of the site take the time to review the applications. You also find some downloadable icons and clip art at ZDnet. You can access it at the following Web address:

`http://www.hotfiles.com/index.html`

Usable Web design

If you're interested in design for the Web, visit *Alertbox*. This site holds a whole collection of columns by SunSoft's distinguished engineer Dr. Jakob Nielsen. Titles include "International Usability," "Top 10 Mistakes of Web Design," "Site Maps," "Why Advertising Doesn't Work on the Web," and so on.

GUI design and Web design overlap in many places — the site offers a column on that, too — so I read *Alertbox* regularly.

You find it at `http://www.useit.com/alertbox/`.

Electronic performance support (EPS)

Performance-centered design and electronic performance support are the subjects of an extensive new Web site, epss.com!. Performance-centered practice in user interface design has some of its roots in training and computer-based training development. Check out the resources at this site if you know a lot about computers and GUI already and would like to strengthen your understanding of how users learn and how to support effective work.

Visit `http://www.epss.com`.

Advanced Reading

As a GUI designer you're often working on your own. A well-supplied book-shelf is a source of new ideas, deeper background information, and alternative opinions to keep your work fresh.

A giant sampler

As long as you have a table to lay it on while you read, the enormous *Human-Computer Interaction: Toward the Year 2000*, written and edited by Baecker, Grudin, Buxton, and Greenberg (Morgan Kaufman Publishers, Inc.), can substitute for an entire library. This 950-page collection of papers, articles, and book excerpts spans both the history and breadth of the HCI field. The volume is clearly intended as a college-level sourcebook. The authors provide an informative introduction to each part. Parts include — among others — "The Process of Developing Interactive Systems," "Psychology and Human Factors," and "Research Frontiers in HCI."

Digging deeper into windows

Alan Cooper's *About Face: The Essentials of User Interface* Design (IDG Books Worldwide, Inc.) is not on my bookshelf. That's because I quote it so often that I keep it on my desk. Author Alan Cooper may be best known as the designer of Visual Basic, but he also writes a witty and straight-talking manifesto for GUI designers. I especially appreciate the chapters that go into detail about each window element, from menus to scroll bars. At the back, you find an overview of design tips and a list of Cooper's pithy axioms — for example, "If it's worth asking the user, it's worth the program remembering." If you've enjoyed *GUI Design For Dummies* and found it useful, *About Face* is the book to continue on with.

What makes an object easy — or hard — to use?

This book was originally published under the title *The Psychology of Everyday Things*, but later editions of cognitive psychologist Donald Norman's classic are titled *The Design of Everyday Things* (Doubleday). Norman uses cognitive and experimental psychology to explain why you and I trip up whenever we try to use everyday objects such as glass doors, light-switch panels, and telephones. If you'd like to go deeper into the psychology of product design but you don't want to read about rats, Donald Norman is a great author to start with.

International interfaces

Modern technology may be shrinking the world to a global village in some ways, but so far, I know of no technology that erases differences in language and culture. Those problems wind up in the hands of international user-interface designers. Jakob Nielsen and Elisa M. del Galdo have edited and contributed to an anthology of articles on the issues that arise as you design interfaces for an international user group or try to transplant interfaces from one culture to another: *International User Interfaces* (John Wiley & Sons).

You can see the table of contents for this book at the following Web site:

`http://www.useit.com/jakob/intluibook.html`

Cost-justifying usability

Randolph G. Bias and Deborah J. Mayhew have edited and contributed to the collection *Cost-Justifying Usability* (Academic Press, Inc.), which is nothing more nor less than ammunition for dealing with those who make decisions as if value equals money — period. The articles are well-documented, and the book includes realistic cost/benefit models and case studies. I'd call this book advanced material rather than fun reading, but the book is definitely heaven-sent if you're in a working situation where you need good arguments for usability work.

Icons

William Horton's *The Icon Book: Visual Symbols for Computer Systems and Documentation* (John Wiley & Sons, Inc.), is a valuable resource for designers who must specify, select, or draw their own icons. *The Icon Book* is concrete, clearly written, and heavily illustrated. Horton covers both theory and practice: why icons work, how they work, how to figure out what to draw, and how to draw them. He describes the icon development process in detail and includes forms for specifying and testing the work. The navy-blue-and-white illustrations in my 1994 edition look a little crude at first glance, but in fact, they enable you to more easily see how pixels are used in each example. My only complaint is that this book was published before the 256-color palette became an acceptable minimum.

Two visual communication classics

Edward R. Tufte, a professor of political science and statistics, got thoroughly fed up with newspaper graphs that told visual lies about the numbers they purported to represent. In 1983, he founded his own publishing company and published his own book: *The Visual Display of Quantitative Information* (Graphics Press). Beautifully illustrated and lucidly written, this book is a joy to read for its own sake and an invaluable guide if you're making an application that presents numerical data in charts and graphs.

Tufte's second book, *Envisioning Information* (Graphics Press), has received numerous awards. Much of the visual design literature is dominated by advertising, where the goal is to create sensory or emotional experiences. Instead, Tufte shows and explains many examples of excellent visual communication by experts and scientists: the communication of quantities, relationships, abstract ideas, and steps. Tufte has very little to say about graphical user interfaces, but his work is still profoundly relevant to a GUI designer. Besides, just turning the pages of this book is a delight!

Publications

I consider any day to automatically be a good day whenever I find one of these two publications in my mailbox.

Interactions

Interactions is a quarterly magazine on interactive systems development published by the ACM (Association for Computing Machinery). This magazine is colorful and well-produced. Most issues maintain a good balance between technology-oriented articles and people-oriented material. You can write for information about the magazine at the following address: ACM, 1515 Broadway, New York, NY 10036. You can also e-mail interactions@acm.org for subscription information or visit the Web site at http://info.acm.org/pubs/magazines/interactions/.

Complimentary copy of Eye for Design

I just renewed my subscription to *Eye for Design*, a bimonthly newsletter from the Massachusetts firm, User Interface Engineering, Inc. (UIE). In 8 to 12 well-illustrated pages, UIE reports interesting findings from usability tests and analyzes new interface design trends. To me, *Eye for Design* is a great value because it contains more information than opinion.

UIE offers one complimentary copy to potential new subscribers. To get yours, send a request with your postal address (that's snail mail, folks) to efd@uie.com, leave your address at the Web site at http://www.uie.com, or write to the following address: User Interface Engineering, Inc., 800 Turnpike St. Suite 101, North Andover, MA 01845.

Places to Go and People to Meet

People and computers usually get along like a Democratic president and a Republican Congress. No wonder so many organizations are devoted to understanding and improving Human-Computer Interaction. Now all we need is a Nobel prize.

Most conferences are moveable feasts. They have new contact addresses and new Web sites each year as they migrate from one attractive venue to the next. For details about upcoming dates and locations, contact the sponsoring organization or search for the conference name on the Internet.

You may want to consider joining one of these professional societies. Of course, you receive discounts on their publications and conferences. If you choose to become an active member, you can meet others who share your professional interests, and you have a chance to put your own pet topics on the agenda.

The CHI conference

CHI is the Conference on Human Factors in Computing Systems and is sponsored by ACM's Special Interest Group on Computer-Human Interaction (ACM SIGCHI).

CHI tends to be a hugely attended conference with an innovative program and lots of activity in addition to traditional papers. To date, CHI has usually taken place in North America. Contact CHI at the following address: ACM Association for Computing Machinery, 1515 Broadway, New York, NY 10036-5701; or try the following Web address: `http://www.acm.org/ sigchi`.

UIST

The Annual Symposium on User Interface Software and Technology, UIST, is jointly sponsored by three ACM Special Interest Groups: SIGCHI, SIGGRAPH, and SIGSOFT.

UIST has a stronger technology profile than the other conferences mentioned here. The program focuses on new interface-building technology and tools. Contact UIST at the following address: ACM Association for Computing Machinery, 1515 Broadway, New York, NY 10036-5701; or try the following Web address: `http://www.acm.org/sigchi`.

INTERACT

INTERACT is an international conference; its organizers traditionally pick exciting venues outside North America. This event is another heavily attended conference with parallel sessions, tutorials, posters, and exhibits. INTERACT is held in odd-numbered years.

The conference is sponsored by IFIP, the International Federation for Information Processing — in particular, the IFIP Technical Committee on Human-Computer Interaction (IFIP TC13). Contact IFIP at the following address: IFIP Secretariat, Hofstrasse 3, A-2361 Laxenburg, Austria.

Usability Professionals' Association

The Usability Professionals' Association gathers members who work with usability issues in a wide range of fields, including computer science and software design. Practitioners have varied backgrounds, from anthropologists and architects through software developers and on to technical writers. UPA activities focus on professional development. The Association holds an annual conference. Contact UPA at the following address: Usability Professionals' Association, 4020 McEwen, Suite 105, Dallas, TX 75244-5019; or check out the following Web address: http://www.upassoc.org.

The Performance Support Conference

Electronic Performance Support is a new and rapidly growing branch of software development. Most EPS systems use GUI or multimedia to support users in learning a new job or performing better in an existing one. This conference, held for the first time in 1995, brings together systems developers and designers, instructional designers, and the manufacturers of EPS authoring tools.

The conference is jointly sponsored by a group of firms offering products or services for EPS, and arranged by the following commercial conference facilitator: RMR Conferences, Inc., 167 Central Street, Holliston, MA 01746. For more information, try the following Web site: http://www.epss.com/.

Appendix

About the CD

Here's some of what you can find on the *GUI Design For Dummies* CD-ROM:

- ✔ A draft project GUI standard or style guide
- ✔ Examples of many of the design documents mentioned in *GUI Design For Dummies*: a design considerations memo, conceptual models, a paper prototype, a test script and test results from sample projects
- ✔ Iconsucker, a freeware utility you can use to capture icons to study
- ✔ Info Spy, a shareware utility to help you keep track of your application's use of memory and resources
- ✔ An evaluation copy of Activity Map, an application you can use to support a brainstorming or conceptual modeling session

System requirements

Make sure your computer meets the minimum system requirements listed below. If your computer doesn't meet these requirements, you may have problems using the contents of the CD.

- ✔ A PC with a 486 or faster processor.
- ✔ Microsoft Windows 95 or Windows NT 4.0 or later.
- ✔ At least 8MB of total RAM installed on your computer. For best performance, we recommend at least 16MB of RAM.
- ✔ Space on your hard drive for each of the programs you want to install. (You need less space if you don't install every program.)
- ✔ A CD-ROM drive — double-speed (2x) or faster.
- ✔ A monitor capable of displaying at least 256 colors or grayscale.
- ✔ For the sample files that have file type .doc, a word processor that can read or import Microsoft Word 6.0 format.
- ✔ For the sample files that have file type .ppt, a graphics program that can read or import Microsoft PowerPoint 4.0 format.
- ✔ For the single sample file that has file type .xls, a spreadsheet program that can read or import Microsoft Excel 7.0 format.

If you need more information on the basics, check out *PCs For Dummies,* 4th Edition, by Dan Gookin, or *Windows 95 For Dummies* by Andy Rathbone (both published by IDG Books Worldwide, Inc.).

How to view or copy sample files

If you want to view or copy one of the sample files from the CD, follow these steps. If you want to install one of the programs from the CD, go to the next set of instructions.

1. **Insert the CD into your computer's CD-ROM drive and close the drive door.**

2. **Click the Start button, click Run, and in the dialog box that appears, type** D:\SETUP.EXE.

   Most of you probably have your CD-ROM drive listed as drive D under My Computer in Windows 95. Type in the proper drive letter if your CD-ROM drive uses a different letter — for example, *E.*

4. **Click OK.**

   A license agreement window appears.

5. **Because I'm sure you want to use the CD, read through the license agreement, nod your head, and then click on the Accept button.**

   After you click on Accept, you'll never be bothered by the License Agreement window again. Next, the setup program shows the CD title page, GUI Design For Dummies.

6. **Click anywhere on the title page to see an overview of the CD contents.**

   On the contents page, you see several categories.

7. **To view a sample file, double-click on the category "Sample Files and Diagnostics".**

   You see a list of the phases in a GUI Design project, corresponding to the parts *in GUI Design For Dummies.*

8. **Click on one of the phases.**

   You see a list of sample files relevant to the project phase you have chosen.

9. **Click on one of the sample files.**

   These files were made with Microsoft Word, Excel, or PowerPoint. If you have the same or a newer version of the program that the sample file was made with, Windows will start the appropriate program and open the file. If you have older versions of these programs, you will not be able to open the sample files (See "System Requirements.")

If you do not have Word, Excel, or PowerPoint, Windows checks the file type extension (.doc, .ppt, or .xls) on the sample file to see if you have previously designated a program to read this type of file. If not, Windows will provide a list of the applications that you may be able to use for reading the sample files. If the sample file you want to read is a text file with the .doc extension, choose your word processor. For a graphics file with the extension .ppt, choose your graphics editor. For a spreadsheet file with the extension .xls, choose your spreadsheet program.

You can save your own copy of the sample file, if you want. After you open the file in your favorite word processing, graphics, or spreadsheet program, choose File⇨Save as from the menu bar and save the file to your chosen hard drive or other media.

You are welcome to make copies of the sample files and to edit them for your own use. You may not publish the sample files in any form or claim copyright to them.

How to install programs from the CD

To install a program from the CD to your hard drive, follow these steps. If you want to view or copy the sample files, go to the previous set of instructions.

1. **Insert the CD into your computer's CD-ROM drive and close the drive door.**

2. **Click the Start button and click Run.**

3. **In the dialog box that appears, type** D:\SETUP.EXE.

   Most of you probably have your CD-ROM drive listed as drive D under My Computer in Windows 95. Type in the proper drive letter if your CD-ROM drive uses a different letter — for example, *E*.

4. **Click OK.**

   A license agreement window appears.

5. **Because I'm sure you want to use the CD, read through the license agreement, nod your head, and then click on the Accept button.**

   After you click on Accept, you'll never be bothered by the License Agreement window again.

   Next, the setup program shows the CD title page, GUI Design For Dummies.

6. **Click anywhere on the title page to see an overview of the CD contents.**

   On the contents page, you see several categories such as "Icon Stuff" and "Sample Files & Diagnostics."

7. **To view the programs within a category, click the category's name.**

   A list of the programs in the category appears.

8. **For more information about a program, click on the program's name.**

   You see a brief explanation of what the program can do and, in some cases, special installation instructions you need to follow.

9. **To install the program, click the Install button; if you don't want to install the program, click on the Go Back button to return to the previous window.**

   The CD begins installing the program that you chose. You may be asked to confirm or select a directory where the installation will take place.

   After the installation is completed and if you want to install something else from the CD, you may need to click `GUI Design` on the Task bar in order to bring the CD window to the front again.

10. **To install other items, repeat Steps 7 through 9.**

11. **When you finish installing programs, click on the Quit button to close the interface.**

    You can eject the CD now. Carefully place it back in the plastic jacket of the book for safekeeping.

Sample files on the CD

The sample files consist of design documents from sample projects as well as blank forms and reusable templates for memos, logs, prototypes, and the like. You find one or more documents relating to the work described in each part of *GUI Design For Dummies*:

✔ **Part I: Identifying Goals and Constraints**

- Blank design considerations memo: `desncon.doc`

- Project description for a library project: `projdesc.doc`

- Sample invitation to stakeholder meeting for a library project: `mtg_inv.doc`

- Sample design considerations memo for a library project: `desconex.doc`

✔ **Part II: Surviving the Early Design Phase**

- Re-usable paper prototype construction: `protkit1.ppt`

- Sample conceptual model for library use: `conmod1.doc`

- Sample conceptual model for library search function: `conmod2.ppt`

- Sample Navigation model for library project: `navmod1.ppt`

- Sample paper prototype for library interface: `protoex.ppt`

- Draft project GUI standard (any Windows 95 business application): `gui_std.doc`

✔ **Part III: Designing GUIs that Work**

- Sample interview request letter for library project: `int_req.doc`

- Sample interview findings report for library project: `int_find.doc`

- Sample interview consent form for library project: `consent.doc`

✔ **Part IV: Designing Windows**

Draft project GUI standard (any Windows 95 business application): `gui_std.doc`

✔ **Part V: Doing Reality Checks**

- Re-usable Testers Bill of rights: `billofri.doc`

- Sample interview/test consent form for Library project: `consent.doc`

- Blank observation log: `obs_log.doc`

- Blank Observation log with timestamp macro and autofill for category: `timelog.xls`

- Sample test script: `testscri.doc`

- Sample test results from test of Library prototype: `testres.doc`

Programs on the CD

To install programs from the CD or view more information about them, see the section "*How to install programs from the CD.*" The programs consist of freeware, shareware and evaluation copies of utilities or applications that I have found helpful in my work as a GUI designer. When you run the setup program on the CD, you can find the programs in these categories:

✔ **Icon Stuff**

- Icon Edit: a shareware icon editor from Elliot Mehrbach.

- Icon Extractor: a shareware icon collection and management utility from NeoSoft Corporation.

- Icon Sucker: simple freeware from Copsey Strain, Inc., to extract icons from executable files and save them as .ico files.

✔ **Concept Mapping**

- Activity Map: This application from Time/system international is useful in documenting brainstorming sessions, planning sessions, or for doing quick diagrams of the relationships between ideas.

- Inspiration for Windows: Use Inspiration from Inspiration Software, Inc. when you're in creative mode to capture your thoughts and work with relationships between ideas.

✔ **Sample Files & Diagnostics**

- InfoSpy from Dean Software Design: This program enables you to see exactly what your application is doing within Windows; a big help when you are working with application performance-related issues.

- Sample Files: Clicking this item on the interface lets you quickly install a copy of the sample files to your hard drive.

If you have problems (of the CD kind)

I tried my best to compile programs that work on most computers with the minimum system requirements. Alas, your computer may differ, and some programs may not work properly for some reason.

The two likeliest problems are that you don't have enough memory (RAM) for the programs you want to use, or you have other programs running that are affecting installation or running of a program. If you get error messages such as `Not enough memory` or `Setup cannot continue,` try one or more of these methods and then try using the program again:

✔ **Turn off any anti-virus software that you have on your computer.** Installers sometimes mimic virus activity and may make the anti-virus program incorrectly believe that the computer is being infected by a virus.

✔ **Close all running programs.** The more programs you're running, the less memory is available to other programs. Installers also typically update files and programs. So if you keep other programs running, installation may not work properly.

✔ **Add more RAM to your computer.** This is, admittedly, a drastic and somewhat expensive step. However, if you have a Windows 95 PC, adding more memory can really help the speed of your computer and allow more programs to run at the same time.

If you still have trouble with installing the items from the CD, please call the IDG Books Worldwide Customer Service phone number: 800-762-2974 (outside the U.S.: 317-596-5261).

Index

(continued)

IDG Books Worldwide, Inc., End-User License Agreement

READ THIS. You should carefully read these terms and conditions before opening the software packet(s) included with this book ("Book"). This is a license agreement ("Agreement") between you and IDG Books Worldwide, Inc. ("IDGB"). By opening the accompanying software packet(s), you acknowledge that you have read and accept the following terms and conditions. If you do not agree and do not want to be bound by such terms and conditions, promptly return the Book and the unopened software packet(s) to the place you obtained them for a full refund.

1. **License Grant.** IDGB grants to you (either an individual or entity) a nonexclusive license to use one copy of the enclosed software program(s) (collectively, the "Software") solely for your own personal or business purposes on a single computer (whether a standard computer or a workstation component of a multiuser network). The Software is in use on a computer when it is loaded into temporary memory (RAM) or installed into permanent memory (hard disk, CD-ROM, or other storage device). IDGB reserves all rights not expressly granted herein.

2. **Ownership.** IDGB is the owner of all right, title, and interest, including copyright, in and to the compilation of the Software recorded on the disk(s) or CD-ROM ("Software Media"). Copyright to the individual programs recorded on the Software Media is owned by the author or other authorized copyright owner of each program. Ownership of the Software and all proprietary rights relating thereto remain with IDGB and its licensers.

3. **Restrictions on Use and Transfer.**

   (a) You may only (i) make one copy of the Software for backup or archival purposes, or (ii) transfer the Software to a single hard disk, provided that you keep the original for backup or archival purposes. You may not (i) rent or lease the Software, (ii) copy or reproduce the Software through a LAN or other network system or through any computer subscriber system or bulletin-board system, or (iii) modify, adapt, or create derivative works based on the Software.

   (b) You may not reverse engineer, decompile, or disassemble the Software. You may transfer the Software and user documentation on a permanent basis, provided that the transferee agrees to accept the terms and conditions of this Agreement and you retain no copies. If the Software is an update or has been updated, any transfer must include the most recent update and all prior versions.

4. **Restrictions on Use of Individual Programs.** You must follow the individual requirements and restrictions detailed for each individual program in the "About the CD" section of this Book. These limitations are also contained in the individual license agreements recorded on the Software Media. These limitations may include a requirement that after using the program for a specified period of time, the user must pay a registration fee or discontinue use. By opening the Software packet(s), you will be agreeing to abide by the licenses and restrictions for these individual programs that are detailed in the "About the CD" section and on the Software Media. None of the material on this Software Media or listed in this Book may ever be redistributed, in original or modified form, for commercial purposes.

5. **Limited Warranty.**

    (a) IDGB warrants that the Software and Software Media are free from defects in materials and workmanship under normal use for a period of sixty (60) days from the date of purchase of this Book. If IDGB receives notification within the warranty period of defects in materials or workmanship, IDGB will replace the defective Software Media.

    (b) **IDGB AND THE AUTHOR OF THE BOOK DISCLAIM ALL OTHER WARRANTIES, EXPRESS OR IMPLIED, INCLUDING WITHOUT LIMITATION IMPLIED WARRANTIES OF MER-CHANTABILITY AND FITNESS FOR A PARTICULAR PURPOSE, WITH RESPECT TO THE SOFTWARE, THE PROGRAMS, THE SOURCE CODE CONTAINED THEREIN, AND/OR THE TECHNIQUES DESCRIBED IN THIS BOOK. IDGB DOES NOT WARRANT THAT THE FUNCTIONS CONTAINED IN THE SOFTWARE WILL MEET YOUR REQUIREMENTS OR THAT THE OPERATION OF THE SOFTWARE WILL BE ERROR FREE.**

    (c) This limited warranty gives you specific legal rights, and you may have other rights that vary from jurisdiction to jurisdiction.

6. **Remedies.**

    (a) IDGB's entire liability and your exclusive remedy for defects in materials and workmanship shall be limited to replacement of the Software Media, which may be returned to IDGB with a copy of your receipt at the following address: Software Media Fulfillment Department, Attn.: *GUI Design For Dummies,* IDG Books Worldwide, Inc., 7260 Shadeland Station, Ste. 100, Indianapolis, IN 46256, or call 800-762-2974. Please allow three to four weeks for delivery. This Limited Warranty is void if failure of the Software Media has resulted from accident, abuse, or misapplication. Any replacement Software Media will be warranted for the remainder of the original warranty period or thirty (30) days, whichever is longer.

    (b) In no event shall IDGB or the author be liable for any damages whatsoever (including without limitation damages for loss of business profits, business interruption, loss of business information, or any other pecuniary loss) arising from the use of or inability to use the Book or the Software, even if IDGB has been advised of the possibility of such damages.

    (c) Because some jurisdictions do not allow the exclusion or limitation of liability for conse-quential or incidental damages, the above limitation or exclusion may not apply to you.

7. **U.S. Government Restricted Rights.** Use, duplication, or disclosure of the Software by the U.S. Government is subject to restrictions stated in paragraph (c)(1)(ii) of the Rights in Technical Data and Computer Software clause of DFARS 252.227-7013, and in subparagraphs (a) through (d) of the Commercial Computer–Restricted Rights clause at FAR 52.227-19, and in similar clauses in the NASA FAR supplement, when applicable.

8. **General.** This Agreement constitutes the entire understanding of the parties and revokes and supersedes all prior agreements, oral or written, between them and may not be modified or amended except in a writing signed by both parties hereto that specifically refers to this Agreement. This Agreement shall take precedence over any other documents that may be in conflict herewith. If any one or more provisions contained in this Agreement are held by any court or tribunal to be invalid, illegal, or otherwise unenforceable, each and every other provision shall remain in full force and effect.

Installation Instructions

*T*he CD stuck to the back of this book contains helpful programs and sample files related to GUI Design.

Installing programs from the CD

Follow these instructions to get more information about the programs or to install them. These instructions assume that your computer has Windows 95 or NT version 4.0 or later, at least 8MB of RAM, and a CD-ROM drive with a minimum speed of 2X. To access the programs on the CD, follow these steps:

1. **Insert the CD into your CD-ROM drive.**

2. **Choose Start⇨Run.**

   The Run dialog box appears.

3. **Type** D:\SETUP.EXE **in the Open text field and press Enter.**

   If your CD-ROM drive uses a different letter than D, please replace D with the correct letter.

4. **Follow the directions on the screen.**

   You must agree with the licensing agreement in the initial window in order to continue the installation program.

Viewing sample files on the CD

These instructions assume that your PC has applications capable of reading or importing the following file formats: Microsoft Word 6.0, Microsoft PowerPoint 4.0, and Microsoft Excel 7.0. To access the sample files on the CD, follow these steps:

1. **Insert the disk into your CD-ROM drive.**

2. **Start the Windows Explorer.**

3. **Click on the name or icon of the CD-ROM drive to display its contents.**

4. **Double-click on the name of the sample file you want to view.**

You are welcome to make copies of the sample files and modify them for your own use. You may not publish the files in any form or claim copyright to them. If, after following these instructions, you still have problems installing the utility programs from the CD attached to this book, please call the IDG Books Worldwide Customer Service phone number: 800-762-2974 (outside the U.S.: 317-596-5261).

IDG BOOKS WORLDWIDE REGISTRATION CARD

Visit our
Web site at
http://www.idgbooks.com

ISBN Number: 0-7645-0213-1

Title of this book: **GUI Design For Dummies®**

My overall rating of this book: ❑ Very good [1] ❑ Good [2] ❑ Satisfactory [3] ❑ Fair [4] ❑ Poor [5]

How I first heard about this book:

❑ Found in bookstore; name: [6]   ❑ Book review: [7]

❑ Advertisement: [8]   ❑ Catalog: [9]

❑ Word of mouth; heard about book from friend, co-worker, etc.: [10]   ❑ Other: [11]

What I liked most about this book:

What I would change, add, delete, etc., in future editions of this book:

Other comments:

Number of computer books I purchase in a year: ❑ 1 [12] ❑ 2-5 [13] ❑ 6-10 [14] ❑ More than 10 [15]

I would characterize my computer skills as: ❑ Beginner [16] ❑ Intermediate [17] ❑ Advanced [18] ❑ Professional [19]

I use ❑ DOS [20] ❑ Windows [21] ❑ OS/2 [22] ❑ Unix [23] ❑ Macintosh [24] ❑ Other: [25]_____

(please specify)

I would be interested in new books on the following subjects:

(please check all that apply, and use the spaces provided to identify specific software)

❑ Word processing: [26]   ❑ Spreadsheets: [27]

❑ Data bases: [28]   ❑ Desktop publishing: [29]

❑ File Utilities: [30]   ❑ Money management: [31]

❑ Networking: [32]   ❑ Programming languages: [33]

❑ Other: [34]

I use a PC at (please check all that apply): ❑ home [35] ❑ work [36] ❑ school [37] ❑ other: [38] _____

The disks I prefer to use are ❑ 5.25 [39] ❑ 3.5 [40] ❑ other: [41]_____

I have a CD ROM: ❑ yes [42] ❑ no [43]

I plan to buy or upgrade computer hardware this year: ❑ yes [44] ❑ no [45]

I plan to buy or upgrade computer software this year: ❑ yes [46] ❑ no [47]

Name: Business title: [48]   Type of Business: [49]

Address (❑ home [50] ❑ work [51]/Company name:)

Street/Suite#

City [52]/State [53]/Zip code [54]:   Country [55]

❑ **I liked this book!** You may quote me by name in future
IDG Books Worldwide promotional materials.

My daytime phone number is _____

IDG™
IDG
BOOKS
WORLDWIDE
THE WORLD OF
COMPUTER
KNOWLEDGE®